Radical Antiquity

"Despite humanity's egalitarian origins, hierarchical societies must depict anarchism as chaotic and unworkable. Unearthing the ancient world's anarchist cultures, Zeichmann presents a compelling argument that authority may itself have always been the real aberration. Highly recommended."

—Alan Moore, writer, activist, performer

"An inspirational masterpiece. This breathtakingly original account of experiments with anarchy in the ancient world will transform the way you think about the Classical world, about history in general, and about the possibilities for human liberty."

—William Arnal, Professor, Department of Religious Studies, University of Regina

"Anarchy is not a dream but a way of life. Zeichmann provides fascinating accounts of these ancient anti-hierarchical movements and communities, while never losing his critical edge. Wonderfully informative and a pleasure to read."

—Uri Gordon, editor, *Freedom*

"A rigorous, engaging history of communities and movements throughout the ages that resisted dominant ruling orders and organized themselves around more egalitarian principles. This history is essential for anyone seeking to understand the breadth of humanity's yearning for emancipation and solidarity."

—Roman A. Montero, author of *All Things in Common: The Economic Practices of the Early Christians* and *Jesus's Manifesto: The Sermon on the Plain*

Radical Antiquity

Free Love Zoroastrians, Farming
Pirates, and Ancient Uprisings

Christopher B. Zeichmann

PLUTO PRESS

First published 2025 by Pluto Press
New Wing, Somerset House, Strand, London WC2R 1LA
and Pluto Press, Inc.
1930 Village Center Circle, 3-834, Las Vegas, NV 89134

www.plutobooks.com

Copyright © Christopher B. Zeichmann 2025

The right of Christopher B. Zeichmann to be identified as the author of this work has been asserted in accordance with the Copyright, Designs and Patents Act 1988.

British Library Cataloguing in Publication Data
A catalogue record for this book is available from the British Library

ISBN 978 0 7453 5039 4   Paperback
ISBN 978 0 7453 5041 7   PDF
ISBN 978 0 7453 5040 0   EPUB

This book is printed on paper suitable for recycling and made from fully managed and sustained forest sources. Logging, pulping, and manufacturing processes are expected to conform to the environmental standards of the country of origin.

Typeset by Stanford DTP Services, Northampton, England

Simultaneously printed in the United Kingdom and United States of America

EU GPSR Authorised Representative
LOGOS EUROPE, 9 rue Nicolas Poussin, 17000, LA ROCHELLE, France
Email: Contact@logoseurope.eu

Contents

List of Figures	vii
Dedication	viii
Acknowledgments	ix
Abbreviations	x
Chronology by Region	xi
Map of the Ancient Mediterranean World	xii
Introduction: Radical Potential within Ancient Democracy	1
1. The Quest for Freedom: Spartacus and the Slave Community at Thurii	22
2. Communities of Jewish Radicalism: The Therapeutae and the Essenes	51
First Interlude. Anatolian Anarcho-Primitivists: The Region of Phrygia	75
3. Against a Dog-Eat-Dog World: Cynic Philosophers	85
4. Zoroastrian Polygamists: The Mazdakites	109
Second Interlude. Life in the Northern Periphery: The Sámi People	140
5. "Forgive Us Our Debts": The Circumcellions	147
6. Self-Governance on the Open Sea: Cilician Pirates	172
Third Interlude. Living in the Ruins: The Fall of Rome in Britannia	197

Conclusion: The Ghost of Spartacus   205

Discussion Questions   230
Notes   236
Index   288

List of Figures

1 Map of the ancient Mediterranean world   xii
2 Coin minted by Eunus/Antiochus (135–132 BCE)   29
3 Claudius preparing to kill Britannia (50–65 CE)   45
4 The execution of Mazdak and his followers
 (1330 CE)   120
5 Reconstruction of the *Orbis Terrarum* (20 CE)   144
6 Roman coffin depicting an enslaved ship crew (third
 century CE)   177
7 Pirates in a Roman mosaic (third century CE)   190

For my parents,
who unintentionally taught me to question authority.

BBBWS

Acknowledgments

This book would not exist without the important help of a few people. Kieren Williams, Nathanael Romero, Kevin McGinnis, Koom Kankesan, Bryn Jennings, and Cindy Chan all offered valuable feedback on earlier drafts of the research. Their comments helped refine the ideas and phrasing, resulting in a stronger manuscript. My thanks also go out to the anonymous peer reviewers for their helpful suggestions. David Castle, who serves as Editorial Director at Pluto Press, has been an incredible advocate since I first proposed the book. David, Patrick Hughes, Sandy Balfour, and others have made working with Pluto Press a fantastic experience. Naira Antoun's copyediting deserves special mention—her keen eye and strong intuitions have helped improve the prose.

I offer my gratitude to those who contributed in other ways. Cindy continually proves to be the partner I have wished for since I was young. My love for her exceeds any words I could find to express it. My dachshund Luba provided Cynic-style mischief while I was working on this project, for which I think I am grateful, though I'm not quite sure. Thanks also to Toronto Metropolitan University's History Department and to the Canadian Union of Public Employees 3904 Units 1 and 2 for reimbursing some expenses incurred while working on this book.

Abbreviations

All translations are the author's own, unless otherwise indicated. "LCL" refers to translations from the Loeb Classical Library.

Scholars of antiquity commonly abbreviate references to papyri and inscriptions. This book uses the standard abbreviations, which can be found via papyri.info and *Supplementum Epigraphicum Graecum*.

Chronology by Region

Greece
Archaic Period   776–480 BCE
Classical Period   480–336 BCE
Hellenistic Period   336–30 BCE
Byzantine Empire   330–700 CE
The Byzantine Empire persevered long beyond 700 CE, although its influence outside Asia Minor waned.

Rome
Roman Monarchy   753–509 BCE
Roman Republic   509–27 BCE
Roman Empire   27 BCE–476 CE
Post-Roman Europe   476–800 CE

Persia
Neo-Babylonian Empire   626–550 BCE
Achaemenid Empire   550–334 BCE
Hellenistic Empires   334–248 BCE
Parthian Empire   248 BCE–224 CE
Sasanian Empire   224–651 CE
Umayyad Caliphate   651–750 CE

General
Classical Antiquity   776 BCE–235 CE
Late Antiquity   235–750 CE

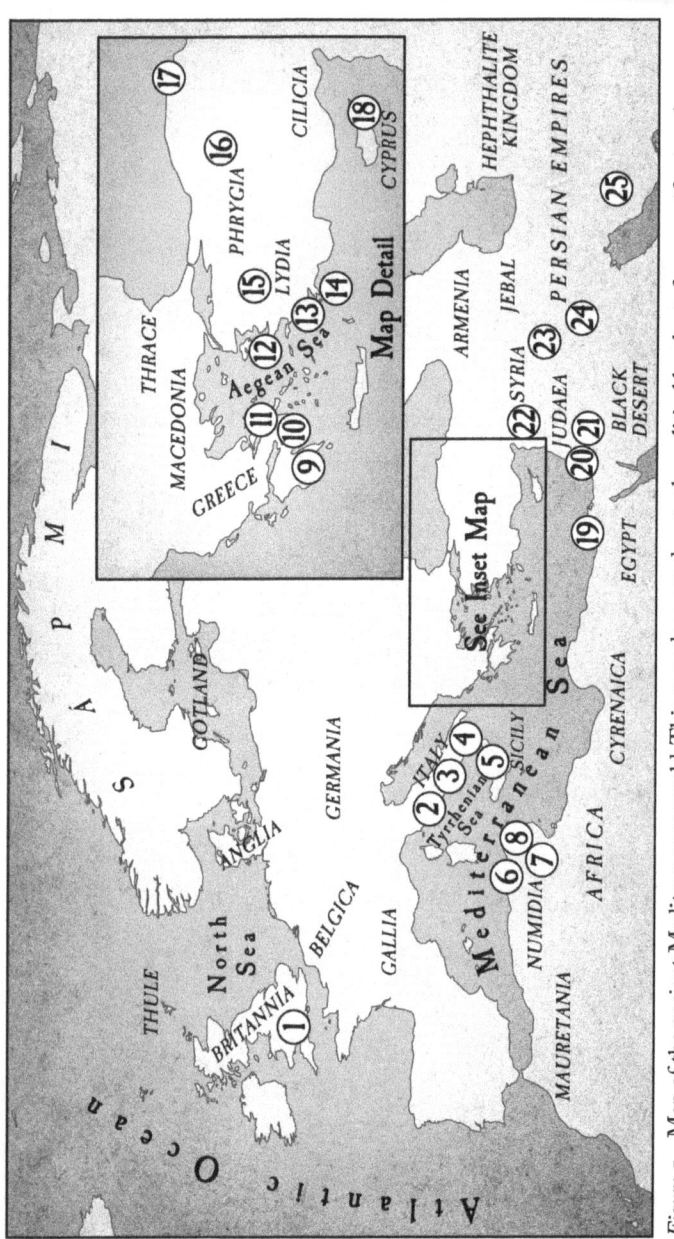

Figure 1 Map of the ancient Mediterranean world. This map does not denote the political borders of any specific time, but indicates locations mentioned throughout this book. Cities are identified by number. (Image by Christopher B. Zeichmann)

1. Bath, 2. Rome, 3. Capua, 4. Thurii, 5. Lipara, 6. Hippo, 7. Bagai, 8. Carthage, 9. Sparta, 10. Salmis, 11. Athens, 12. Chios, 13. Cnidus, 14. Rhodes, 15. Blaundos, 16. Gordion, 17. Sinope, 18. Citium, 19. Alexandria, 20. Jerusalem, 21. Qumran, 22. Emesa, 23. Ctesiphon, 24. Madharaya, 25. Fasa

Introduction: Radical Potential within Ancient Democracy

A Brief Portrait of a Dissatisfied Slave

Ancient works of history provide a limited perspective on antiquity. Sometimes we are left with just fragments—a name, an event, a brief remark in a text. But behind those traces were real people, living lives full of choices, struggles, and moments that were never recorded. The following scene is based upon the life of a real person named Erotis, about whom we know very little. In fact, she features just as a single name on an inscription listing the roster of an ancient club that gathered on the Greek island of Salamis. This portrait imagines her life, built on what we can infer and filled in with what might have been. While we may not know how the details of her life played out, I offer here one possibility.[1]

Erotis, born around 335 BCE in Persian Syria, never knew her parents. As an infant, she was taken captive by the army of Alexander the Great and sold to a slaver. After moving around the Mediterranean for a few years, she ended up on the Greek island of Salamis, just a half-hour boat ride from Piraeus, the port of Athens. But it was a strange time. Athens was no longer the famed site of democracy nor was it the maritime-merchant empire that it had been a few decades earlier. Athens and the surrounding cities had been reduced to a shadow of their former glory under the thumb of Alexander's successors.

On Salamis, Erotis was a slave in the household of Epicles, a coppersmith who purchased her to handle household chores. He spent most of his retirement at home, complaining to Erotis about the Macedonian occupation, also often waxing lyrical about the good old days back in Athens and about his commercial accomplishments during his smithing days. He reminisced about the years when he felt he had a meaningful say in civic affairs, a far cry from his powerlessness under the ongoing Macedonian occupation. The irony of Epicles complaining to his slave about feelings of political impotence was not lost on Erotis. She probably suppressed the urge to roll her eyes whenever he brought up his perceived victimization, but the lofty ideals of Athens in its prime piqued her interest. Rather than being ruled by a far-off king with no accountability to the people, the men of Athens had formed a government that prevented anyone from accumulating too much power. Athenian politics were built around the consensus of the Popular Assembly, which included all of the city's citizens. A "citizen" of course, was a limited concept in Athens and elsewhere in antiquity. It did not include women, slaves, or immigrants. The Popular Assembly, made up of those who were accorded citizenship, regularly convened to discuss new decrees drafted by the City Council. Members of the City Council had been chosen at random from among the citizens and Epicles liked to point out that this ensured that he and other metalworkers had as much a chance to lead as the aristocrats—that is, the wealthiest men in the city, who wielded considerable economic and political influence. Once the City Council prepared a decree, it was presented to the Popular Assembly for a show of hands: unanimity was required to ratify. If anyone objected, the matter was debated within the

INTRODUCTION

Popular Assembly and any resulting proposal was put to a blind ballot, in which a modified proposal might find agreement. Though Epicles never served on the City Council, he was especially proud of a speech he once gave that opposed special rights for an opportunistic landlord who had in-laws on the council. The men of the Popular Assembly vetoed the proposal and Epicles was eager to take credit for the decision.

Erotis' interest grew when Epicles spoke about the time a priestess had gained admittance into the more localized District Assembly on a legal technicality. Erotis wasn't sure she understood how this happened in the first place, but she could see that the incident continued to irritate Epicles who, decades later, spoke of it as an affront to the civic order. Erotis' relationship with Epicles was never close, but he was thoughtful enough that his will ensured she was freed upon his death. Since Epicles had no heirs, she also received a modest sum from his estate.

Life wasn't much easier as a freedperson, but Erotis found kinship with another former slave named Aitherion—they worked as housemaids for the same wealthy family and quickly formed a friendship. They attended the theater together and gossiped after working long days. Aitherion soon introduced Erotis to a club of Athenian expatriates who had moved to Salamis and who met regularly, often discussing the golden age of their hometown. Neither Erotis nor Aitherion had ever lived in Athens, but both their former masters had regaled them with enough tales of the city's past that they found it easy to blend in. In fact, the club modeled its own governance on that of Athens, altered to fit the particulars of its membership. The club held its own Popular Assembly during which members ate, discussed the day's news, debated organizational policies, and offered sacrifices to their patron goddess Athena Polias (naturally, since she protected the city of Athens). The club's membership of 124 people paled in comparison to Athens' 30,000 citizens, but unlike Athens, its version of the Popular Assembly was open to women, foreigners, and even former slaves such as Erotis and Aitherion. Erotis regularly attended these meetings, contributed what donations she could, and participated in this alternative vision of society. She made new friends and connections, and spoke in its Popular Assembly about various proposals under consideration. Mutual aid was central to the group's purpose, since the club collected funds to help members pay for unexpected expenses like funerals. This community became a source of vitality and respite from the powerlessness Erotis felt in most other aspects of her life.

Despite the group's ideals, members' prejudices occasionally surfaced. Some of the men proposed policies designed to marginalize Erotis and Aitherion within the club. These efforts failed, thanks in part to the compelling speeches she and her allies delivered to the Popular Assembly. The group eventually celebrated Erotis' financial contributions and unwavering commitment to the club. She and Aitherion were both voted recipients of the Golden Crown, an award mimicking that same honor bestowed upon many great Athenians. The club's regulations dictated that the monument celebrating the Golden Crown list them last of all, since they were both women and former slaves. Nevertheless, Erotis fondly recalled that day for the rest of her life.

This tale of Erotis is in some ways imaginary. She was a real person. We do not know the details of her thoughts, but we do know that she was a former slave, knew Aitherion, and this association awarded her the Golden Crown. Her life warrants reflection because there is a common tendency to think of Athens as an imperfect and rigid society. Men had rights; women and slaves did not. But the mere fact that an Athenian Assembly permitted a priestess to attend its sessions, suggests that the Athenian system was more flexible than Epicles wanted to acknowledge. And the fact that its ideas could be adopted—and adapted—in microcosm on Salamis by a club which included former slaves, women, and foreigners suggests that more radical conceptions of democracy were in wide circulation. I would go further: the story of Erotis tells us that there are lessons to be learned from antiquity that can inform our own debates about democracy, self-governance, and the characteristics of a free life.

Athens, Direct Democracy, and Anarchism

Erotis and her fellow Athenians wanted a system that allowed them to thrive. This led them to experiment in ways that both imitated and critiqued the state.[2] Although democracy in Classical Athens served the interests of the city's citizens, it excluded women, children, slaves, and immigrants. About one in six people inhabiting Athens held "citizen" status, so only a small portion of its residents could participate in the Popular Assembly.[3] But even citizens living at the city's periphery had difficulty participating, since it could be troublesome to reach the Athenian Acropolis, where the Popular Assembly gathered. Participation was never what it could have been, as it was easier for the wealthy (with their leisure time and centrally located homes) to attend than it was for the farmers and paupers who lacked such conveniences. People responded in various ways, often joining clubs, as Erotis did. These responses adopted the model of an imperfect state to produce something better suited to their needs—but they failed to address the flaws inherent to the Athenian city-state: such clubs did not end slavery, patriarchy, or xenophobia, all of which Greek and Roman states enshrined in their constitutions. Innumerable laws, norms, and rituals ensured that political power was concentrated with a small portion of the population: freeborn adult men with citizenship. Whether in Athens, Rome, Sparta, Alexandria, or elsewhere, these sorts of clubs could never solve the problems that affected people like Erotis.

This was a deeply flawed system, but there is something appealing about Athens' participatory democracy.[4] What might Athens' direct and consensus-based democracy offer to people disillusioned by today's governments? What potential lies untapped in its flawed system? After all, more recent organizations have used Athenian direct democracy as a model for their own decision-making processes, one of the better-known examples being the General Assemblies of the Global Occupy Movement in 2011.[5] Direct democracies are rare today, since most governments opt for representative and majoritarian rule: it only takes a simple majority of politicians to impose unpopular laws or a plurality of the vote to elect a divisive official. By contrast, ancient Greeks preferred consensus-based decision-making, effectively mandating that all citizens agree upon a proposal.[6] If no consensus emerged, then the Popular Assembly took suggestions, refined the measure in search of a more agreeable outcome, and put it to a majority-rule vote as a last resort. Greek democracy emphasized individual participation and collective deliberation, which the citizens found exhilarating. Athens' most famous politician, Pericles (495–429 BCE), noted how the people enjoyed the conversations, debates, and compromises that were central to its direct democracy. "Instead of considering discussion an impediment to action," he declared, "we regard it as a necessary preliminary to any reasonable action."[7] Politics did not take place "over there," where a handful of elected politicians did their thing, but "among us," where all citizens could participate.

The Athenian system was strengthened by various checks to ensure power-hungry men could not exploit loopholes to undermine the people's interests. Rather than electing officials who would become lifelong politicians with a vested interest in the system, the Athenian Constitution laid out a sortition procedure wherein magistrates were randomly selected to serve a one-year term. There was no need to campaign, since there was no election, and the term of office was too short to warrant the formation of political parties. A leatherworker had the same chance of becoming a politician as did an old-money aristocrat. Athenians also developed the legal process of "ostracism" through which it was possible to temporarily expel anyone who posed a threat to democracy. Once a year, Athenians could name someone they believed presented a danger to the city and if at least 6,000 citizens agreed, that person was banished for ten years. Many of these ballots survive to the present day, giving us a sense of why citizens thought someone should be ostracized. Athenians banished the general Themistocles around 471 BCE, with Greek historians citing his arrogance and accumulation of power.[8] Some of the surviving ballots provide a citizen's reasoning. "Themistocles, who loves money," "Themistocles, a pollutant in our land," or "Themistocles, on account of his reputation."[9] One ballot dispenses with any diplomacy: "Themistocles son of Neocles, huge asshole."[10] Ostracism served as a check on aristocratic efforts to rework Athenian laws in their favor. This system helped to ensure that the people determined the city's politics and prevented Athens from degenerating into a plutocracy.

And, to be sure, many influential men wanted to transform the city into a plutocracy. Consider the philosopher Plato (427–348 BCE), who had nothing good to say about Athenian democracy. Plato was an aristocrat who characterized democracy as a system in which the poor accumulated too much power and used it to punish the wealthy.[11] Plato lamented how the city's uneducated played as significant a role in governance as he did, that every citizen was free to do as they pleased, and that men of disparate social status were treated as equals. Heaven forbid! Plato wanted to replace Athenian democracy with a strong state grounded in a strictly stratified system that assigned people a role based on a single skill. Plato thought the government should regulate sexual relationships to develop a system of eugenics to maintain the purity of the guardian class and institute a monarchy that, unsurprisingly, was ruled by aristocratic philosophers like himself.[12]

Plato's criticisms were hardly unique. Aristocrats loathed democracy, consistently opposing the idea that common people should have meaningful political power. It was also they who produced the vast majority of literature in antiquity. Thucydides, Tacitus, Polybius, Cicero, and many others wrote about how democracy empowered the incompetent and spiteful masses. The voices of these aristocrats dominate the historical record. There are zero endorsements of Greek democracy in the written record. Every written text from the ancient world that discussed democracy was critical of it, consistently preferring some form of oligarchy.[13] But rather than take their criticism as grounds to discard democracy, we might interpret it in an opposing manner: although Athenian politics excluded many people and bore an imperialist inflection, *some* democratic potential must lie within it, given how much democracy's empowerment of the lower classes frustrated the wealthy.

This radical potential becomes clearer when one observes how Greek writers connected democracy with the word *anarchia*. Anarchy did not necessarily denote the disorder that the word colloquially means today. Rather, ancient Greeks used the word as a neutral term that referred to situations of leaderlessness: *an* + *archia* (without + leadership). For instance, the philosopher Aristotle (384–322 BCE) and the historian Xenophon (430–355 BCE) both described the years when Athens failed to elect a magistrate (*archon*) as a "year of anarchy."[14] When a Greek city-state did not have a recognized *archon*, it was anarchy, even if it was otherwise governed as usual. And even before then, the historian Herodotus (484–425 BCE) had used the word to describe a Persian cavalry unit whose commander died, rendering them leaderless; the soldiers cooperated perfectly well, making decisions collectively until they returned to the main camp.[15] Greeks tended to use the word *anarchia* in a value-neutral sense, often to designate peaceful times of leaderlessness.

Anarchy was not an inherently pejorative word for the people of Classical Athens. Only later did people associate the term with chaos. Even so, aristocrats took particular issue with the anarchistic aspects of democracy. Plato complained about how democracy encouraged people to bring anarchy into their households, leading them to equate democracy with liberty.[16] This love of egalitarian freedom was dangerous in Plato's mind, and he suggested that all children be taught to respect authority in order to prevent them from getting too comfortable with such freedom.[17] Plato did not think of anarchy as a distinctive variety of politics, but as a type of democracy.

It is this meaning of anarchy—cooperative leaderlessness—that is the radical idea behind this book. We will consider a range of people who not only dreamed of a better way to organize society but who made that dream a reality in how they lived and governed themselves. These were people for whom the anarchistic aspects of democracy were not impediments to be overcome, but sources of exciting possibility. There wasn't a single, universal cause that prompted all of these communities to form. Rather, people responded in diverse ways to the problems they faced. Some of these radical democracies emerged in deliberate opposition to the state (e.g., Cynics, Therapeutae, Cilician pirates), whereas others simply had limited contact with the state (e.g., Sámi). Sometimes this involved people creating new visions of alternative societies and in other cases people hearkened back to more familiar ways of life before the encroachment of imperial states.

This book concerns anarchist communities during classical and late antiquity. For our purposes, this refers to the regions surrounding the Mediterranean Sea from the first Olympic Games in 776 BCE until the fall of the Umayyad Caliphate in 750 CE, although our discussion sometimes extends to more distant peoples described in Greek and Roman literature. These groups ranged from communities of escaped slaves to religious sects living in isolation, and to large regions where people obstructed powerful empires. Some of these stories are well known, such as those of Spartacus and the Cynic philosophers. Others, such as those concerning the Therapeutae and the Mazdakites, may be less familiar.

Graeco-Roman Imperialism: Was There No Alternative?

Today, every inch of landmass on the globe is claimed by one or another nation-state. We often assume this is an entirely natural way of doing things. Sometimes, we even assume this is the *only* way of doing things. To tweak the phrasing of cultural theorist Mark Fisher, it is easier for most people to imagine the end of the world than to imagine the end of the state as a political institution.[18] Many people think the demise of the state would require an apocalypse of some sort, leading to Mad Max-style chaos in which everyone fends for themselves.

Despite the prevalence of these assumptions today, many people of antiquity found the state an encumbrance that could be readily discarded in favor of something more equitable and empowering. They recognized that the empires of the day held only a fraction of the power they claimed. Governments had little impact beyond the sight and earshot of state officials, and laws were difficult to enforce outside urban centers. These empires exerted minimal influence in rural and peripheral regions. Back then, governments had difficulty performing rudimentary functions such as introducing money to the economy, maintaining a basic quality of life, or preventing revolts. Life was remarkably free for anyone more than half a day's walk from a city. For most people, daily life didn't involve money, patrolling soldiers, lawcourts, bureaucrats, or meaningful consequences for flouting laws. The state's loose hold on the population suited some people better than others. Archaeologists have recovered dozens of letters written by moderately affluent people living in the Egyptian countryside, each petitioning a Roman military officer to intervene because of some perceived injustice—theft, violence, vandalism, and the like.[19] Often, these crimes were committed by the very soldiers that were supposed to protect them! No doubt those people would have preferred the state to provide greater oversight to ensure the security of their wealth.

Meanwhile, many people took the state's weakness as an opportunity to live more freely, doing so in defiance of the reigning empire. After the Roman emperor Diocletian (reigned 284–305 CE) restricted the autonomy of the North African provinces, inhabitants exploited legal loopholes to retain local independence. People living in the provinces of Numidia and Mauretania Caesariensis devised a system that allowed them to elect their own bishops, who in turn sheltered them from Rome's political abuse.[20] They leveraged the Christian Church to create semi-autonomous lawcourts that technically upheld Roman law, but whose rulings were issued by people chosen by the local population rather than the Roman magistrates. This was not exactly a secret: Africans erected monuments publicly announcing their defiance of imperial edicts and their bishops preached sermons that denounced Rome's abuse of laborers and debtors.[21] Of course, this wasn't quite the same as anarchy. Rather, these North Africans created a more democratic counter-state that outmaneuvered the Roman Empire. Ancient states' legitimacy was never entirely secure, even over lands that were a short voyage from the imperial capital. The

INTRODUCTION

Greek, Roman, and Persian empires struggled to impose their rule everywhere beyond their seats of power.

Under such conditions, it was nearly inevitable that autonomous societies would arise, both within and alongside formal empires. Various populations inhabited the lands that remained unclaimed by any state at all. For instance, the nomadic tribes of the Black Desert (stretching across modern-day Syria and Jordan) were largely herders who relocated their goats, sheep, and camels in annual cycles to areas most conducive to pasturing.[22] Their lives involved considerable freedom, as they were beholden to neither the Romans to their west nor the Parthians to their east. Rather than settling in one spot, this nomadic population sowed cereal grains and returned a year later to harvest. They developed expertise in astronomy and achieved a higher literacy rate than nearby empires. Though they occasionally raided settled populations for resources and sometimes acted as mercenaries, there is no indication that their daily lives involved any more violence than sedentary populations in neighboring empires. Particularly striking is the presence of Roman and Greek names (e.g., Titus, Claudius, Gregory) in their inscriptions. Evidently, some Romans preferred the nomadic life over the empire's purported "civilization."[23]

It is sometimes assumed that once a society is introduced to the concept of a state, the inhabitants will recognize its benefits as a matter of course, and develop statehood soon after. But this narrative is contradicted by the historical record. Anthropologist Pierre Clastres shows that even in our time, many supposedly "primitive" societies decisively reject this form of governance.[24] Such people are well acquainted with the state, but they know that states facilitate inequality and encroach upon communal democracy. In short, they recognize that adopting the state would impede their democracy, liberty, and happiness.[25] And the people of antiquity were no different, with many refusing the state to instead form societies lacking a market economy, social stratification, military surveillance, and centralized power structures. People said "no" to the state in sustained ways—whether that refusal arose from deep embeddedness in stateless institutions or from a preference for older ways of life that preceded state encroachment. Even the weak states of antiquity were too intrusive.

A Word of Clarification: Anarchy, Not Anarchists, Nor Anarchism

Throughout this book, the phrases "radical democracy" and "stateless society" serve as synonyms for the more provocative term "anarchy." To the extent that historians have discussed statelessness in antiquity, they have tended to focus on anarchists and anarchism. This book focuses on *anarchy*, meaning a condition of radical leaderlessness, in which the dominant political idea is that of communal democracy and autonomy.

This book does not discuss "anarchists." It generally avoids focusing on individuals, and rather it focuses upon groups, communities, and societies. This is partly because it avoids the "great man" variety of history—a way of narrating the past that emphasizes the achievements of and conflicts between a few great men, figures like Julius Caesar, Augustus, Leonidas, and so on. Great man histories assume that you can only understand why things happened the way they did by paying attention to a handful of important people with exceptional courage, leadership, or intellect. It is a way of telling history that essentially limits human agency to a few aristocratic

INTRODUCTION

men, and so is hard to reconcile with democratic principles.[26] This book will focus on the experiences of less well-known people, people like Erotis in the story above. Historians call this "history from below," an approach that centers the experiences of ordinary folk to the greatest extent possible. Thus, Chapter One discusses the thousands of anonymous slaves who revolted in the Third Servile War rather than the famed Spartacus. Many scholarly books discuss Spartacus, so rather than adding to an already extensive corpus, it might be more productive to reflect on what escaped slaves found attractive about the revolt and how they lived as a community. Such an approach will help us develop accounts about groups and communities that scholars of antiquity have neglected.

Because I am not focusing on "anarchists," this book will devote little space to individual anarchist thinkers. The philosopher Zeno of Citium (334–262 BCE) was a Stoic philosopher who urged people to follow their moral intuitions in the hope that it would render the state and its laws unnecessary. Unfortunately, all his writings have been lost, and what survives are a few quotations found in the treatises of later philosophers. Most important among Zeno's works was his *Republic*, where he described his political philosophy.[27] Peter Kropotkin summarized Zeno's politics with detectable admiration:

> [Zeno] repudiated the omnipotence of the State, its intervention and regimentation, and proclaimed the sovereignty of the moral law of the individual—remarking already that, while the necessary instinct of self-preservation leads man to egotism, nature has supplied a corrective to it by providing man with another instinct—that of sociability. When men

are reasonable enough to follow their natural instincts, they will unite across the frontiers and constitute the Cosmos. They will have no need of law-courts or police, will have no temples and no public worship, and use no money—free gifts taking the place of the exchanges.[28]

Zeno's ideal government had no laws, no philosopher-king, no military hierarchy, and no eugenics. Many philosophers have interpreted Zeno's *Republic* as an attack on Plato's utopia, which celebrated a state that verged on fascist totalitarianism.[29] It is easy to see why Zeno is an important figure within the history of anarchism, but he will play little role in our discussion of anarchy. Though Zeno's philosophy was practical, it remains in the realm of ideas as distinct from actions, practices, and communities.[30] Zeno never got to live in the stateless society that he imagined. Similarly, the philosophies of anarchist thinkers like Aristippus (435–356 BCE) and the Christian heretic Epiphanes son of Carpocrates (second century CE) sit outside the scope of this book.

This also means the book will not discuss fictional anarchies. The Roman poet Ovid (43 BCE–17 CE) speculated about humanity's golden age—a time when the only ruler was the god Cronos, who dwelled far off in the heavens.

> Golden was that first age which unconstrained,
> with heart and soul, obedient to no law,
> gave honor to good faith and righteousness.
> No punishment they knew, no fear; they read
> no penalties engraved on plates of bronze;
> no suppliant throng with dread beheld their judge;
> no judges had they then, but lived secure.[31]

INTRODUCTION

This "golden age" was glorious and much of that was because of its anarchistic qualities. Everyone could trust their neighbors, there were no rulers, there were no regulations or punishments, and there were few limits on a person's freedom. Ovid had much to say about how we fell from the comfort of this innocence into a life of toil and misery. But most ancient literature did not depict anarchy positively. Consider, for instance, the poet Homer's description of life among the cyclopes in *The Odyssey* (written in the eighth century BCE):

> They hold no councils, have no common laws,
> but live in caves on lofty mountaintops,
> and each makes laws for his own wife and children,
> without concern for what the others think.[32]

Although the absence of laws and governments might sound like freedom, the men unilaterally imposed rules on their families and showed indifference to their neighbors. This was not so different from Thomas Hobbes' characterization of life without government as "nasty, brutish, and short."

Ovid and Homer depicted states of anarchy, offering their tales in the shape of myth with no pretensions of historical accuracy. Numerous authors depicted fictional anarchies, some as utopias, others as dystopias.[33] Good or bad, these societies did not actually exist. In turning our attention away from fictional examples, this book will address one common critique of anarchism: that life apart from the state is either impossible or results in an everyone-for-themself society, as Homer described the cyclopes.

This book focuses on anarchistic communities. But this raises another question.

RADICAL ANTIQUITY

What Is "Anarchy"?

People use the word anarchy in very different ways. Since we are thinking about antiquity, it would be appropriate to consider how Greeks used the word to denote leaderlessness. This is not quite how most people understand the term today, as it usually refers to statelessness or non-hierarchical forms of governance. This book attempts to align ancient usage with more recent understandings of "anarchy." I would identify three characteristics common to such forms of governance: they were leaderless, were not modeled upon the state, and promoted a relatively egalitarian social order.

"Leaderlessness" refers to groups without a leadership structure capable of concentrating power in a handful of political offices. When discussing radical democracies, we should permit exceptions for ceremonial leadership and contextually limited power. This might include religious specialists, military commanders, and elders who transmitted knowledge. Although such people held some authority, their power remained formally limited and circumscribed. If someone was a military commander, they were not also a judge, a religious official, or a legislator. The reason for allowing such exceptions is simple: every society distributes power unevenly, but these groups decentralized authority, thereby limiting anyone's accumulation of power.

In refusing the model of the state, these groups structured power in a way that prevented their officials or governing councils from coercing others. Scholars distinguish between three types of power: persuasive power (the use of words to influence behavior), normative power (the use of social norms to influence behavior), and coercive power (the use of force to influence behavior). Whatever the mechanisms and processes these societies developed to govern themselves, they did not rely upon coercive power to compel behavior.[34] I would suggest that the decision to reject coercive power served as a rejection of the state itself, since the state's monopoly on violence has long been recognized as one of its essential characteristics. The sociologist Max Weber defined the state as "that thing which claims a monopoly on the legitimate use of physical force within a given territory."[35] The state not only wields this power coercively, but relies upon the perception that this is a legitimate means of enforcing behavior within its borders. Although many of these groups rejected state violence, we should not suppose that everyone mentioned in the following pages was a pacifist; in fact, very few were. This book explores democratic societies founded upon an aversion to coercive power. These were voluntary associations founded upon direct action.

Finally, the egalitarian social order that these societies instituted indicates that they tried, insofar as they were able, to create social forms which were free of hierarchy. Slavery, patriarchy, citizen-foreigner distinctions, plutocracy, and other inequalities were incompatible with these values. Within these communities, material resources (such as food and clothing) and symbolic resources (such as power and authority) were distributed in a manner that ensured a relatively non-exploitative social order. We might think of these groups as engaging in a prefigurative praxis—living out, in the present, the values that a group hopes will characterize the future—that helped prevent inequality from emerging within their various institutions. Egalitarianism is essential to this book's understanding of anarchy. The radical democracies discussed here implemented some form of mutual aid and created a classless society.

To summarize, throughout this book, radical democracy refers to any group that *was* leaderless, implemented measures to *remain* leaderless, and *valued* leaderlessness. The book advances a conception of democracy that has nothing to do with majoritarian voting or electing representatives, but everything to do with political systems that ensured freedom, the even distribution of power, a generally egalitarian atmosphere, and institutions that were open and responsive to the needs and desires of the populace. These were "horizontal" social arrangements that organized people in non-hierarchical ways, as opposed to the top-down structures that prevailed in most governments, workplaces, religious communities, and homes. The anarchistic principles mentioned above—decentralized authority, direct action, mutual aid, and a classless society—will be particularly useful in examining their values, practices, and self-understandings throughout this book.

This understanding of anarchy is intentionally vague, because it allows intriguing questions: How did these people live? How did people implement and preserve a non-hierarchical society? How did they relate to neighboring communities that did not live by these principles? How did they adapt to changing situations while retaining their commitment to leaderlessness? How might more recent history help us understand ancient groups? Rather than supposing these questions can all be answered with appeals to one or another grand theory, we can examine how different groups negotiated these exciting but challenging issues. We will see that governance varied significantly, arising from the specific combination of the group's needs and resources.

INTRODUCTION

Still, democracy remained available to those who seized the opportunity. These groups were radical. In using this word, I mean they operated with a mode of politics that did not seek to revise or reform the state, but to establish a new political order founded upon leaderlessness and egalitarian ideals. "Radical" overlaps with, but is distinct from "rebellion," which while also oppositional, is not necessarily animated by the same anarchistic politics.

We set off on this journey through antiquity to see if, in contrast to the main narrative of ancient "democracy," we can find evidence of radical lives, lived radically. The evidence is there. People, often under extreme pressure, found radical solutions to the question that faces all those who challenge power: if not me, then who? In answering that question, they found ways of living that empowered those who had been left out of the political regime and ensured that no one could appropriate the community for personal benefit. This book will offer a small taste of how various groups functioned, in the hope of fostering an appreciation of the wide range of ways people created communities, without presuming one is inherently preferable to another. Readers interested in more information about a given community can consult the section on further reading that concludes each chapter. Topics for group conversation can be found at the end of the book before the Subject Index.

With all that said, let us begin our tour of antiquity.

⚜ I ⚜

The Quest for Freedom: Spartacus and the Slave Community at Thurii

The name of the philosopher Epictetus (50–135 CE) translates into English as "acquired," a name given to him because he spent the first decades of his life as a slave. As a young man, Epictetus was enslaved to a wealthy freedman named Tiberius Claudius Epaphroditus who had himself been a slave of the emperor Claudius before Nero (Claudius' successor) freed him and hired him as a court secretary. When Epictetus was freed, he didn't choose a life of political intrigue the way his former master did, but pursued philosophy, which he had begun studying while still a slave. Epictetus is renowned today as one of the most influential philosophers of the Stoic school. Like other Stoics, Epictetus thought the key to living virtuously was understanding what we can and cannot control in the world around us. He determined that the only thing that we have true control over is our own mind—how we feel about things and how we think about the world. He concluded, for instance, that there is no benefit to feeling angry after our rival insults us. If we indulge in these feelings, we become complicit in our rival's provocations. But if we let go of our desire to control the uncontrollable, then we become profoundly free.[1]

It is easy to see why somebody who is enslaved might find it helpful to think about the world this way: although Epaphroditus legally possessed Epictetus' body as property and could command his slave to do as he pleased, Epictetus retained control of his own mind and thus considered himself free. Although he rarely mentioned Epaphroditus in his lectures, Epictetus appeared remarkably indifferent about his former master, expressing no resentment and mostly describing him as a man preoccupied with the wrong things in life: groveling to people he did not respect, sympathizing with the greedy, and being subjected to mockery.[2] Epictetus did not linger on any unpleasant feelings toward Epaphroditus, despite his low opinion of the man.

Epictetus is a rare example of a (former) Roman slave whose ideas have been well preserved and he occasionally expressed his thoughts about the institution of slavery itself. Slavery often functioned as a negative metaphor in his teaching—he discouraged people from being "enslaved" to the opinions of others, for instance. At one point, Epictetus used the runaway slave as a metaphor for the human quest for freedom. Epictetus noted how a slave fleeing her master depends only upon herself; she has no wealth and cannot count on others to find her freedom.[3] This was a remarkable way of making his point, since the metaphor implied sympathy for fugitive slaves. This might have made contemporaries suspicious that Epictetus harbored subversive politics—especially since he was a former slave himself. After all, escaped slaves faced the possibility of execution if apprehended and anyone harboring them received a punishment ranging from fines (for the wealthy) to corporal punishment (for the poor and non-citizens).

There is ample evidence of slaves fleeing their owners during antiquity. Archaeologists have discovered many "wanted" posters to aid the apprehension of escaped slaves from Graeco-

Roman Egypt. These posters bore written descriptions of the slaves who had fled. One such poster advertised a bounty for a fugitive slave named Horos, "who does not know how to speak Greek, a tall man, thinnish, clean-shaven, who has a scar on the left side of his head.... A weaver by occupation, he struts around arrogantly, speaking in a harsh voice. About 32 years old."[4] Whether Horos was apprehended or managed to achieve freedom is unknown: his wanted poster was found in an ancient garbage dump.

There were also slaves who sought freedom through violent means, even armed rebellion. Although slaves revolted numerous times, power-hungry leaders usually blunted the radical potential of these insurrections. Thus, rather than instituting an exciting new social order, these revolts often ended up with a slave claiming kingship and maintaining hierarchies similar to those that slaveowners had put in place. Things may have been a bit better for the slaves, but they still had another "lord" whom they had to obey.

One rebellion stands out against this tendency: the Third Servile War (73–71 BCE), initiated by a former gladiator named Spartacus. This revolt was noteworthy in its implementation of radical democracy, creating a society free of money, free of any true leader, and free of sexual violence. Rather than focusing on military combat between the escaped slaves and the Roman legions or the life of Spartacus himself, this chapter will offer a new reading of how the rebels governed themselves, during and after the rebellion, in the Italian city of Thurii (Italian in the sense that it is in both the Roman region of Italia and modern-day Italy). The daily life of the rebels deserves our attention, since they spent only a small portion of that period in combat. Free from the constraints of Roman society, how did these former slaves create a community that served their long-neglected needs?

* * *

Romans conceptualized slaves as distinct from freeborn people in numerous ways. Ancient writers thought that slaves were legally, socially, and even biologically different from the rest of the population. Crucially, slaves were also distinct from people who were merely poor. This is not to downplay their commonalities. Both slaves and the poor experienced physical violence, food scarcity, discriminatory treatment, legal restrictions, among other forms of abuse, but the legal and ideological distinctions between free and slave presented an insurmountable barrier to forming bonds of solidarity no matter how much their material and political interests converged. The Roman politician Tiberius Gracchus (163–133 BCE), famous for his demand that public lands be reallocated to poor Roman citizens, argued for this redistribution on the grounds that slaves were untrustworthy. He cited an ongoing slave revolt (the First Servile War, discussed below) as evidence that Rome would benefit from having freeborn citizens work upon and profit from public lands, rather than allowing the idle rich to hold these estates and force resentful slaves to perform this same agricultural labor.[5] Gracchus, a man lauded for his class consciousness among historians of the left today, was far from an abolitionist. He understood slaves as a liability to the flourishing of impoverished, but *freeborn*, Romans.

There was an inherent tension between the enslaved and the free, and slaves found creative ways of resisting their owners. This sometimes involved malingering—pretending to be ill. The Roman physician Galen (129–216 CE) wrote about a slave who rubbed his skin with a poisonous flower to create a rash to get some time off work, for example.[6] Others, like Horos noted earlier, fled their owners in hopes of living a life of freedom. Some even chose death over enslavement: around 250 CE, some 400 young captives on a ship drowned themselves to avoid being sold to Roman brothels.[7] Details of the voyage are slim, but when the Jewish children realized they were going to be sold into sexual slavery, they quickly agreed it was preferable to die by their own accord—first the girls gathered and leapt into the sea as a group, then the boys.

Violent acts of collective resistance, though, were much less common. As crucial as the slave–free status distinction was in Roman society, there is little evidence that slaves understood themselves as sharing much in common with each other. Keith Bradley observes that "there never developed among the slave population a sense of collective identity—or class consciousness."[8] We find virtually no calls for abolition in antiquity, whether by the free or the enslaved.[9] Although slaves were the primary participants in the three Servile Wars of the late Roman Republic, these wars were not fueled by a sense that slaves shared a common identity or even common interests.[10] The First Servile War (135–132 BCE) was led by a Syrian slave named Eunus, who claimed to be a prophet and who united thousands of agricultural workers (largely, but not exclusively slaves) across Sicily. The Second Servile War (104–100 BCE) also took place in Sicily, when the Roman consul reneged on his pledge to free slaves who had allied with Rome, which prompted confusion about which slaves were freed, leading to rebellion. The Third Servile War— the topic of the present chapter—began in the Italian city of Capua and mostly involved enslaved Gauls, Germans, and Thracians. That is, the First Servile War was fought by agricultural slaves, the Second by slaves whose freedom was revoked, and the Third was largely an ethnic rebellion. There was no sense that "all slaves" should unite as against the injustice of slavery.

Even in the context of "slave revolts," enslaved people apparently did not think of slavery as something inherently unjust. This was particularly evident in the slave revolt of Drimachus (third century BCE). After leading a rebellion on the Greek island of Chios near Turkey, Drimachus negotiated with local slaveowners and assured them he would only offer refuge to mistreated slaves—if Drimachus did not find an escaped slave's tale of abuse compelling, he sent them back to their owner.[11] There is no evidence that any of these rebellions sought the end of slavery. These were situational revolts that addressed specific injustices and drew together a small portion of the slaves in the region.

The community that emerged within the Third Servile War, alongside Spartacus, tried something different. This society of escaped slaves claimed safe harbor in (or near) the Italian town of Thurii. Despite some early conflict between the escaped slaves and the city's freeborn residents, they quickly found a way to live peacefully alongside each other. Rather than focusing on the tactics and battles of the Third Servile War itself, we will examine the radically democratic society these slaves created, and how those who did not see combat—women, children, disabled people, and those otherwise unwilling to fight—lived freely as part of this rebellion. For present purposes, "Thurii" serves as a shorthand for the slave community that emerged amid the Third Servile War.[12]

At Thurii, these former slaves imagined and put into practice a new political order, inaugurating a democratic way of life that prevented anyone from acquiring too much power within the community.

* * *

Though we might admire the courage of those who rebelled during the First and Second Servile Wars, the rebelling slaves created profoundly undemocratic structures. Indeed, their leaders created monarchic states of their own. Before Eunus instigated the First Servile War, he was a slave who entertained his owner's guests with fire-breathing, magic tricks, and oracles from the gods. Eunus told the more generous guests that he would reward them once he became king.[13] Those who attended these parties assumed Eunus was joking, but evidently he was serious: other slaves regarded him as a prophet and once the revolt commenced, Eunus crowned himself king and took the regnal name "Antiochus." The name Antiochus was common among Syrian royalty at the time and Eunus/Antiochus endeavored to create a state to rival Rome.[14] He implemented a legal system, including trials, and expected other slaves to swear fealty, with little distinction between him and his slave-kingdom.[15] Eunus/Antiochus also preserved the existing system of economic exploitation, as the rebels "neither burned slaveowners' houses nor destroyed their property and crops."[16] Eunus/Antiochus went so far as to ensure that the economy of Sicily remained monetized, even minting coins that proclaimed himself "King Antiochus" (see Figure 2). E. S. G. Robinson argues that Eunus/Antiochus' slave kingdom "was not a merely destructive or anarchical institution," but an effort to create a new state.[17] Although Robinson uses the word "anarchy" in the sense of "chaos," his

SPARTACUS AND THE SLAVE COMMUNITY AT THURII

argument also works with the meaning of the term in this book: this kingdom was far from leaderless. Eunus/Antiochus mostly continued business as usual, merely substituting his own monarchy for the Roman Republic.

The leaders of the Second Servile War attempted to do the same thing Eunus/Antiochus had. Salvius, who instigated the Second Servile War, also declared himself king and adopted the regnal name Tryphon, once again taking the name of a Syrian king.[18] Even after Salvius/Tryphon died in battle, the rebels chose a Cilician slave named Athenion as his successor. Both the First and Second Servile Wars revolved around the leaders' personal charisma and claims of supernatural knowledge: Eunus/Antiochus was regarded as a prophet, Salvius/Tryphon interpreted sacrificial entrails, and Athenion studied astrology.[19] These supposed connections to supernatural forces no doubt legitimized their claims.

Figure 2 Coin minted by Eunus/Antiochus (135–132 BCE). The obverse depicts the goddess Demeter–Atargatis, the deity who supposedly conveyed prophecies to Eunus/Antiochus. The reverse depicts a stalk of grain and reads in Greek (*not* the Roman language of Latin): "King Antiochus," which was Eunus' regnal name. The coin is a low-value bronze issue minted at Enna in central Sicily, a city known for its temple of Demeter. (Image by Christopher B. Zeichmann, after E. S. G. Robinson)[20]

Turning to the Third Servile War, Spartacus himself had been a Thracian warrior before the Roman legions captured him in battle and sold him to a gladiatorial school in the Italian city of Capua. Many other gladiators fought in the Third Servile War on the side of the rebels.

A gladiator's life was unpleasant. Injury was a matter of course and death was common. Daily routines involved military-style discipline that entailed grueling training regimens, unappetizing food, and little contact with any prospective romantic partners. The choice of captured warriors as gladiators had obvious benefits: the games were far more enjoyable if the combatants knew how to fight and these men were seasoned in battle. Gladiatorial games were a fairly recent innovation in Spartacus' day. Rome had identified them as an effective medium for conveying imperial ideology: the games featured the re-enactment of famous battles, provided a chance to parade and slay exotic animals captured by the legions, and cultivated a society where the death of foreigners became a matter of entertainment and even celebration. All of this encouraged the audience of Roman civilians to identify with imperial violence. The arena was a site of retribution, where a bloodthirsty audience applauded the humiliation of old foes, punishing them for daring to stand up to Rome's might. When people cheered for the execution of war captives through ritualized combat—hoping to witness foreign bloodshed in the arena as a memorial to their own greatness—they became profoundly Roman.[21]

The Third Servile War revealed the shortsightedness of enslaving foreign warriors for martial entertainment. When gladiators revolt, they might just prove an overwhelming force. And the gladiators at Capua proved more formidable

SPARTACUS AND THE SLAVE COMMUNITY AT THURII

than the legions expected. The rebellion grew quickly. Historians of the time disagreed on how many slaves participated in this insurrection: Eutropius and Livy said there were nearly 60,000 rebel soldiers in the final battle of the Third Servile War. Appian claimed it was twice that and Velleius Paterculus doubled Appian's number.[22] Ancient authors are notorious for embellishing figures, but the rebels' repeated military success suggests that their troops must have been considerable—we can safely suppose that several thousand escaped slaves fought in the rebel army. This was enough to rival a legion.

The community of escaped slaves at Thurii included thousands of enslaved women, children, and men who were unable to fight, but were nevertheless invested in the revolt. Although these particular rebels did not raise arms, they were integral to the community. The slaves even welcomed some freeborn civilians into the community.[23]

The Third Servile War lasted three years, sufficiently long for the rebels to create an alternative society, with its own political systems, values, rituals, and social life. Rome violently brought this revolt to its end in 71 BCE, but that did not mark a definitive end to the way of life the rebels had forged. Many fled and continued to live in isolated communities in the hinterlands of southern Italy for at least another decade.[24]

* * *

Ancient authors were uniformly hostile to the escaped slaves at Thurii, perhaps saving a few kind words for Spartacus' ability to mobilize such a motley crew.[25] The primary sources for understanding the Third Servile War and the community at Thurii were written across antiquity: Sallust (first century BCE), Livy (first century BCE), Diodorus Siculus (first century CE), Plutarch (second century CE), and Appian (second century CE) provide the earliest accounts. But these authors were neither neutral nor eyewitnesses. Some wrote hundreds of years after the war occurred and much of what they said was certainly fictional. When Roman historians wrote about Thurii, they usually limited their focus to the military aspects of the Third Servile War. Their writings offer only glimpses of daily life in Thurii and their histories reveal their contempt for the rebels. The historian Orosius wrote nearly 500 years after the Third Servile War, but he nevertheless felt strongly enough that his scorn for Spartacus is unmistakable. Orosius claimed that the rebels at Thurii not only raped a woman who then committed suicide in shame, but that they forced captive (but freeborn!) Romans to fight as gladiators at her funeral.[26] Orosius depicted Spartacus as the mastermind behind a terrifying society, where slavish tyrants did not respect venerable institutions that structured honor, but wielded their newfound authority with malice. For Orosius, the mock-gladiatorial games emasculated the Roman fighters: the funeral only took place because Roman citizens had failed to protect this woman and their unwilling participation in a gladiatorial game ridiculed a tragic moment.[27]

Orosius wanted to convince his readers that Spartacus was a dictator and that sadistic slaves were eager to torment freeborn Romans. To what extent should we take this account seriously? It is indeed plausible that the former slaves at Thurii appropriated imperial values for their own benefit, since systems of spectacular violence were deeply ingrained within Roman society. Certainly, other slave revolts were not immune to simple reversals of power, where the "oppressed became the oppressor." After all, Eunus/Antiochus created a new state

SPARTACUS AND THE SLAVE COMMUNITY AT THURII

during the First Servile War, maintaining the existing systems of exploitation, but freeing the slaves who recognized his royal claim. Eunus/Antiochus engaged in exactly this kind of violence, murdering freeborn men, women, and even infants in Sicily.[28] Or one might consider Drimachus, also mentioned above: his slave rebellion preserved the system of slavery, as he collaborated with slaveowners, merely asking that they treat their slaves a little better.

What about the Third Servile War? Even if literary accounts of cruelty at Thurii are plausible as hypotheticals, we have reason to doubt that Orosius' tale ever happened. Not only does his account of Thurii align suspiciously well with his biases against slaves, but it is unlikely that his shocking tale of rape and humiliation would be first told half a millennium later, if it had actually happened. If other historians had known about it, they certainly would have recounted it with similar fervor. The anecdote is plainly fictitious and, like most other ancient historians' tales about life at Thurii, is more akin to propaganda than reliable history. These texts reveal more about the aristocratic anxieties of their authors than about the lives of escaped slaves that they purport to tell.

What information about life within the community at Thurii can we extrapolate from such contemptuous texts? Oddly enough, it is helpful that Roman authors were so hostile to the slaves, since their testimonies show little evidence of romanticism. Given that our sources for the Third Servile War uniformly vilify the slaves, there is no reason to suppose that ancient authors were concocting flattering details. Once we rummage through these hostile sources, we arrive at three tentative insights about community life at Thurii: a ban on money, the absence of leadership, and a ban on sexual violence.

RADICAL ANTIQUITY

* * *

Let us start with how these former slaves did away with money and the accumulation of wealth. The Roman historian Appian declared that Thurii "prohibited merchants from importing gold and silver, nor would they allow soldiers to keep it from the loot," a detail that Pliny also mentioned.[29] Though Appian connected this ban on gold and silver with a preference for more militarily useful metals (iron and brass), there is reason to think that the prohibition on precious metals concerned something deeper. For instance, Appian observed that plunder was divided equally after battle and that "unnecessary goods" were discarded.[30] A collection of biographies known as the Historia Augusta similarly noted Spartacus' contempt for wealth.[31] The people at Thurii operated with a sense of financial value that appears to have been quite different from that of the Roman Republic.

The rebels were undoubtedly aware that they would never be reincorporated into Roman society. This was clear from the bloody suppression of the previous Servile Wars. In that case, why use money at all? Because the people of Thurii had no aspirations to create a state-like government, coinage and precious metals were no more practical than other tokens of exchange within the community. Since slaves were usually destitute and the community at Thurii was isolated from the rest of Roman society (legally, socially, ideologically, geographically, etc.), they concocted an alternate economic system.

Ancient writers offer little insight into Thurii's economy, but we can get a sense of how it worked.[32] Thurii's moneyless society differed from the kingdom of Eunus/Antiochus, which minted the coin depicted above (Figure 2).[33] When the people at Thurii rejected a monetized economy and prohibited precious metals, they were probably trying to do things differently from both the Roman Republic and the kingdom of Eunus/Antiochus. We might look to Graeco-Roman participation in the "military-coinage-slavery complex" to understand why.[34] This phrase refers to how military and economic systems were inextricably related to slavery in antiquity. The "Roman army" of the late Roman Republic is perhaps best understood as several distinct armies, each under the authority of one aristocrat or another. These aristocrats borrowed massive quantities of money to fund their personal military ventures, conquering foreign lands in the name of the city and paying the soldiers' wages out of their own pockets. In the process of such campaigns, these aristocrats typically accrued debt, which they repaid in one of two ways. The first was the sale of captives into slavery, ranging from foreign warriors, who would become gladiators, to women and children who would be sold to brothels. Human chattel was profitable and there was little that defeated populations could do about their own enslavement. The second way of dealing with debt was the transformation of metal plunder into coins.[35] Victorious armies pillaged valuables from foreign temples and the treasuries of wealthy individuals, smelting such artifacts and transforming them into official coinage. Captured slaves might also work in the gold, silver, and copper mines as captives to extract metal that could be minted as coinage.

Conquest and coinage were inseparable: the Achaemenid Empire invented the first coins in Persia so they could pay mercenaries (610 BCE).[36] Soon after, Greeks started minting coins for the same purpose (545 BCE); Romans used Greek coins for a few decades before creating their own system to fund their wars (323 BCE). Coinage spread slowly, and it was centuries before the use of coins was widespread. A system of coinage required massive loads of precious metals, mints to produce the coins, viable markets, and willful political administrations. This was a slow and uneven process—although coins may have been produced in any given region, populations often resisted adopting them as a medium of transaction. In fact, it was not until the end of the first century CE that coins were commonly used in all of Rome's provinces and, even then, people in rural areas continued to avoid cash.

People resisted coinage for many reasons, but particularly important was their awareness of how monetization exacerbated social inequality by facilitating the extraction of wealth, whereas exploitation proved much more difficult in non-monetized economies. This was because coinage presented an efficient way to transport large quantities of wealth, especially relative to most material goods. Before monetization, farmers tended toward subsistence agriculture, producing goods that they themselves consumed with little participation in broader economies. A given farm might produce enough dairy, wheat, and fruit for the family to remain largely self-sufficient. Even in lean years, neighbors could assist each other with little need for recourse to the market. Evidence suggests that farmers operated with informal systems of credits and favors. The peasant economy was structured around subsistence and the reciprocity of mutual aid. When subsistence farmers interacted with local markets for new clothes or tools, the value of these goods may have been calculated in monetary terms (denarii or drachmas), but people nevertheless tended to exchange via credit and gift: if a farmer needed to rent a backhoe from a neighbor, he might spare some surplus grain, write an IOU, or simply call in a favor.[37] Renters even paid their leases with livestock and grain.[38]

Landlords and the government both preferred that peasants pay their rent, debts, and taxes with cash. This is because the wealthy found it impractical to collect payment "in kind"—that is, paying with harvest (e.g., grain, fruit, oil) rather than money. Transporting large quantities of harvest was incredibly inefficient even over short distances, as the need to feed any beast of burden transporting produce could render it a zero-sum enterprise: the heavier the load and the further from the storage silo, the more often cattle needed to rest and consume the very grain that they were transporting.[39] In rural areas, tax collectors traveled unpaved roads to collect cumbersome loads that lost value the further they trekked. All this rendered tax evasion relatively easy in rural areas, especially those off the trodden path: there was little reason for tax collectors to bother stopping by if it was unprofitable. Coinage was far easier to collect and required only a purse to transport it. Considering how money worsened life for everyone but the rich, we might think of the ban on precious metals and equal division of spoils at Thurii as an effort to mitigate inequality—these measures prevented too much wealth (and the accompanying social power) from accumulating in anyone's hands.

In their former lives as slaves, the people at Thurii experienced firsthand the dehumanizing effects of money, since they had been assigned a precise monetary value and sold as chattel on the market. Beyond this, many had seen the process of monetization and its effects in their earlier lives. Shortly before the Third Servile War, the Thracian government not only imported Roman denarii in massive quantities, but convinced the occupying Roman power to construct mints to produce coinage in Thrace.[40] Rather than introducing small denomination coins that could have been used for daily purchases, Romans and their Thracian puppet kings injected high-value coinage into the economy. The coins' exorbitant value made them suitable only for aristocratic status rituals: elaborate gift-giving, dowries for royal weddings, and so on. Thracian coinage was intended less for spending and more as something akin to extravagant jewelry—useful for a public ostentatious display of wealth and power. Coinage served a similar function in Gallia. The Gallic chieftain Lovernius (second century BCE) would ride through the fields in his chariot and scatter gold and silver among the crowds following him.[41] Most of the slaves in the Third Servile War were either Thracian or Gallic, so even before they were enslaved they had experienced monetization as a form of showboating—often by their native leaders who reaped the benefits of their alliance with Rome. The slaves' distaste for coinage was understandable. The ancient Gauls and Thracians saw through such transparent efforts at purchasing loyalty and subservience. The majority of slaves in the Third Servile War were from Gallia and Thrace—many of them had witnessed these incidents with their own eyes.

Thurii's ban on precious metals and money resulted from a mix of necessity, practicality, and political ideology. The prohibition on the private ownership of valuables indicates that precious metals were used for strictly public gain at Thurii, especially since they traded such goods away to traveling merchants. Those living at Thurii were prohibited from possessing valuables that might enable them to exert influence over other community members, but merchants—who had no lasting connections to the rebels at Thurii—continued to participate in the market economy. Practical commodities were kept and used, but loot that was toxic to the group's egalitarian ambitions was traded away. This arrangement made a great deal of sense, given the lack of trust between the two parties. Merchants understandably regarded this community, consisting of Rome's declared enemies, as a risky bet for a long-term investment. They were surely aware that merchants who had been holding unspent coins (or IOUs) of Eunus/Antiochus felt like fools after Rome suppressed the First Servile War, since the money became worthless. Likewise, the former slaves at Thurii probably knew they were easy to take advantage of and wanted to avoid trading away anything necessary for survival.[42] In a situation where there was little trust, precious metals—plunder that was outlawed within Thurii, but valuable everywhere else and thus attractive to merchants—provided a viable medium of exchange.

This leads us to the second point: that Thurii was an anarchist society in the most literal sense of the word—there was no formal leader. To the extent that Spartacus led the community at Thurii, evidence suggests it was in two capacities: as an instigator of the revolt and as one among several military commanders. Spartacus never took on the role of a king (unlike Drimachus, Eunus/Antiochus, Salvius/Tryphon, or Athenion), nor is there any indication that he acted as a political leader. No ancient accounts give us serious reason to think that Thurii operated with a mode of governance that required a head of state. Instead, all evidence suggests that the community was leaderless outside of battle.

One might object that military leadership most certainly is a form of leadership, with generals sitting atop an authoritarian command structure. But here, the idea of "justified leadership" within radical democracies may prove helpful. Anthropologists characterize justified leadership as the *power to* organize people who voluntarily follow, as distinct from inherent *power over* other people.[43] Justified leadership is voluntarily accepted, situational, and limited to specialist expertise. For instance, a professional electrician practices justified leadership when instructing an apprentice about how to wire a complex motor; likewise, a conductor leading an orchestra. In each case, people voluntarily recognize the authority of the "leader," within strict contextual limits. Musicians have no reason to defer to their conductors' demands in other situations. Spartacus and the other generals had power, but this was simply the power to command the military action of the rebels who willingly took up arms. They did not hold any inherent authority over others at Thurii.

Ancient authors give no reason to think that the people at Thurii used coercive power in their institutions. There is no evidence of a court system that might punish those who committed crimes. It seems that life at Thurii permitted considerable freedom, and perhaps it should be self-evident why former slaves wanted to live with such liberty. The exceptions to this freedom were a few prohibitions that ensured that no one accumulated enough power to bend the community to their will—what anthropologists call "leveling mechanisms" that preserve egalitarian structures.

It requires considerable effort to ensure that non-hierarchical societies remain that way, and communities thus often develop leveling mechanisms as rituals to preserve their egalitarianism. Perhaps the most famous example comes from anthropologist Richard Borshay Lee's encounter with the !Kung people in southern Africa during the 1960s. Lee hoped to celebrate Christmas with his !Kung friends and brought them a large, meaty ox for a feast. But upon seeing the animal, they proceeded to mock Lee's gift, despite his great pains to acquire it. They complained that the ox was thin, old, and no more than a "bag of bones," insulting the beast to Lee's face. Needless to say, Lee was taken aback and asked his !Kung friend Tomazo why his gift was being ridiculed. Tomazo responded that Lee's gift was arrogant:

> When a young man kills much meat, he comes to think of himself as a chief or a big man, and he thinks of the rest of us as his servants or inferiors. We can't accept this. We refuse one who boasts, for someday his pride will make him kill somebody. So we always speak of his meat as worthless.[44]

The !Kung diligently undermined anyone's effort to exert power over others within the community. The former slaves at Thurii had similar concerns about people with ambitions of power and so imposed leveling mechanisms to ensure their community remained devoid of coercive power. The !Kung used a reactive ritual to ensure the playing field remained level; we have seen that by prohibiting money and wealth, the people of Thurii opted for a more preventative approach. How they implemented these prohibitions is entirely unclear, but nothing in the record suggests that they were drafted by a representative legislature or imposed by a head of state. One presumes, however tentatively, that they made decisions with an informal consensus, since the rebels otherwise agreed on foundational matters of civil society.

All of this casts Spartacus' role in a new light. Although he instigated the revolt, Spartacus held equal standing with the other generals (Oenomaus, Crixus, Gannicus, and Castus) in the rebels' military command.[45] They focused their military efforts on distinct geographic areas independently of each other, forming a confederation of distinct escaped slave communities and armies. Ancient writers attributed nearly everything done by the community at Thurii to Spartacus himself. But this was typical of Graeco-Roman historians' chauvinism—as a rule, ancient historians regarded common folk as devoid of agency and unworthy of interest. Plutarch, for instance, depicted Spartacus as a leader in the vein of Graeco-Roman aristocrats, albeit one who fell into slavery by tragic happenstance: "He not only possessed great spirit and strength, but he was more intelligent and nobler than his fate, and he was more Greek than his Thracian background might indicate."[46] These historians were simply explaining away their military defeats at the hands of foreign-born slaves: the Romans had such a hard time dealing with the revolt because Spartacus was Greek *in spirit*, if not ethnicity. This fixation on Spartacus' greatness allowed Romans to reassure themselves that the slaves only found success because of his individual genius, not because slaves might have been capable. In most instances, when ancient texts say that "Spartacus did such and such," they usually deploy his name as shorthand for the rebelling slaves. We might therefore read many of the accounts that focus on Spartacus as discussions of the people at Thurii more broadly. Spartacus' duties appear to have been limited to commanding one of the rebel armies and acting as a spokesperson in negotiations with outside parties.

SPARTACUS AND THE SLAVE COMMUNITY AT THURII

What did Thurii's radical democracy entail? What exactly did non-combatant escaped slaves do? Thurii was a complex society. Ancient texts indicated the different roles slaves played: gladiators served in the military, some women served as priestesses, weavers crafted useful implements like baskets and makeshift shields, and former agricultural slaves sustained the community's food supply. No doubt there were many others—Roman slaves had a wide range of skills, from acting to writing to crafting wares. One can only assume that they were also eager to contribute to the democratic experiment at Thurii.

We can get a sense of the kind of society that they wanted to create when we consider the prohibition of sexual violence, the third aspect of community life at Thurii. Of course, the rebels were willing to use physical violence in combat. All sources not only speak to the armed insurrection, but many rebels' enslavement as gladiators before the revolt—sometimes hinting that they were warriors before being apprehended as war captives. But according to Sallust, the earliest source for the Third Servile War, Spartacus prohibited sexual violence, even in the context of battle.[47] This is quite striking, since sexual violence was a regular part of warfare at the time. In the Greek and Roman empires, conquering armies sexually violated civilians. The Roman historian Tacitus described the scenes at the Second Battle of Bedriacum (69 CE): "Whenever a young woman or a handsome youth fell into soldiers' hands, they were torn to pieces by the violent struggles of those who tried to secure them."[48] This violence was so common that people not only assumed it occurred as a matter of course, but publicly announced such in imperial artwork.[49] Consider one sculpture discovered at Aphrodisias in modern

43

Turkey (Figure 3). It depicts the emperor Claudius preparing to deliver the coup-de-grâce upon a woman whose clothes have been torn off. The position of their bodies implies that Claudius had either just raped her or was about to before killing her. The sculpture's base reveals the woman's identity: Britannia, a personification of the British people. Claudius had conquered Britannia in 43 CE and the statue announced the treatment his forces meted upon the civilians who resisted his might. A few years later, Romans erected a similar sculpture in that same city, this one depicting the emperor Nero and the personification of Armenia. Rome had conquered both Thrace and Gaul shortly before the Third Servile War, so many inhabitants of Thurii either witnessed sexual violence or experienced it personally as a part of the conquest that led to their enslavement.

Rape was a common experience for slaves. The Roman writer Seneca the Elder offered a maxim: "Sexual depravity is a crime for the freeborn, a duty for the freedman, and a necessity for the slave."[50] Although sexual misdeeds were punishable crimes for Roman citizens, former slaves were expected to show their gratitude to their former masters by submitting to their advances, and slaves were required to satisfy the sexual urges of their owners. In one Roman work of fiction, an attendant reminds a love-struck slaveowner, "You are her master, with full power over her, so she must do your will whether she likes it or not."[51] The idea that masters were entitled to use their slaves for sexual pleasure was pervasive in antiquity.[52] While Roman writers did not characterize intercourse with slaves as "rape," they nevertheless acknowledged that the consent normally required for morally acceptable intercourse did not apply to slaves and captives (whose enslavement was

Figure 3 Claudius preparing to kill Britannia (50–65 CE). The emperor Claudius (reigned 41–54 CE) is partially dressed as a soldier, but is mostly naked in a "heroic nude" style. He stands over Britannia, the personification of the region, who is stripped of her clothing. The relief commemorates Claudius' military victory in Britannia and its annexation to the Roman Empire. The statue was erected in the Asian city of Aphrodisias, located in present-day Turkey. (Photograph by Steve Kershaw)

imminent). Slaves, especially women and young people, were common targets of sexual violence. It makes sense then that sexual abuse was a concern for the people at Thurii, given their experience of rape in their former lives as slaves and as witnesses to Rome's wars.[53]

These three features of life indicate that the former slaves at Thurii experimented with a radical mode of living.[54] This is quite the contrast from the First and Second Servile Wars, during which various slave-kings implemented monarchic states that offered only modest liberties to the escaped slaves, expecting them to remain subservient to leadership. The escaped slaves at Thurii experimented with a social system that was designed precisely to impede the accumulation of power:

1) the absence of a monetized economy and prohibition of precious metals prevented an uneven distribution of material resources;
2) its political system indicated no head of state or formalized leadership other than situationally limited cases requiring specialized skills (e.g., military command, trade negotiations, religious rituals); and
3) the prohibition on sexual violence freed people from one of the most frequent abuses they had experienced as slaves.

The resulting picture is striking. People, having been kidnapped and enslaved, created their own society, one that actively impeded the unequal distribution of power. This might be contrasted with the supposed equality of Roman democracy, which only enfranchised the small portion of the population which were citizens. The community at

SPARTACUS AND THE SLAVE COMMUNITY AT THURII

Thurii regarded the experiences of those whom these states excluded—women, slaves, and foreigners—as the building blocks of their civic order, developing a social system that prevented the emergence of the very exploitations that hindered their participation in Roman society.

* * *

The former slaves at Thurii developed their society in deliberate contrast with the Roman Republic. Let us imagine, for a moment, what a couple of days of life there might have looked like, perhaps a few months into the rebels' occupation of the city. A couple of days after Spartacus and his soldiers returned from a battle against the legions, bloodied but victorious, the community had an opportunity to survey their spoils. The army's haul included high-quality armaments seized from the legionaries, but also culinary delicacies and luxury goods left behind when the merchant caravan absconded. All of this was welcome, since the Roman steel provided much-needed replacements to the makeshift swords and shields that the rebels had been using. Let us imagine this was the day the former slaves celebrated their military victory: the priestesses of Dionysus offered sacrifices of gratitude at their altar, with the aroma of roasting meats and incense filling the neighborhood. Thick clouds rose into the sky, the priestesses' fingers tracing spirals in the air, while they chanted in low, rhythmic tones. One closed her eyes and started trembling, her voice rising in prophecy—a warning, perhaps, or a blessing—her words were difficult to decipher. This ritual was followed by a communal meal and dance, where everyone in town was welcome, including the freeborn population who lived in Thurii before the rebels had arrived. The quality of the food and music rivaled that of a senator's banquet: most cooks and musicians were slaves, after all, and their expertise was plentiful at Thurii. The same could be said of many other occupations: physicians, educators, metalworkers, artisans, actors, accountants, etc. All in all, life was remarkably comfortable, once people settled into a rhythm of sharing their skills.

We can further imagine that a handful of recently escaped slaves arrived at Thurii the next morning, bringing several carts of wheat they had stolen from their former master. The community welcomed them, but called a public meeting to discuss what to do with the grain. These meetings adapted a system suggested by some Germanic slaves, based on their traditions: a public assembly in which all were invited, proposals were taken, and something approaching consensus was required to implement a given plan—all of this being moderated by the priestesses. Three options gained traction in this particular assembly: sowing the grain now, trading it to merchants, or preparing it for bread production. There was disagreement about the total grain required for the upcoming winter, so the assembly decided to reconvene in a few days. The freeborn residents of Thurii watched from the periphery of the meeting, finding the proceedings a bit confusing: these assemblies had little in common with the legislative bodies they were familiar with, lacking both the formality of the Roman Senate and the aristocratic charisma showcased within city councils. Why didn't Spartacus simply dictate policy? He clearly held everyone's respect, yet no one was deferential toward him. The freeborn locals also noticed how the slaves put a peculiar emphasis on the process of decision-making itself. It was definitely a time-consuming way of doing things, but it had many benefits. Even the people who didn't get what they wanted left the meeting with their honor intact and unlikely to harbor grudges. As the evening drew to a close, some residents noticed distant lights upon the sea: news of their victory had spread and merchant ships neared Thurii's port, eager to take the gold, silver, and other valuables off their hands the following morning. The timing could not be better: weeks earlier, the assembly decided that upcoming trades should prioritize the acquisition of construction materials; hundreds of escaped slaves from nearby villages had found refuge at Thurii in the past few weeks. In short, the city's current population was starting to exceed its capacity.

In imagining this scenario, we should not suppose that Thurii was a utopia. Historians reported human sacrifice.[55] Menstruating women were kept apart from everyone else. The community was always vulnerable to attack: the Roman army pursued the rebel slaves, and outside forces took advantage of them. Pirates, for example, claimed they would help spread the revolt to Sicily by transporting some of Thurii's rebels to the island for a fee, only to abscond with Thurii's down payment.[56] It was a precarious existence that relied upon occasional raiding to acquire resources that they could not produce on their own. Like many other radical communities in antiquity, the people at Thurii were subject to much slander by ancient historians. Even so, we might take seriously the radical ideas that proved foundational to their society, how they lived as though they were already free.

Further Reading

Schiavone, Aldo. 2013. *Spartacus*. Translated by Jeremy Carden. Harvard: Harvard University Press.

Shaw, Brent. 2001. *Spartacus and the Slave Wars: A Brief History with Documents*. Boston: Palgrave.

Strauss, Barry. 2009. *The Spartacus War*. New York: Simon and Schuster.

Urbainczyk, Theresa. 2008. *Slave Revolts in Antiquity*. London: Acumen.

Brent Shaw's book translates nearly all ancient texts discussing the Third Servile War and other slave revolts of Roman antiquity into English—reading what Appian, Sallust, and others wrote would be helpful to anyone interested in the Third Servile War. Barry Strauss' book is well considered, even if he argues that Spartacus was not a "political" figure. More willing to interpret Spartacus as a man invested in democracy is Aldo Schiavone, who does so convincingly. Spartacus has been a beloved figure in popular culture, though this has rarely translated into interest in the community that emerged around him—these are almost invariably "great men" versions of history. That said, Theresa Urbainczyk compares slave revolts across Graeco-Roman antiquity with compelling insights.

2

Communities of Jewish Radicalism: The Therapeutae and the Essenes

Patriarchy, like slavery, was so integral to life in antiquity that few people conceived of a world without it. Tales about the death in the second century CE of Beruriah, a Jewish woman who was a scholar of the Torah, reveal much about the pervasive sexism of the time.[1] Although most ancient rabbis extolled Beruriah's devotion to Judaism, some saw her femininity as a liability. In what is certainly an apocryphal tale—the earliest account was not written until nearly a millennium after she lived—one author wrote about her death:

> Once Beruriah mocked how the sages said "Women are flighty." Her husband, Rabbi Meir, said to her, "By your life! You will eventually concede the correctness of their words." To make his point, he instructed one of his disciples to seduce her. The disciple flirted with her for many days, until she slept with him. When she became aware of the deception, she hung herself, while Rabbi Meir fled the region in disgrace.[2]

In a perverse effort to prove to his wife that women lacked men's steadfast wisdom, Rabbi Meir convinced one of his students to seduce Beruriah, culminating in her suicide. Historians agree this did not happen, but the existence and circulation of the story indicates how well-educated women inspired anxiety in many men. According to this misogynistic tale, even women as devout and intelligent as Beruriah were susceptible to their feminine passions;[3] a wise man should never trust any woman.

This chapter will consider the Therapeutae (in Egypt) and the Essenes (in Judaea), two Jewish sects that took on patriarchy in different ways. The Therapeutae and the Essenes renounced the ownership of slaves, private property, and even the comforts of life to create a relatively egalitarian community conducive to theological reflection. To do so, both groups moved away from the city, where they could organize themselves more democratically. Surviving evidence about these communities is limited, so we cannot definitively say when they were founded or when they folded, but it is clear that they flourished during the first century CE. Particularly interesting, though, were their wildly different approaches to confronting patriarchy. The Therapeutae segregated men and women but ensured equality, whereas the Essenes entirely prohibited women from their community. At first glance, neither of these appears particularly consistent with gender equity, let alone anarchy: the Therapeutae's approach invites comparison with America's racist "separate but equal" policies and the Essenes could be understood as creating an exclusionary patriarchy. This chapter suggests that both groups challenged chauvinism, albeit in distinct ways. Let us begin with overviews of these groups before considering their unique approaches to gender, as these groups are best understood in contrast with each other.

* * *

If it is difficult to say much about the escaped slaves at Thurii because ancient authors denigrated them, then the Therapeutae present a challenging case for inverse reasons: only one ancient text even mentions them (Philo of Alexandria's *On the Contemplative Life*, written 41 CE) and that text is so effusive in its praise that its reliability is questionable.[4] Despite some apprehensions, historians agree that the Therapeutae were Jewish philosophers living along the northwestern shore of Lake Mareotis, about ten miles away from the Egyptian metropolis of Alexandria. Lake Mareotis was sufficiently far from the city that few passersby bothered them, but not so far that those interested could not find them. Their name, "Therapeutae," was a Greek term meaning "the attendants (of god)" or "the healers."[5] Life among the Therapeutae involved the intense study of Jewish scripture and the elimination of worldly distractions.

The Therapeutae lived in isolation from the outside world. Newcomers renounced all their property and abandoned relationships with parents, spouses, and siblings, but when they joined, they received their own home within a new community. These houses were humble; adherents were expected to live frugally, focusing their lives on divine wisdom rather than material pleasures. Community members contributed to meals consisting of basic staples like bread and salt, while many Therapeutae fasted as an act of religious devotion. Prayer, philosophical meditation, and the composition of hymns to their God were regular parts of the schedule. Central to all of this was a sophisticated reading of scripture, interpreting it as a symbolic tale about the divine principles at work in nature. For instance, they believed that when the Torah discussed Jewish customs of cleanliness (e.g., kosher diet, objects to avoid touching, how to worship), what looked like rituals were in fact allegories for how to clean the human soul.[6] Therapeutae typically studied the Bible in solitude, but community members gathered for a robust philosophical discussion weekly. In such meetings, comprehension was prioritized, rather than efforts to impress one another—clear communication was preferable to dazzling others with a novel interpretation.[7] These discussions cultivated relationships of intense listening intended to deepen the community's philosophical habits and nourish one's soul. The number seven was significant within Jewish theology; every seventh week, the community engaged in a symposium that combined theological discussion and frugality. Though abundant wine was a cornerstone of Roman philosophical symposia, the Therapeutae thought the intoxicating effects of alcohol disrupted their inner clarity. They instead drank water while they conversed and celebrated their God.

The group hierarchy—a concept at odds with leaderlessness—wasn't much of a hierarchy at all, since they had no centralized authority. The longer that someone had been a member of the Therapeutae, the earlier they could speak at the symposia, and they were served food sooner when dining. Notably, this did not correspond to someone's age: if someone was 50 years old but a new initiate, they could proffer their insights only after a 30-year-old who had been in the community for several years. There were other traditions which suggest that the Therapeutae's social structure did not concentrate power or authority. For instance, serving meals was considered an honor, but they also preferred that newer members have this opportunity, should they desire it. The Therapeutae were intensely critical of power discrepancies. Perhaps most telling was their reason for prohibiting slavery: they declared that inequality (*anisoteta*) was the root of all evil.[8]

COMMUNITIES OF JEWISH RADICALISM

The Therapeutae's commitment to leaderlessness was apparent in their housing customs. Group members lived in identical homes. These were arranged in a circular formation. No one resided in the center of this settlement and each house was devoid of adornment that might indicate the prominence of its resident. This setup contrasted with typical urban planning of the time, in which neighborhood designs tended to emphasize or consolidate status. Travel and guest–host relations were inseparable from the social dynamics of power and prestige. Who visits whom? And how might the resulting center and periphery reinforce the distribution of power? In the city of Rome, neighborhoods consisted of concentric circles, where the wealthy lived at the center and their dependents lived at a distance corresponding to their diminishing importance.[9] The wealthy thus maintained their power and status by being centrally located in relation to the retinue of clients who sought them out—these aristocrats were eager to be seen as important people whom those of lower status traveled to visit.[10] Conscious of how power maps onto spatial arrangements, the Therapeutae placed their houses in a circle to mitigate against social hierarchies. No one's home was more accessible or important than anyone else's.

* * *

The Essenes were contemporaries of the Therapeutae and the two sects had much in common. Both groups banned private possessions, practiced pacifism, prohibited slavery, shared their property, and lived as a relatively isolated community.[11] Like the Therapeutae, the Essenes spent a great deal of time worshiping the Jewish deity. And we can catch a better glimpse into the community life of the Essenes than we can the Therapeutae. The Essenes adopted a democratic process for decision-making, wherein its adherents elected the people to handle finances and they probably voted on important matters as well—quite the contrast to the kings and imperial governors ruling Judaea at the time.[12] Philo (20 BCE–50 CE) emphasized Essene collectivity: "They live together in the same place, making clubs and societies, agreements with each other, and keep the good of the community in mind with everything they do."[13] Essenes had two options for work: they could do volunteer labor directly within the community or they could seek employment in nearby villages for pay. Those employed outside the community handed over their wages to the treasurer, who pooled their resources to purchase life's necessities.[14] This led to a humble life, devoid of luxury: Essenes ate plain bread and drank only water at their meals. Their lives were peaceful, as they prohibited the forging of weapons and armor within their community.

Our knowledge about the Essenes derives from three ancient historians, Philo, Pliny the Elder (24–79 CE), and Flavius Josephus (37–100 CE).[15] Philo and Josephus were both Jewish, so their accounts offer far greater detail and show familiarity with the rituals and customs of the Essenes. Contrary to popular belief, Essenes were probably not responsible for writing the Dead Sea Scrolls, a collection of Jewish texts found at Qumran in the West Bank in 1946. While many scholars have sought to harmonize the Scrolls with the testimonies of Philo, Josephus, and Pliny on the Essenes, there are major discrepancies between ancient accounts of the Essenes and what the Dead Sea Scrolls reveal about their authors. For instance, "the Copper Scroll" found at Qumran is a treasure map for gold and silver stockpiles, which is hard to reconcile with Essene frugality. Further, the Dead Sea Scrolls never actually use the word "Essene," instead referring to their own group as Yachad, a Hebrew word meaning "community." The authors of the Dead Sea Scrolls indicated that they owned and traded slaves, contrasting with Philo's insistence that there was "not a single slave" among the Essenes.[16] The Dead Sea Scrolls were discovered at a military fortress, which contradicts all evidence that the Essenes were pacifists. Ancient writers declared that the Essenes remained celibate, whereas the Dead Sea Scrolls indicate that members of Yachad married. These and other factors have led some scholars to doubt that Essenes composed the Dead Sea Scrolls.[17]

The Essenes present further complications for historians. Doron Mendels argues that Josephus and Philo were both influenced by utopian fiction when they depicted the Essenes, calling into question the reliability of their accounts.[18] Mendels notes the remarkable parallels between descriptions of the Essenes and Iambulus' (third century BCE) mythical "Islands of the Sun," allegedly located off the eastern coast of Africa, near the equator. Iambulus' depiction of the island featured in a novel that narrated the author's fictitious journey to a long-lost island inhabited by an idyllic community: the people living on the Islands of the Sun shared property, owned no slaves, ate meals in common, and dressed identically.[19] Josephus and Philo attributed these same features to the Essenes, which might cause some concern about their depictions also being fictional. But there were even more bizarre things about the island, which is where it becomes clear that Iambulus wrote a myth, not a travelogue: the islanders had forked tongues, which allowed them to carry on two conversations simultaneously. They also verged on immortality, living 150 years and died only because they committed ritual suicide at that age. And this is not to mention the environmental wonders and bizarre animals with multiple heads that were also found on the island. That is to say, the Islands of the Sun fit well with the sort of fantastical geography that people associated with the edge of the known world, places where mapmakers might write, "Here be dragons."

It is clear that the Essenes formed a real historical community. First off, Josephus, Philo, and Pliny drew upon distinct sources of information; they did not copy each other or use the same sources. This means there are three independent witnesses to the Essenes' existence, which are broadly consistent in their depictions. Second, there is nothing particularly incredible about their portrait of the Essenes, unlike Iambulus' islanders: the Essenes were Jewish sectarians (rather than long-lost people) living in a well-known region (rather than lost islands) with normal human bodies (rather than being nearly immortal and having forked tongues). Third, we might also observe the literary genre: Iambulus wrote in the mode of fiction, unlike the ethnography of Josephus, Philo, and Pliny.

There were also social differences between the Essenes and the fictional inhabitants of the Islands of the Sun. Foremost among these was the question of hierarchy and inequality. Iambulus claimed that the islanders governed through a number of micro-monarchies based on age: the patriarch of each clan acted as a king who required strict obedience. The Essenes, by contrast, denounced inequality (*isoteta*) as an injustice.[20] Equality was so important to the Essenes that they developed numerous customs to prevent anyone from consolidating power, such as eliminating private property and using standardized clothing. Though uniform clothing can stifle expression and creativity, it served as a status equalizer for the Essenes. Then as now, clothing could entrench status inequalities: people exhibit their status through clothing.[21] Clothing was also a means of social differentiation within the Roman Empire, since the color of someone's toga reflected their age, rank, and even convict status.

* * *

The Therapeutae and the Essenes were remarkably similar in their contempt for hierarchy.[22] Another commonality would include their asceticism—a lifestyle that discourages worldly pleasures, typically in favor of spiritual concerns. Asceticism can be an effective means of resisting the powers-that-be. Religious studies specialist Richard Valantasis describes asceticism as a set of practices intended to bring about "an alternative culture, to enable different social relations, and to create a new identity."[23] Ascetics develop this alternative identity in distinction from prevailing norms. People are often encouraged to enjoy certain activities, such as nice food, new clothing, sexual intercourse, the company of others, and physical comfort, but if someone rejects the prevailing standards for what constitutes legitimate pleasure, then a radical new world awaits them.

The Essenes and the Therapeutae were hardly the only people in antiquity to renounce wealth and comfort. There were many ancient Christian priests who took vows of poverty. Laws passed in the fourth century CE allowed priests born into wealthy families to avoid serving on city councils.[24] These councils planned local budgets, collected taxes, and worked closely with the magistrates. If there was a budget shortfall, city council members were personally responsible for funding the deficit. Poverty might sound beneficial and even self-serving in this context, since it meant they would no longer be on the hook for such costs. But priestly vows of poverty also meant that they lost the legal privileges that came with wealth, so priests were now treated as members of the poor—a legally defined population known as *humiliores*. The *humiliores* were liable to corporal punishments including beating and torture, inflicted by the city council magistrates. Thus, when priests gave up their aristocratic lives of comfort, they also refused to partake in the violence that these very city councils perpetuated. Priests who took vows of poverty renounced a world that demanded their cruelty and created another in which they were no longer complicit in such violence. Ascetics insist that it is possible to summon a new world into existence by living out the conditions of its possibility, that one's actions—what one refuses and demands—can sow seeds that will bear the fruit of another world.

What were the Essenes and the Therapeutae renouncing in their own ascetic practices? Sources agree that both sects gave up private property and various comforts of life, preferring simple clothing, housing, and food.[25] They also regarded inequality as contrary to nature and this was probably a guiding principle of their societies. These give some strong hints as to the alternate identity that they cultivated through their asceticism—the new person and new world that might emerge from the fertile soil of these communities. Their practices of mutual aid and their strong emphasis on equality were not enforced through the state, but in opposition to it. These communities were located at the periphery of Roman influence, in areas of isolation: in the extreme heat of the Judaean desert (Essenes) and a full day's walk from the Egyptian metropolis of Alexandria (Therapeutae). The act of separating from the rest of the world was itself ascetic, as group members limited their contact with outsiders who might not share their commitments. This isolation ensured that the Roman Empire had little influence on their lives. In this sense, the very existence of these groups was a form of anti-Roman protest: they showed that life apart from the Roman state could provide communal, philosophical, and theological pleasures. They believed that Roman culture—its theaters, bathing complexes, brothels, literature, politics, and so on—offered only superficial gratifications.

It is no coincidence that these groups emerged shortly after Rome annexed both Egypt and Judaea (30 BCE and 6 CE, respectively).[26] No ancient texts detail the origins of these groups—no founding figures, no sense of beginnings and growth, nor even founding myths. Yet the social crises that prompted their formation can give us some sense of how they defined themselves against the Roman state.

The Therapeutae resided in Egypt, just outside of Alexandria. Within that metropolis, there was a widespread sense that Rome favored the Jewish population, particularly in contrast to the city's "Greek" population. The *Acts of the Pagan Martyrs* are a collection of ancient texts that present the trials and executions of Alexandrian pagans over the period 30 BCE–216 CE.[27] These were fictionalized accounts of the arrest and prosecution of Alexandria's Greek nobility, presented as though they were the transcripts of real court trials. These texts narrated the purported schemes of the Romans and their Jewish allies to rid the city of its Greek character. "Greek" was not an ethnic designation, but a social one, referring to people who participated in the city's Hellenistic institutions. This distinction is important because many Alexandrian Jews also identified as "Greek": Alexandrian Jews spoke the Greek language, studied Greek authors, read the Bible in Greek translation, and participated in symposia, etc. The *Acts of the Pagan Martyrs* were propaganda, but they do give some insight into the resentments of Alexandria's Greek aristocracy around the time of the Therapeutae. When Rome annexed Egypt in 30 BCE, Alexandrian Greeks lost much of their power and autonomy; their city was no longer an independent Greek *polis* with its own constitution, and the new Roman government replaced Greek institutions with Roman ones. The city's Greeks looked for someone to blame for this change and Alexandria's Jewish population made easy targets.

The *Acts of the Pagan Martyrs* spoke to a widespread *perception* of Jewish encroachment on Greek ways of life within Roman Egypt, even though Jews had lived there for centuries. Rome accommodated the Jewish aristocracy of Alexandria by allowing them certain legal exemptions from public service. These pretty innocuous allowances permitted them to rest on the Sabbath and avoid rituals to foreign gods that were incompatible with Jewish monotheism. The other Roman reforms allowed Jewish nobles to exert more power over the local Jewish population, which was more in the aristocrats' interests than the rest of the Jewish population. The majority of Alexandria's Jews lived humble lives and had no such privileges. Even so, the emperor Augustus erected a monument recording the rights he afforded the city's Jews and later emperors intervened on their behalf as well.[28] As Greek aristocrats felt their own power decline, they looked for someone to blame and it was the newly prominent Jewish families who captured their attention. The aristocracy quickly scapegoated the city's broader Jewish population.

The animosity between Alexandria's Greeks, Jews, and Romans largely came down to squabbling between different aristocratic factions, fighting about power and privilege without much concern for bettering the lives of ordinary folk. But the Greek nobles successfully stoked animosity within the general Greek population. In 38 CE the Greeks engaged in a violent anti-Jewish riot that left many beaten, homeless, and dead. Two years later there was further anti-Jewish violence. Both riots were instigated by aristocrats who regarded Rome's accommodation of Jews as a direct threat to their material and political interests.

We do not know precisely when, but the Therapeutae left Alexandria and created their commune shortly before these riots. The Therapeutae consisted of Greek Jewish intellectuals who were unhappy with the encroachment of Roman politics upon a way of life that had previously allowed for more freedom and autonomy. It probably mattered little to the Therapeutae whether the aristocrats exercising power over them were Jewish or pagan—neither shared the Therapeutae's desire for a simple life of study and discussion. The only thing aristocrats seemed to care about was consolidating their own power. Rather than attempting to reform the political system, the Therapeutae preferred to opt out of Alexandrian life by forming an alternative society.

This was also true for the Essenes, who felt the hustle-and-bustle of Jerusalem was no place to live a moral life—they thought of the city as a site of disorder. But the Essenes focused more on communal self-sufficiency than the Therapeutae. Whereas the Therapeutae welcomed donations from sympathetic outsiders, the Essenes took up farming and other crafts to form a more autonomous community.[29] Although the Therapeutae mainly consisted of disaffected intellectuals, the Essenes had a broader demographic that included peasants and laborers. The Essenes created their community as a place where social status played no role and any man was welcome to engage in philosophical reflection of the Jewish scriptures, learning together how one might live an ethical life. It is significant that this ethical life was practiced at some distance from the city, where one could avoid the restraints of the Roman state and the inequities it fostered. Of course, Philo, Josephus, and Pliny were all Roman citizens and sympathetic to Rome, so it is hardly surprising that they say little about the anti-Roman aspects of Essene life. Indeed, it is likely that it never even occurred to them that a group like the Essenes could be both anti-Roman and peaceful.

* * *

The Therapeutae and Essenes developed democratic interpretations of Judaism, in part by turning their religious practices away from the Jerusalem Temple and toward the study of scripture. Although Jewish scripture claims that King Solomon oversaw the construction of the Jerusalem Temple in the tenth century BCE, many archaeologists have come to doubt this account, instead arguing it was only built a few centuries later.[30] Regardless, this Temple was destroyed during the Babylonian conquest in 587 BCE, but with the support of the Achaemenid Empire in Persia, the Jewish population built a new temple to continue worship. The Jewish priests consecrated the Second Temple in the year 516 BCE, though construction and renovation continued for centuries

COMMUNITIES OF JEWISH RADICALISM

afterward. The Second Temple was the economic, political, and ritual center of Judaism at the time of the Essenes and Therapeutae.[31] Its priesthood was a semi-hereditary system that passed through able-bodied Jewish men from the tribe of Levi. Many Jews were frustrated with the priestly aristocrats that the Romans appointed to run the Temple, since these priests wielded their influence in support of projects that served Rome's interests, rather than those of their fellow Jews. Many people formed new sects around this time, creating more democratic forms of their religion—the Yachad at Qumran, the Pharisees, the Zealots, and the Christians.[32] The Therapeutae and Essenes should be understood in this context. Both groups attempted to democratize Jewish society through literacy: the Therapeutae channeled the frustrations of Hellenized intellectuals, while the Essenes created a society where members could enjoy the benefits of literacy regardless of their social background. The Essenes' approach was bold, since only about five percent of the Jewish population at the time qualified as "literate."[33]

A consideration of how the Therapeutae co-opted and subverted the symbols of the Temple reveals much about their actual practice of Judaism, away from the Temple and the Roman sympathizers who ran it. They modeled their society as an alternative to the Temple. Traditionally, the Jerusalem Temple was the place where most Jews offered sacrifices and took part in rituals described in the Torah. Many engaged in annual pilgrimages to participate in Jewish holidays. The Therapeutae, however, read those parts of the Torah differently from most other Jews, instead interpreting them as allegories for the mysteries of the divine and how to build a better society. They thought this allegorical understanding of a symbolic temple offered deeper meanings than one could find in Jerusalem. The Therapeutae constructed a building that served as an imitation temple with a "Holy of Holies," where they performed rituals evocative of those in Jerusalem. Moreover, each Therapeut had their own "sacred room" in their house, where they engaged in ritualized readings of scripture. In other words, their homes acted as substitute temples, with the act of reading serving as a substitute sacrifice. The Therapeutae rendered themselves an alternative to the Jerusalem Temple, an alternative that was more accessible to the masses: women, non-Levites, those hostile to Rome, and even those who weren't ethnically Jewish could fully participate in the Therapeutae's community and devote their lives to the Jewish God.[34] Someone like Beruriah would be welcome among the Therapeutae. Whereas the Jerusalem Temple centralized religious power and authority, the Therapeutae created a system in which anyone could partake in Judaism's most profound mysteries. The Therapeutae thought that the Jewish God was more accessible in his relationship with humanity, not caring about priestly qualifications. "Therapeutae" was itself a Greek term designating non-priestly laborers at a temple: the Therapeutae imagined themselves as true devotees, working diligently to better understand God's will and live out a divine way of life, but requiring no specific qualifications to do so.[35] Not only were there no leaders within these communities, but they also diffused and decentralized power away from the Jerusalem Temple.

The Therapeutae and the Essenes came up with readings of the Jewish scriptures that were quite idiosyncratic as far as most Jews were concerned. The Essenes and Therapeutae read scripture with the assumption that it contained cosmic secrets that could be uncovered if understood correctly. This was quite different from most Jews of the time, who read the Torah as a collection of historical tales about Moses and the Jewish patriarchs that also elaborated upon Jewish customs (e.g., kosher regulations, ritual instructions). But the Therapeutae and Essenes believed that Jewish scriptures contained much deeper meanings, such as insights about the soul, God's mystical qualities, and how cosmic powers related to each other, among other heavenly mysteries. These meanings were apparent only if someone read the Torah through a set of highly technical questions. Their interpretation sidelined the Jerusalem Temple, instead suggesting that the Jewish God preferred people contemplate the enigmas found within holy texts.[36] As far as they were concerned, God didn't really care all that much about the rituals and sacrifices at the Temple. Their interpretations may have involved simple numerology or the elaboration of sophisticated allegories; we don't know, since none of their texts survive and ancient descriptions are rather vague. Philo was neither a Therapeut nor an Essene, but he put his own spin on this mode of reading. He articulated a complex allegorical interpretation of the creation narrative in Genesis, finding numerous cosmic mysteries revealed within it: Genesis 2:2 refers to God resting on the seventh day, but Philo thought that this passage offered profound reflections on human life coming to completion (symbolized through the number six) by God's choice to imbue mortals with divine morality (symbolized through the number seven).[37] The Essenes and the Therapeutae probably read the Torah in a manner similar to Philo. This way of relating to scripture through textual mysteries was common among the well-educated in antiquity, as strange as it might seem to us and to the vast population of antiquity that was illiterate—many learned pagans, Jews, and Christians read their own scriptures this way.[38]

The populism of the Therapeutae was nevertheless limited. Common folk often found religion based on this sort of allegorical interpretation absurd, perhaps because very few people could read in those days. They were convinced that this was overthinking and overanalyzing in hopes of finding some meaning that wasn't really there.[39] After all, it was much simpler for most people to offer a sacrifice at the Temple than to spend decades getting an education to be able to read and interpret in this way. In a context where literacy was rare, these readings provoked polarized reactions.

* * *

For all the Therapeutae and the Essenes had in common, they could hardly have differed more in their handling of gender. Patriarchy was ubiquitous and thoroughly integrated into nearly all social institutions of antiquity. Both the Essenes and the Therapeutae expected their members to remain celibate, since many people found abstinence, as an ascetic practice, to be a powerful way of resisting patriarchy. But the Essenes were a "boy's club" that prohibited women, while the Therapeutae were a mixed-gender community.[40] Both approaches addressed the role of sexual desire within patriarchal power relations, in a quest for authentic equality.

In antiquity, women were largely defined by their relationship with men, with a married woman's husband being most important in this regard, as he claimed possession of her chastity and honor.[41] In the Greek and Roman empires, the proper exercise of power over another human being rendered a sexual act acceptable: the penetrating partner in any sexual act should have more social power than the penetrated partner. Thus, the penetrating partner should be male, freeborn, older, wealthier, and a citizen; anyone penetrated should be "less" than him in these regards: woman or effeminate, slave or freedperson, younger, poorer, or a non-citizen. The act of intercourse both affirmed the existing relationships of power and was an act of domination in its own right.

Yet within any power dynamic, the subordinate party can always find ways of resisting and the women of antiquity exercised their sexual agency in compelling ways. A famous tale of such resistance can be found in Aristophanes' comedic play, *Lysistrata* (first performed in 411 BCE), in which Greek women refuse to sleep with their husbands until the men end the Peloponnesian War. Other women rejected marriage altogether. A Christian work of fiction called *The Acts of Paul and Thecla* (second century CE) depicted a young woman finding independence and autonomy through chastity: by refusing to marry her fiancé, Thecla also refused a patriarchal system that subordinated her to this man.[42] Marriage provided innumerable mechanisms for centralizing masculine power, as it ensured legal authority over family members within the patriarch's household. The general perception of marriage as inherently "good" also meant that people were socialized into understanding these relations as natural and even desirable. Almost everyone—men, women, children, slaves—was convinced that concentrating familial power in the hands of a single patriarch was the normal way of doing things. Both the Essenes and the Therapeutae refused this system. If sexual intercourse was primarily about power in antiquity, then celibacy meant refusing to understand people through such power-relations.

The Therapeutae, though open to people of all genders, preferred gender segregation and sexual abstinence. Philo described the women within the group as "elderly virgins" who, unlike the priestesses of the Greek temples, chose abstinence rather than having celibacy imposed upon them. Philo implied that the women presented themselves as elderly, desexualizing themselves as much as possible, as women ascetics often valued "modesty" in appearance.[43] Their choice of uniforms also hints at this practice, as it refused members' ability to differentiate on the basis of gender. The Therapeutae limited contact between men and women, as they lived in individual houses and were segregated at meals, worship, and symposia. This segregation was one way of preserving equality within the community; it prevented sexist prejudices from interfering with their egalitarian way of life. In a culture where patriarchy rendered masculine power inescapable within any gendered interaction, removing such contact provided a guaranteed way to sidestep that power imbalance. Patriarchy cast women as temptresses who bore responsibility for any lust men might feel. The Therapeutae rejected this explanation and, in doing so, ensured women could participate more fully as equals in the life of the whole community.

The Essenes took a much more direct approach to preventing patriarchy from compromising their Jewish democracy. Only men were allowed in their community, which meant that sexist prejudices and sexual entanglements were less likely to arise in the first place. Philo claimed that Essenes prohibited marriage because the presence of feminine selfishness would undermine their communal spirit, but this may reflect Philo's misogyny more than the Essenes' own reasoning.[44] It seems just as likely that they chose to form a single-sex community because they were aware that patriarchy created the inequalities they loathed. Both explanations are plausible: that Essenes were sexist and banned women because of conflict they might cause, or that they disliked patriarchy and, being aware that sexism was unavoidable, believed that prohibiting women could prevent inequality from arising.

The Therapeutae were appealing to Jewish women of the first century CE. Let us imagine a young woman called Shelamzion, who grew up in a relatively wealthy family in Alexandria. She found the idea of marriage repulsive; men's interest was more nuisance than anything else. She felt that every man who wasn't her immediate family wanted to snuff out the flame of her curiosity and just sleep with her. The only man she trusted was the pedagogue that her parents had hired to tutor her and her brothers. Shelamzion was fortunate to receive a good education, studying the Torah and reading the works of Greek philosophers. Her teacher mentioned how some of his former pupils had left the city after the anti-Jewish riots and hiked over to Lake Mareotis to join a group there. Out of curiosity, she ventured there a few times, donating food whenever she arrived in hopes of meeting her teacher's former students. On the third visit, she finally managed to meet them and the experience was a revelation for her. They conversed for hours about the mysteries of the Torah, the corrupting force of the city, the accessibility of God, and how the Jerusalem Temple was simply a human construction. But what intrigued her most was their report about community life among the Therapeutae: the freedom to study and reflect, extensive periods of group discussion, and a prohibition on sexual relationships.

After this, Shelamzion began visiting the Therapeutae on a weekly basis and even provided them with livestock from her family's estate after she found out that bandits had stolen a few of theirs. After much reflection and a heated argument with her father, she opted to join the Therapeutae and leave everything behind, including the possibility of a significant inheritance. After a year-long initiation process, she was given her own home and invited to study with the rest of the group. Although life was regimented, and even strict, there was a remarkable freedom to it all: the emphasis on discussion, the absence of authorities, a strong community of care, and no sexual overtures. Between the pleasures of study and conversation, they labored together in the fields, milling barley, or baking bread, with the Sabbath a welcome rest; even their cattle had the day off. Among the Therapeutae, Shelamzion not only found a place to study, but somewhere her wisdom was celebrated.

* * *

The Therapeutae and Essenes both despised inequality, yet their religious practices were not accessible to all. Although the Therapeutae created a space for women's participation, the Essenes excluded women from participating in their community. And while the Essenes made a concerted effort to include uneducated peasants, the Therapeutae did not, a significant gap in their quest for equality. There is no reason to think that the Therapeutae's esoteric reading of scripture was founded upon an elitist exclusion of less educated people, but rather that they found ritualized reading essential to their group identity and group purpose. These were, after all, *experiments* in radically democratic Judaism.

The attempts to create new gender relations echo strongly today. Whether intentionally or not, the Essenes and the Therapeutae invited queer people into their communities: men and women who did not find married life appealing. Like many queer people today, they abolished the family unit and built something new from its remains. Queer theorist M. E. O'Brien encourages us to think of family abolition as "a commitment to making the care necessary for human flourishing freely available throughout society."[45] In a queerer society—in a more ethical society—we would no longer depend upon personal relationships, since "access to care could be built into the social fabric of our collective lives." Across history, many gender non-conforming people have created "chosen family" and so did the Therapeutae and the Essenes. They implemented new systems of care and meaning that opposed the hierarchical forms of Judaism. Within their communities, they found space to study, work, reflect, and live in ways where the exploitations of patriarchy were far from their minds—a place where someone like Shelamzion or Beruriah could flourish.

Further Reading

Mendels, Doron. 1979. "Utopia and the Essenes." *Harvard Theological Review* 72: 207–22.

Taylor, Joan E. 2003. *Jewish Women Philosophers of First-Century Alexandria: Philo's 'Therapeutae' Reconsidered*. Oxford: Oxford University Press.

Taylor, Joan E. and David M. Hay. 2021. *Philo of Alexandria: On the Contemplative Life. Introduction, Translation and Commentary*. Leiden: Brill.

VanderKam, James C. 2012. "The Common Ownership of Property in Essene Communities." Pages 359–75 in *'Go Out and Study the Land': Archaeological, Historical and Textual Studies in Honor of*

Hanan Eshel. Edited by Aren Maer, Jodi Magness, and Lawrence Schiffman. Leiden: Brill.

Joan Taylor's book provides the best starting point for research about the Therapeutae, discussing the range of historical issues at play in ascertaining how they lived; her commentary (co-authored with David M. Hay) on Philo's *On the Contemplative Life* is also valuable. Scholars have written more extensively about the Essenes, but most assume that the Essenes were responsible for the Dead Sea Scrolls, which seems doubtful. The articles by Doron Mendels and James VanderKam both discuss the utopian qualities of the Essene community, though they presume the relevance of the Dead Sea Scrolls.

First Interlude.
Anatolian Anarcho-Primitivists:
The Region of Phrygia

The philosopher Synesius (373–414 CE) lived in Cyrenaica, located in northern Africa. In a letter to a friend, Synesius discussed the distance between his homeland and the Byzantine capital Constantinople—not just geographic distance, but political distance, too; Synesius claimed that the people of Cyrenaica were oblivious to Byzantine power:

> No doubt people here know that there is an emperor, since tax collectors remind us about this every year. But *who* he is, that's not very clear. Some people here assume that Agamemnon, the great king who battled against Troy, still rules us. We have heard "the king" called by this name since childhood and some of us know him only by that name.[1]

Although the shepherds of Cyrenaica were aware that there was an emperor in Constantinople, he did not rule them in any practical sense. Agamemnon, the nearly mythological king of Mycenae who was known for fighting in the Trojan War almost two millennia earlier, played a more significant role in their lives. The people of Cyrenaica recounted Agammemnon's deeds when they recited epic poetry, at least.

Cyrenaica was not unique in this regard. The poet Phaedrus (15 BCE–50 CE) told a fable with a similar point, observing how regime fluctuations meant little to the rural peasantry.

Whether their land was claimed by Rome or one of Rome's enemies, their lives remained the same: "Will they lighten this load I need to carry?" "Nope." "Then I don't really care who our new king is."[2] The ancient state was remarkably weak and easily shrugged off. With modest effort, large populations could elude its grasp.

Archaeological evidence suggests that people in the region of Phrygia disregarded imperial power just as much as the people of Cyrenaica. Various empires and states of antiquity could not impose their rule. Phrygia sits in the western part of Asia Minor (see Figure 1), encompassing a grassy plateau, with a largely arid climate. This environment rendered living conditions harsh: hot summers and cold winters, with little tree cover to offer protection. The climate made it difficult to grow the most profitable crops, so Phrygians tended to use the land for animal husbandry and were often nomadic. The region never fully urbanized, with settlements mostly consisting of small towns and villages. And yet within these groups, there were some radical ideas. The analysis of Peter Thonemann supplies the basis for this interlude.[3]

* * *

To understand why Thonemann believes Phrygia was stateless, it may help to go via the work of anthropologist James C. Scott.[4] Scott argues that large regions can evade state control, taking Zomia (an Asian region stretching from southeastern Vietnam to Bhutan) as his case in point. He identifies three reasons for Zomia's success in remaining stateless.

1) Highland regions are inherently more difficult for states to govern, due to dispersed population, inaccessibility of travel, and agricultural complications;

ANATOLIAN ANARCHO-PRIMITIVISTS

2) The population of Zomia largely comprises people who have taken refuge from the surrounding lowland regions who do not hold deep connections to their former homelands;

3) Most importantly, the various peoples of Zomia have developed a democratic way of life that both thwarts external efforts of governments to assimilate Zomian structures and prevents state-like entities from emerging internally.

One way people have prevented states from emerging is by rejecting literacy. But rather than being pre-literate people who have not yet developed a writing system, Zomians are post-literate in that they were previously capable of writing but have willingly abandoned it. As anthropologist Pierre Clastres notes, "writing directly bespeaks the power of the law, be it engraved in stone, painted on animal skins, or drawn on papyrus."[5] The people of Zomia gave up literacy because it gave rise to the intellectuals and bureaucrats who facilitated exploitation. These three factors foster the conditions that have allowed Zomians to live with minimal state intrusion. Thonemann observes that all three points apply to ancient Phrygia:

1) the region is a plateau;
2) there was a large population in ancient Phrygia who had taken refuge from surrounding areas; and
3) as we will see, they actively impeded the efforts of the occupying power to integrate the region into their own networks of power.

Thonemann sees something useful in Scott's idea of an intentionally stateless region—that a government's claim to power over an area might be flatly contradicted by life on the ground. What might initially look like an "underdeveloped economy" could be reconceptualized as the successful, large-scale evasion of state power—something we find with both modern Zomia and ancient Phrygia. And there was good reason that ancient Phrygians evaded such power. Phrygian statelessness provided a modest but sustainable quality of life, marked by a degree of freedom and a generally egalitarian culture. There was no compulsion to participate in exploitative economic systems. For much of antiquity, the people of Phrygia lived without significant interference from the Persian, Greek, or Roman empires.

Centuries before this statelessness began, they were governed by the Phrygian kingdom, lasting roughly 950–620 BCE. This kingdom was sophisticated: there is evidence of luxurious palaces, intricate religious structures, widespread writing, and a system of hereditary kingship, all maintained by a powerful class of bureaucrats. Archaeologists have uncovered, for instance, a massive palace complex, including living quarters for about 300 laborers. These laborers attended to the elites in the city of Gordion, Phrygia's capital at the time. The neighboring kingdom of Lydia conquered Phrygia in 620 BCE, but the Lydian conquest hardly interrupted this state of affairs. Palaces continued to spread throughout Phrygia, reaching a zenith in the sixth century BCE, with numerous monumental structures throughout the region. Lydian rule proved generous to Phrygian elites. The imperial power sponsored extensive building projects at the already impressive site of Gordion.

However, by the time of Alexander the Great's conquest in 330 BCE, the Phrygian state seems to have disappeared, with its decline beginning around the time the Achaemenid

Empire conquered the Lydian kingdom in 540 BCE. The Phrygian economy, managed by the bureaucrats laboring within that network of palaces, had collapsed, alongside a significant decline in the urban population. Independent workshops replaced the centrally organized system that had flourished under the Phrygian and Lydian kingdoms. The social hierarchy flattened around this time too, with evidence of wealth disappearing. For example, the aristocratic custom of burial in funerary mounds ceased, reflecting elites' inability to generate enough wealth to distinguish themselves from the peasantry.[6] But Phrygia did not experience any large-scale catastrophe. Instead, Thonemann observes that palaces gradually fell out of use and Phrygians began to exercise greater autonomy in the areas of life previously controlled by the state. The Phrygian language disappeared from the written record after the Achaemenid conquest: the language was commonly found on earlier monuments, but nearly all Phrygian writing under the Achaemenid Empire took the form of graffiti. This suggests that the once extensive class of bureaucrats responsible for taxation, legislation, and running the courts—the people who taught and maintained the Phrygian language—had vanished. The absence of written Phrygian became even more conspicuous in the Hellenistic period: in the years after Alexander the Great's conquest, there is only one instance of the language's use in writing until its revival nearly half a millennium later. For several centuries, Phrygian became a strictly oral language.

One possible explanation for the decline of the Phrygian language, bureaucracy, and its palatial network is that it was a side effect of the destructive conquests in the region. After all, many previously impressive centers of cultural and economic activity throughout western Asia collapsed on account of the devastating invasion of Achaemenid Persia. Likewise, several other languages declined after Alexander's conquest, as Greek replaced them as the language of bureaucracy and prestige. But Thonemann notes that these factors cannot explain the Phrygia case, since the Phrygian language had been declining centuries before Alexander's conquest. Moreover, other Persian regions that had collapsed in the wake of the Achaemenid invasion bounced back within a few years, thriving under both the Persians and Greeks. Phrygia, by contrast, never really recovered; the people of Phrygia had neither a state nor a written language.

Thonemann suggests that the people of Phrygia resisted the Achaemenids and their Hellenistic successors by dismantling their own social systems, including literacy without which exploitative bureaucracy could not function. The Achaemenid Empire often appropriated existing social structures to extract wealth from conquered populations. For instance, Egypt had long been divided into districts called "nomes" and extracted wealth through this system—taxes were collected in-kind as grain by the district's nomarch, who then conferred most of it to the chiefs of the granaries, who, in turn, conferred most of it to Egypt's palace treasurer.[7] The Achaemenids saw no need to meddle with this efficient system of extracting wealth within Egypt and allowed it to continue with a few modifications so that Persian royalty could take their cut. Likewise, the Achaemenids helped the Jewish people rebuild the Jerusalem Temple, which the Babylonians had destroyed in 587 BCE. The Achaemenids knew this bit of generosity would pay for itself through the goodwill it generated among the Jewish aristocracy and it didn't take long for it to pay dividends: the biblical book of Isaiah proclaimed the Achaemenid King Cyrus as the Messiah for this reason![8] The Persians found it much easier to commandeer existing systems of power and exploitation than to create new ones. Thonemann suggests that the people of Phrygia were aware of this and dismantled their social systems, such that far-off kings and their bureaucrats found it challenging to take advantage of them. Moreover, by abandoning literacy, they prevented exploitative systems from re-emerging—with few potential bureaucrats around, any government would have difficulty finding locals to manage the Phrygian population. Of course, this does not mean that all hierarchy was absent; even so, the concentration of wealth and power diminished.

This situation in Phrygia persisted well beyond Alexander's conquest. It was a "post-state zone" while it was under Hellenistic (330–130 BCE) and later Roman (130 BCE–330 CE) domination. Although Hellenistic and Roman rulers technically governed the region, Thonemann notes that "the Phrygians were, in real and tangible senses, 'freer' than the inhabitants of an autonomous Greek city-state."[9] There was effectively no centralized government to enforce laws, start wars, or exacerbate inequality in Phrygia. Phrygians operated with a largely moneyless economy until the mid-second century BCE and even then, coinage remained rare outside of cities. The people occasionally abandoned palatial sites like Gordion entirely, only to move back into its dilapidated ruins a century or two later. Without money or a state, Phrygians were freer to work and relax as they desired. There were no lawcourts, bureaucrats, or soldiers that could punish people who fell behind on rents, fines, or taxes.

This didn't stop the Greek and Roman empires from claiming control of Phrygia and attempting to establish colonies there. Graeco-Roman colonists and native Phrygians drew sharp distinctions from each other—the former being urban and the latter rural.[10] Greece and Rome founded several mini-cities, humble in size but impressive in their architecture and planning: Romans founded the "urban" site of Blaundos, but found it difficult to convince people to live there. Less than 1,000 people populated it at any given time. A handful of similar cities were sprinkled throughout the region, with little effect on how native Phrygians lived. Urban populations consisted almost entirely of Greek and Roman colonists. Phrygians showed little interest in these cities and preferred to live away from these sites of "culture." To take only one example, the population of Blaundos was a quarter of that in the surrounding countryside. Although some native Phrygians were drawn to the grandeur and opportunity within the mini-cities, such people were few. Consequently, these mini-cities had difficulty establishing authority and the state's power continued to be negligible. Phrygian populations remained itinerant and these mini-cities failed to form meaningful networks. Phrygians did not produce majestic monuments or cities of marble and little evidence of their more modest dwellings has survived to the present day.

But this doesn't mean that life in Phrygia was monotonous. Phrygian culture had flourished before they developed a written language and there is every reason to think this continued after they abandoned literacy. Most people in the Mediterranean couldn't read or write anyway, as their cultures relied more upon oral storytelling than the written word. It

ANATOLIAN ANARCHO-PRIMITIVISTS

simply means their tales, artwork, and poetry have been lost to time.

* * *

Historians have generally accepted Thonemann's arguments that Phrygia was stateless for most of antiquity, though some find it hard to believe that Phrygians actively chose to dispose of the state's supposed luxuries.[11] Some scholars doubt that anyone would want to live the way Phrygians did. But their skepticism presumes a trajectory of social development, with the state as the natural pinnacle of human social evolution. This assumption is precisely what Peter Thonemann, James C. Scott, Pierre Clastres, and others have called into question: the state is just as optional as any other human institution. Clastres' research is particularly instructive, as he observes the multiple reasons why many Indigenous peoples do not have a state apparatus with centralized power and coercive laws.[12] Though most scholars long supposed that such peoples were stateless because they were unfamiliar with the state, Clastres argues that many Indigenous people saw the state, chose not to embrace it, and continued their lives without it.

Phrygia was a remarkable example of a widespread effort to evade state power over the course of centuries. Phrygians shared a distaste for the state, recognizing its exploitative nature. But life was not always easy: lacking any organized system of defense meant that Phrygian civilians were occasionally kidnapped and sold into slavery. Their aversion to literacy is indeed unusual. Though governments have often used anti-intellectual policies to oppress a subset of the population (e.g., anti-literacy laws targeting the enslaved in the United States), Phrygians found that illiteracy offered a refuge from exploitation. The absence of a literate culture and the incidental risk of violence from neighboring peoples were a modest price for freedom. It is easy to imagine Phrygians living like the shepherds of Cyrenaica mentioned above: yes, they knew that a king claimed Phrygians as his subjects, but his power over them was meaningless. Like the shepherds of Cyrenaica, Phrygians were probably more familiar with the kings of local legend—Midas, Otreus, and Mygdon—than the real-world monarchs of the Achaemenid, Hellenistic, and Roman empires.

3
Against a Dog-Eat-Dog World: Cynic Philosophers

The story goes that when Crates (365–285 BCE) finally grasped the profundity of Diogenes' teachings—Diogenes of Sinope (404–323 BCE) being a famous Cynic philosopher—his reaction was melodramatic.[1] Realizing that property was a burden upon his soul, Crates ran into the streets and started giving away all his possessions. In a particularly theatrical act, he announced, "Crates hereby grants Crates his freedom," a formula used whenever owners manumitted their slaves. For Crates, relieving himself of his belongings amounted to emancipation, as he was now liberated from his enslavement to social conventions. Although he was never a slave, Crates was now free to live an ethical life. The question was, what did this entail?

Graeco-Roman philosophy always had practical matters at its heart. By ascertaining the nature of the universe, God, and justice, the philosopher was better positioned to understand the principles of a moral life. Numerous schools of thought flourished during Classical antiquity, including Plato's Academy, the Epicureans, the Stoics, and the Pythagoreans. Of particular interest for this book is Cynicism, a school of thought founded in the fifth century BCE that continued to be practiced into the sixth century CE. Cynic philosophers lived anarchistic lives, prizing self-sufficiency and a bold critique of power. This stance toward the world was supported by an ascetic practice that renounced the pleasures of Graeco-Roman civic life in favor of cosmopolitanism. Cynics preferred a simple lifestyle without the accoutrements of civilization: the unnecessary finery, the insincere rituals of deference and status, the polite euphemisms, and similar contrivances. Cynicism confronted Greek and Roman culture and its hypocritical chauvinism. Cynics were reputed for their voluntary poverty, indifference to their public reputation, simple living, and quest for virtue. These were not merely philosophical ideals, but matters of practice in their anarchistic lives.

* * *

The city-state (*polis*) was the central social institution in Classical Greece (480–336 BCE). It formed the basis of everyone's identity, being the place where one's reputation, loyalties, and political sympathies were forged. The city-state was governed by the small portion of the population holding citizenship—typically, freeborn sons of lawful citizen marriages. Citizens received numerous privileges, ranging from tax exemptions to legal assurances to networking opportunities with other citizens (for political, business, romantic, or other purposes).[2] Each city had its own initiation rituals for young men on the path to citizenship, preparing them to participate fully in the city's social and political life. Throughout the Classical period, roughly 15 percent of the people inhabiting Athens were citizens. Women, children, slaves, and foreigners were denied this privilege. This was typical of Classical Greece. Other city-states had citizenship rates of around 5 to 20 percent.

Although the benefits of citizenship were considerable, the flaws with this system were sufficiently obvious that various people sought alternatives. Diogenes and other Cynics adopted a radical approach that rejected the Hellenic conception of citizenship. They discarded civic affiliations altogether, asserting that true citizenship was found in the *kosmopolis*—the worldwide city of all humanity.[3] Diogenes described himself as "a homeless exile (*apolis*), dead to his homeland, a wanderer who begs for morsels of bread."[4] Cynics regarded political borders as constructs and declared that no city's laws were more virtuous than those of any other. Laws and customs meant little outside the city-state enforcing them. Who cared if Athenians said that you shouldn't eat certain foods or disrespect the city's temples? Diogenes noted that people in foreign lands did these things and it was clear that the gods didn't care, since they never punished any of those people for it. Antisthenes (446–366 BCE), the first Cynic philosopher, espoused a similar attitude: "The wise man does not conduct his life by civic laws (*nomoi*), but by the law of virtue."[5] Cynics concerned themselves with the laws of virtue, attempting to understand goodness as something distinct from the arbitrary social conventions governing society.

What did it mean to live according to the laws of virtue, rather than the laws of the city-state? To answer this, it is important to understand the Graeco-Roman preoccupation with honor and shame. Honor was the social recognition of someone's public standing, a standing that people acquired in part through their behavior—taking up a respectable occupation, properly fulfilling gender norms, living up to one's duties, abiding by social rituals, etc. Honor and shame were part of an inescapable game whereby a person's status affected nearly every social interaction. To whom do you show deference? Who shows deference to you? Whom might you marry? From whom might your club solicit a donation? How might you repair your reputation if you were suspected of military desertion? How might you respond to rumors that your spouse had an affair? This "game" revolved around the rules governing society and respect for authority, so it inevitably entrenched social inequalities. Much of this came down to playing the proper role in society: being obedient to the right people (boss, landlord, king, etc.) and eliciting subservience from others (wife, children, slaves, the homeless, etc.). Articulating the game succinctly, the philosopher Aristotle concluded that honor inherently favored the powerful: "Virtues and actions are more honorable when performed by those who are naturally worthier, for instance, by a man rather than by a woman."[6] It was a rigged game designed to reward people already at the top and penalize those at the bottom.

Cynics had little interest in playing this game, deeming it more virtuous to live shamelessly. Cynics not only rejected efforts to exert power over them, but also insisted that the rules governing the game were entirely arbitrary. The philosopher Socrates once asked his friends what they were most proud of. Some were proud of their good looks, others of their ability to memorize poetry, and still others of their family. Antisthenes' answer shocked the room, "My wealth. Oh, and I don't have a penny to my name."[7] Antisthenes continued by shamelessly bragging about how his commitment to poverty ensured he had everything he needed to be happy: he did not need to worry about work, he was free to do what he wanted with his time, and was in debt to no one, either financially or socially. Antisthenes confronted his friends with a different set of assumptions than the prevailing ones about the correlation between wealth, happiness, and honor.

"Cynic" means "dog-like," and these philosophers adopted many canine values: loyalty, resourcefulness, contentedness, and the freedom to do what they pleased. We should also remember that dogs are known for licking their crotches, urinating where they like, and having sex whenever they want. Cynics developed a reputation for their shameless sexual behavior, having little regard for marriage as a venerable institution. We saw in Chapter Two how marriage perpetuated patriarchy: the institution limited women's agency, granted men much greater sexual freedom than women, and ensured most resources (money, honor, etc.) only circulated among men. Patriarchs surveilled and regulated the sexual activities of women within their households. Women's sexuality was seen as more of a liability to familial honor than anything else: wives should be impeccable in their marital faithfulness and daughters should remain steadfast in their virginity to preserve the family's reputation.

Cynics disregarded these sexual and gender norms, as they bound people within slavish relationships of power and obligation. Crates and Hipparchia were exemplary in their Cynic rejection of a conventional marriage. Hipparchia was born into a wealthy family and, impressed by his Cynic lifestyle, fell in love with Crates. When she proposed marriage to Crates—which itself went against patriarchal norms—he stripped naked and said he would only marry her if she also lived a Cynic life.[8] He exposed his body, with an impaired leg and curved spine, far from the ideal physique that Greeks celebrated in their sculpture and art. To her family's horror, she married Crates and the two formed an unusual relationship built upon their refusal to abide by social norms. He insisted that she should be able to attend events reserved for men and she soon became a renowned Cynic in her own right. But refusing gender discrimination was only the tip of the iceberg. The two of them would copulate in public and later encouraged their son to marry a sex worker.[9] Crates and Hipparchia had no interest in generating or preserving familial honor, nor did they have any interest in finding their son an "honorable" wife. If their son was happy with someone, then that was all that mattered. These were not juvenile acts of rebellion. By undercutting the system of honor and shame, Crates and Hipparchia enacted a radical new social order that rendered social hierarchies unintelligible. Within their world, one marriage was no more respectable or legitimate than any other. This in turn undermined the genealogical chauvinism that helped legitimize the aristocracies of ancient Greece.

Other Cynics were just as brazen in their sexuality. Antisthenes declared that men shouldn't be too picky about finding the perfect spouse, but should just marry someone eager to sleep with them.[10] Diogenes masturbated regularly in the marketplace.[11] Family values be damned! Cynics' sexual liberality put them in conflict with Greek, Roman, and eventually Christian values.[12] All of this was part of a larger critique of honor and shame. Cynics partook in something like performance art: they satirized their society's values by living (theatrically) within a committed ethical framework.[13] By rejecting Greek preoccupations with status, Cynics rebuffed the *polis* as a political system; the relationships that were pivotal to life in the city-state were of no particular concern.

Although Hipparchia willingly abandoned her respected family to become a philosopher, shamelessness was not always a matter of choice for Cynics. People not only acquired honor and shame through their behavior, but were also ascribed these attributes at birth, such that being born into slavery or a disreputable family marked you as shameful for life. You could exceed society's low expectations with your actions, but you could never escape your family background. For Cynics, the fact that people had no control over these things revealed how arbitrary the system was. When King Antigonus Gonatas asked the Cynic philosopher Bion (325–250 BCE) about his family background, Bion spoke without embarrassment: his father was a former slave "who wiped his nose on his sleeve," his mother was an enslaved sex worker, and Bion himself had been sold into slavery along with his parents.[14] "And now you know all about my glorious family background," he quipped. Still others, such as Monimus of Syracuse (fourth and third centuries BCE) and Menippus of Gadara (third century BCE), expressed no shame over the fact they were born of slaves.[15]

Diogenes and Plato were both slaves, if briefly. How each handled the fact that they were sold into slavery reveals much about their attitudes to shame. These men were contemporaries, but the differences could not be starker. In Plato's case, he fell afoul of a Sicilian autocrat who sold him into slavery.[16] Plato was soon ransomed by another philosopher named Anniceris, who granted Plato freedom and helped him return to Athens. Plato found this incident so embarrassing that he never mentioned any of it—not Anniceris, not the Sicilian autocrat, not his enslavement. None of this ever came up a single time in the large corpus of his writings. One would never get the impression that he had been enslaved from his philosophy; it is clear that he regarded slaves as irrational and unworthy of dignity.[17] By contrast, Diogenes the Cynic was taken captive and sold as a slave at auction and, rather than expressing shame or even deference, he warned potential buyers that if they were to buy him, they would not be purchasing a slave, but their new master.[18] For Diogenes, slaveowners may have claimed to own people's bodies, but that was no guarantee that their slaves would respect their owner's authority. Diogenes assured any prospective owners that they would need to show *him* respect, not the other way around. Many people scorned the Cynics, as they refused to express any shame about their supposedly humiliating lives. Cynics thought that social status was a matter of circumstance and therefore had no bearing on one's virtue.

Cynics found virtue in unexpected places. They looked to foreigners, children, and animals as models for a virtuous life, despite their supposedly uncivilized behavior.[19] Building on their cosmopolitan ideals, they adopted an inclusive approach to ethics and insisted that a virtuous world is not beholden to cultural chauvinism. Rather, an ethical society must ensure that democracy is open to all people, respects their natural freedoms, and disregards life circumstances. Many famous Cynics lived in democratic city-states like Athens, Sinope, Thebes, and Syracuse. Here, they witnessed the strengths and shortcomings of Greek governance, gathering insights to push democracy in radical directions. For instance, the Cynic celebration of bold speech (*parrhesia*) arose from their observation of the Popular Assemblies in these cities; citizens should not mince words in deference to those with power, but speak without fear of censure. Cynics radicalized this democracy with their cosmopolitan perspective. The entire world was their *polis*, so any public space became its Popular

Assembly—a place where one's authenticity demanded boldness.

Despite attesting to some of the strengths of democratic city-states, many Cynics were excluded from this political system. Antisthenes' mother was Thracian, Diogenes was from the Greek colony of Sinope in Asia Minor, and Crates was from the Greek city of Thebes, rendering them ineligible to participate in the Popular Assembly. Hipparchia was prohibited on account of her gender. None of them could contribute to the Popular Assembly because Athenian *nomoi* prohibited it. Disillusioned with a supposedly democratic system, Cynics sought to implement a world that better lived up to its own claims.

Cynics adopted a shameless life as part of an effort to redefine the values of their day. This notion of "value" was two-sided. First, what are those values that govern society? And second, what does society regard as valuable? Ideally, these two forms of value would dovetail, but often this was not the case. Diogenes lamented that "valuable things are sold for nothing and worthless things cost the highest prices. For instance, a statue fetches 3,000 drachmas, while barley costs a few little coins."[20] Why do people value a useless monument to one man's ego more than something that nourishes the body? Emblematic of the tensions sparked by this redefinition of "value" was the criminal charge against Diogenes for defacing money in his hometown of Sinope.[21] A common slogan among Cynics thus became "remint the coinage." Diogenes and others meant this literally—that money should be abolished.[22] In another instance, Diogenes said that gold and silver are "worth neither more nor less than pebbles on a beach."[23] But this slogan also had a metaphorical meaning:

people must reassess society's values and put new ones in place. The arbitrary conventions that rendered some behaviors honorable and others shameful were the primary targets for this project. Male/female, citizen/foreigner, honorable/shameful, free/slave, and so on were artificial constructs that caused more harm than good in the eyes of Cynics.

* * *

Cynic mischief lent itself to anecdote. Writers collected various stories about them in short tales of wit and repartee called *chreiai* (singular: *chreia*). *Chreiai* had a distinct formula, grounded in the playful way Cynics contested people's assumptions about honor and shame. *Chreiai* usually began with someone asserting dominance over a Cynic philosopher, attempting to shame them. If you were mocking anyone other than a Cynic, they would likely reject the premise of the affront: "How dare you insult me? I am a man of honor!" But the Cynic did not presume to be anyone's superior. Rather, the Cynic *accepted* the premise of their antagonist ("I did indeed do that" or "Yes, you certainly are wealthier than I") and in this way laid bare their antagonist's flawed assumptions. Ancient students learned to write by composing their own *chreiai* about how they thought Diogenes and others would behave.[24]

Take, for instance, one *chreia* featuring the Cynic philosopher Demonax (first and second centuries CE): "Once, Epictetus was chastising Demonax and telling him that philosophers should marry and start a family, so as to leave a successor. Demonax replied without missing a beat: 'Well then, Epictetus, why don't I marry one of your own daughters?'"[25] That the joke culminates with Demonax's request to marry one of Epictetus' own daughters is funny enough, but this is where the real wit comes in: Epictetus himself was unmarried and childless.[26] By offering to marry Epictetus' daughter, Demonax exposed his hypocrisy; Epictetus did not live up to the standards he imposed upon Demonax!

Chreiai also invited the reader to imagine themselves in similar situations, not only by delighting in seeing rapscallion Cynics humble the arrogant, but also by directly addressing the reader/hearer as "you." *Chreiai* were written so that everyone felt like the Cynic was speaking directly to them.[27] Historians today are skeptical about the historical reliability of these anecdotes, which, full of humor, allowed readers to fantasize about how they might retort to an insult with wit and wisdom. A compilation of Cynic sayings and deeds became an anarchistic handbook. If you want to put your boss, your slaveowner, a conceited aristocrat, or someone else in their place, here is how you went about showing that they were just as shameless as you are.[28]

* * *

Further evidence that Cynic philosophy was a practical lifestyle rather than an intellectual exercise was evident in their clothing. There were three telltale visual signs that someone was a Cynic: their tattered cloak, their handbag, and their staff—they carried nothing else with them.[29] These three items had both symbolic and practical functions. The cloak and staff on the one hand, evoked the demigod Hercules: "Think of your ragged cloak as the lion's skin, your staff as the club, and your pouch as the land and sea that nourishes you." This will ensure that the spirit of Hercules "stirs within you," wrote one Cynic.[30] Hercules evoked self-sufficiency, bravery, and practical wisdom—an appropriate figure for the Cynics to claim as their own. On the other hand, their shabby and minimalistic attire also suited the Cynic contempt for social pretension. The words on Hipparchia's tombstone illustrate the point: "I, Hipparchia, did not choose the lifestyle of luxurious women, but the coarse life of the Cynics. Neither brooch-clasped tunics, nor beautiful shoes, nor perfumed headscarves pleased me. Instead, I lived with only a knapsack and staff, with a rough cloak and the ground for a bed."[31] In a remarkably egalitarian move, Cynics even rejected the idea that clothing should be gendered.

Cynics' rugged clothes announced their simple life. Cynic asceticism meant that they typically found their food by begging and scavenging. The benefits of this life were numerous: you never accumulated more than you needed, you never had to grovel before bosses or politicians, and you never worried about your social status. We might recall the most famous Cynic *chreia*. Alexander the Great had recently conquered Greece and when he visited the city of Corinth, numerous philosophers went out to greet him. Diogenes was conspicuously absent from the welcoming party. Alexander wanted to see Diogenes, heard that he was in a nearby suburb, and went to see him there. Alexander was so excited that he told Diogenes that he would do anything Diogenes wanted. Any gift, any honor, *anything*. Diogenes' reply has become iconic: "Can you just get out of my sunlight?"[32] Not only was Diogenes perfectly content sunbathing on the ground, but the only thing that the most powerful man in the world could offer to make Diogenes happier was his absence.

To live a truly happy life, a person needed to discard human contrivances and return to more natural principles for living.

AGAINST A DOG-EAT-DOG WORLD

Cynics ascertained these principles not only by relying on their intuitions, but looking to animals, children, and barbarians for other ways of doing things—anyone or anything that had not yet been misled by the arbitrary values of the Greek *polis*. In this regard, Cynics resembled the Essenes and the Therapeutae discussed in Chapter Two. All three groups sought to live a truly "good" life, grounded in their own interpretations of divine justice and ethics. But we might also contrast Cynic philosophers with the communitarianism found among the Therapeutae and Essenes. The Therapeutae and Essenes were both emphatically communities: their practice emphasized mutual aid, shared property, and collective worship of the Jewish deity. They lived at a distance from the city and seemed almost monastic in their ways of life. The Cynics, by contrast, were urban and largely independent from each other and broader social groups. Whereas the hungry Essene could attend the community meal to eat, the hungry Cynic had no choice but to beg random passersby for food and coin, having no one else they could depend upon.

The historian Desmond Williams suggests that "the most convenient label for the Cynics is that they were anarchists."[33] Another historian, Marile-Odile Goulet-Cazé, arrives at the same conclusion, determining that Cynics were "pacifist anarchists."[34] Cynics suggested that people shouldn't identify with their city-state or its laws.[35] The citizens of an ethical society bore no allegiance to such arbitrary conventions and instead adhered to natural principles of virtue. One Cynic articulated the matter clearly:

> Law [i.e., *nomos*] uses force against wrong action, philosophy uses persuasion to show us why an action is wrong.

It is superior to the same degree that acting willingly is preferable to acting under compulsion. Which is why I say study philosophy and stay out of government. Knowing how people are taught good behavior is a finer thing than knowing how to keep them from breaking the law.[36]

In this view, laws coerce people to act in accordance with the will of others; it is far better to live authentically in a life of virtue. Cynic hostility toward the state predictably antagonized powerful people and numerous *chreiai* recount their run-ins with authority figures. For instance, not one, but two Roman emperors banished Demetrius the Cynic (first century CE) from the city of Rome![37] Isidorus (first century CE) publicly mocked the emperor Nero for hypocrisy and was promptly expelled from Italy.[38]

* * *

The earliest Cynics were contemporaries of other famous thinkers, particularly those of Plato's Academy. Antisthenes, like Plato, was a student of Socrates. Diogenes was purportedly a student of Antisthenes and a contemporary of Aristotle. They lived in the same city at the same time, so it is little surprise that they were thinking about the same topics and responding to the same social issues. Most notable for our purposes was their shared perception that the institution of the Greek *polis* was in decline and their distinct understandings of democracy's role in this crisis.

We saw in the Introduction to this book that Socrates and the Academics (e.g., Plato, Aristotle) were convinced that Athens was *too* democratic and had fallen into the hands of the masses. They thought that men of leisure—aristocratic intellectuals like themselves—should run the city. Since Athenian democracy let men with disreputable jobs and questionable backgrounds have as much say as the wealthiest, chaos was inevitable. But Athens had experienced several humiliating military losses in the latter days of the fifth century BCE. Athens' situation would get even worse following the conquests of Philip of Macedon and his son Alexander the Great in the fourth century BCE. The city was no longer the political powerhouse that it had been a century earlier, when it was rich from the plunder of recent military victories and dictated the policies of its allies. Socrates and the Academics longed for the return of Athenian dominance and they believed that a state governed by a strong aristocracy was the best way to achieve this. Democracy, as far as they were concerned, impeded the aristocracy's ability to implement the reforms necessary for Athens to flourish once again.

The Cynics were also skeptical of Athenian democracy, but we have seen that they felt this way for entirely different reasons. Far from being too accessible to the Athenian public, this democracy was exclusionary, and indeed many Cynics were personally excluded from democratic institutions because they were foreigners, citizens, or women. They sought a world where everyone could claim citizenship. Whereas Socrates, Plato, and others lamented the decline of Athenian power, for Greek Cynics it was becoming clear that the value of Athenian political dominance could not be taken for granted. They developed ethics for a more cosmopolitan world. To do so, Cynics grounded their philosophy in a distinction between two sources of human behavior: *nomos* (plural: *nomoi*) and *physis*. The Greek city-states were governed by various *nomoi*—human-made laws and customs.

These varied from one *polis* to another, and consisted of the rituals, traditions, and legislation that defined civic identity. Cynics had little use for these. Rather, they claimed that they derived their ethics from *physis*, natural or divine moral principles of universal quality, the basis of a virtuous life.[39] The former were arbitrary and artificial conventions that should be discarded, whereas the values arising from *physis* guided a person toward a life that was harmonious with nature.

The Academics and most other philosophers simply didn't like the people who were getting involved with Cynic philosophy. "Philosophy" was typically the domain of affluent men who spent their ample free time debating abstract concepts like justice and friendship. Philosophers commonly distinguished themselves from "sophists," people who made their living by teaching and speaking about wisdom. Socrates disapproved, characterizing it as a cash grab: in the olden days, men of wisdom never charged anyone a dime for education, but sophists of his own day eagerly profited from instruction.[40] This sounds like a perfectly reasonable concern about an authentic quest for wisdom and frustration with those who were turning that quest into a grift. But in suggesting that no one should make money from teaching or philosophizing, Socrates was really saying that only the independently wealthy could be legitimate philosophers. This sentiment was widespread among philosophers and many singled out Cynics as responsible for convincing ordinary people to pursue wisdom. Lucian of Samosata (125–185 CE) derided Cynics as "slaves and day laborers" who did not have the wealth to study philosophy.[41] The idea that anyone, regardless of education, economic standing, occupation, gender, or even enslavement, might be wise offended many philosophers. They understood their love of wisdom to be a specifically aristocratic enterprise to be undertaken in their leisure time. Cynics were exceptionally universalist in their idea that the illiterate and uneducated could pursue a life of philosophy.

For this reason, scholars today often characterize Cynicism as a "popular" philosophy. There was no need to attend a Cynic academy to learn its doctrinal nuances. There weren't any buildings dedicated to Cynic instruction in the first place! Rather, Cynic philosophy was undertaken by imitating important figures whose deeds were recounted in the *chreiai*: their defense of freedom, shamelessness, self-sufficiency, boldness, and unconventional understanding of virtue. Anybody could live out these values, regardless of identity. These philosophical principles were straightforward, but it required considerable effort to execute a self-consciously shameless life, since it would alienate loved ones and nearly everyone else one encountered. As demanding as Cynicism was, it defied the odds to flourish in Greek-speaking contexts during the fourth and third centuries BCE.

Cynicism flourished in two distinct periods, first finding success in Greek-speaking regions during the fourth and third centuries BCE. Its popularity declined in the following years, before seeing a revival in the first century CE under the Roman Empire, though the philosophy had changed significantly by this time. Cynicism was an odd fit for Rome. This was in part because the Cynic emphasis on cosmopolitanism was stranger for Romans than it had been for earlier Greeks. Cynic cosmopolitanism was articulated as a critique of the Greek *polis*: how the city's institutions encouraged people to not only identify with a specific city-state, but to live a contrived life in obedience of the city's *nomoi*. Citizenship served a very different function in the Roman Empire, as it was not confined to a single city-state as it had been for the Greeks. In some ways, Romans made the privileges of citizenship more accessible. Greeks insisted upon the exclusivity of citizenship, but this was not an issue for Romans, since—with enough money or willingness to jump through the necessary hoops—any man from Hispania to Syria could theoretically acquire citizenship. The interconnectedness of the Roman Empire already lent itself to a form of cosmopolitanism: Athens and Sparta, for instance, were no longer rival city-states, but were located within a single province which was in turn part of a massive empire that encompassed the entire Mediterranean. Romans even awarded many emancipated slaves a form of citizenship, something almost unimaginable in Classical Greece.[42] This isn't to say Roman citizenship was easy to obtain, but there were ways to acquire it, no matter where you came from. This was different from the Greeks, who prohibited foreigners and slaves from ever claiming the privilege. All of this meant that Romans understood citizenship very differently from Greeks. Becoming a Roman had less to do with following the *nomoi* of a specific *polis* and more to do with understanding the Roman conception of the human ideal. It required would-be Roman citizens to develop competence in Roman ways of doing things—how to dress like a Roman, how to cook like a Roman, how to speak like a Roman, etc.[43] This ideal was not a cookie-cutter template, but was all subject to local adaptation and personal preference. What value did Cynic cosmopolitanism hold in a Roman context?

Two distinct strands of Cynicism emerged during its revival under the Roman Empire. Both show concerns with adapting a very *Greek* philosophy to address *Roman* values—one by using the philosophy to challenge Roman values, the other by ensuring Cynicism was consistent with Roman values. Particularly interesting is how they diverged on the issue of shamelessness.[44] Although both claimed to be the legitimate heirs of Diogenes, Crates, and others, these two strands of Cynicism could not have been more different.

On the one hand, many Roman Cynics continued to delight in the shamelessness that they knew from the *chreiai*. Jewish rabbis of the third century CE mentioned Cynics who slept in graveyards and wore torn clothing.[45] Symeon the Holy Fool—a Christian saint, living in the sixth century CE—adopted a Cynic way of life, mingling with sex workers, defecating in public, eating raw meat, and dragging a dog's carcass around wherever he went.[46] The Stoic philosopher Epictetus, living in the first century CE, noted how Cynics of his own day enjoyed farting in public.[47] This vein of Cynicism attracted people from the poor of the Roman and Byzantine empires who felt little need to play the game of honor and shame. People turned to Cynicism because of widespread poverty: the philosopher Dio Chrysostom (40–115 CE) found this variety of Cynicism annoying but admitted that many Cynics shamelessly begged because they couldn't afford food.[48] Much like the Cynics of Classical and Hellenistic Greece, these were poor and enslaved people who found refuge in Cynicism—even if the political situation and questions of citizenship had changed significantly.

But many Romans disliked Cynicism for precisely this reason. A philosophical community consisting of sexual deviants, beggars, and eccentrics was bound to rub some people the wrong way. The Roman politician Cicero (106–43 BCE) had mixed feelings about Cynicism. He found the

Cynic emphasis on self-mastery consistent with his very Roman conception of masculinity, but he took issue with Cynic shamelessness: "It is incompatible with our innate sense of right and wrong; and without that there can be nothing good, nothing honorable."[49] We have already seen that Dio Chrysostom and Epictetus regarded the Cynics of their day as pale imitations of Diogenes.

Emerging from these concerns, another strain of Roman Cynicism developed, this one concerning a respectable manner of philosophizing. In the minds of respectable Cynics, shamelessness had given their philosophy a bad name, and they sought to redeem it by discarding its countercultural elements. For instance, the Roman emperor Julian (reigned 361–363 CE) tried to re-paganize the Roman Empire after his uncle Constantine began to Christianize it a few decades earlier. Julian turned to Graeco-Roman philosophy, regarding it as a viable mechanism for returning to paganism's glory days. But for all Julian's interest in Cynicism, which he regarded as a venerable school of thought, he disliked the homeless people and beggars who practiced it. Julian condemned these Cynics, defending the philosophical school from the disrepute that shameless Cynics brought upon it.[50] These Cynics were "slaves to gluttony, sex, or bodily pleasure in general, people who mock my words and laugh in my face, like dogs that piss in front of schools and law courts."[51] Julian believed the best response to these shameless dog-philosophers was to do what you do with a misbehaving puppy: don't encourage their bad behavior by giving them attention. Julian, however, didn't take his own advice: he wrote two treatises to convince others that Cynicism was better without this kind of shamelessness. Rather, Julian, Cicero, Epictetus, and others believed that Cynicism should be practiced within Roman social values.

This more respectable strain of Cynicism diverged significantly from the radical practices of Diogenes and other Greek Cynics. These "respectable" Cynics had diluted the radical teachings of Greek Cynics and transformed them into the values of Roman aristocracy: asceticism became moderation, self-sufficiency turned into patrician resourcefulness, and boldness of speech evolved into the humiliation of lower-status people. Taking the last of these as a case in point, they composed bigoted *chreiai* in the name of the great Cynics. For instance, one writer concocted a sexist *chreia* and attributed it to Diogenes: "Seeing a woman giving another woman advice, he said, 'Look! A viper is supplying venom to an asp.'"[52] Women were a bunch of snakes and nothing safe could come out of their mouths. Some of these Roman-era "respectable" Cynics also attributed racist sayings to Diogenes.[53] All of this was at odds with the spirit of Cynic cosmopolitanism.

As Christianity spread throughout the Mediterranean, Cynicism declined again in the fifth century CE. Although a few Christians appreciated its asceticism, the popular appeal of the philosophy had diminished by this time.

* * *

Many people find Cynics appealing today, especially those who hold "respectability" in low regard. But others, particularly on the political left, are more suspicious. Given that Cynics did not really live a communal life, those on the left tend to think of them as more libertarian than anything else. In such a view, Cynicism was not exactly radical democracy, but something more like "lifestyle anarchism"—prioritizing individual freedom and happiness over collective liberation. And there is good reason people feel this way. After all, Max Stirner, perhaps the most famous individualist anarchist, looked to the Cynics for inspiration: "What else was Diogenes of Sinope looking for, other than the true enjoyment of life, which he found in having the fewest possible needs?"[54] Stirner regarded the Cynics as advocates for self-oriented individualism; they found freedom in their personal pleasures. And you can see why he understood Cynics this way. What was Diogenes' act of public masturbation if not a defiant act of hedonism? The Cynic value of self-sufficiency also pointed in this direction. Stirner and other individualist anarchists think that Diogenes found pleasure by becoming a fully autonomous individual, dependent upon no one else for happiness. Within this framework, Cynics serve as a model for the autonomous individuals who constitute the irreducible building blocks of a free world.

But this offers a shallow understanding of Cynicism. In fact, this entire understanding of human freedom relies upon a poor grasp of human sociality, unironically adopting the same logic as Margaret Thatcher, when she (in)famously stated, "there is no such thing as a society: there are individual men and women."[55] That is, it is incumbent wholly upon oneself to find happiness, achieve freedom, and become an autonomous human being. This contradicts any reasonable understanding of human social life, though. Only the most superficial analysis would deny that we depend inextricably upon the innumerable people in our lives, not to mention the complex networks of relations that emerge from them.

Although some people today appeal to Cynics to justify their individualist politics, this misconstrues their emphatically social critique.[56] Cynics offered a world where shamelessness did not further marginalize those excluded from the *polis*. Indeed, the very lives of Cynics demonstrated that honor and shame constituted a system of oppression. They showed that a virtuous world means we must refuse to even consider questions of status. The system of honor and shame stacked the deck against most of society, as only a few benefit from this game. Rather than trying to reform honor and shame so as to include these marginalized people, Cynics suggested it was better to throw the whole thing out. The Cynic cosmopolis was thus radically democratic in that it remained open to all, regardless of status. It was a sphere in which everyone could enjoy their freedom.

Further Reading

Desmond, William D. 2006. *The Greek Praise of Poverty: Origins of Ancient Cynicism*. Notre Dame: University of Notre Dame Press.
Desmond, William D. 2008. *The Cynics*. Stocksfield: Acumen.
Dobbin, Robert, translator and editor. 2012. *The Cynic Philosophers: From Diogenes to Julian*. New York: Penguin.
Gardner, Darren. 2022. "Cynicism as Immanent Critique: Diogenes and the Philosophy of Transvaluation." *Polis, The Journal for Ancient Greek and Roman Political Thought* 39: 123–48.
Kalouche, Fouad. 2003. "The Cynic Way of Living." *Ancient Philosophy* 23: 181–94.

Dobbin's volume offers an accessible translation of the most important ancient texts discussing Cynics. Concerning the democratic thought of Cynics, Fouad Kalouche contextualizes Cynic politics with respect to other philosophers of Greek antiquity. There are several excellent studies on Cynic philosophers, ranging from articles on their social criticisms (e.g., Gardner's article) to more comprehensive book-length publications (e.g., Desmond's books). Historians are often reluctant to outright state that Cynics practiced a form of anarchism, even if it is often implied. For a useful discussion of Cynic anarchism, see Desmond, *Cynics*, 184–208.

4

Zoroastrian Polygamists: The Mazdakites

This chapter considers a religious group living in the region east of the Greek and Roman Empires, turning to what is today Iraq and Iran. The Mazdakites (later called the Khurramis) were a radical Zoroastrian sect founded under the Parthian Empire in the third century CE, rose to prominence under the Sasanian Empire (224–651 CE), and lasted centuries into the Islamic caliphates of the seventh century and beyond. Ancient texts were consistent in their allegations: Mazdakites were libertine peasants who revolted against the nobility, practiced non-monogamy, raised their children in a communal fashion, and held property in common. Mazdakites were widely condemned as heretics. Their practices offended even Christian and Muslim writers who were otherwise unconcerned with questions of Zoroastrian orthodoxy— Zoroastrianism being the religion dominating Persian social and political life for about a millennium until the rise of Islam. No Mazdakite texts survive, which would have been immensely helpful in assessing the claims of their detractors.[1] However, it is possible to weed through the defamatory claims, and to catch a few glimpses of how Mazdakites lived.

Mazdakites generally avoided violence, shared goods with each other, and ate a vegetarian diet. Most striking is how they practiced fraternal polyandry—a marital system wherein one woman can marry several men who are related to each other. This in itself might grab our attention, since polyandrous societies are rare historically. An obvious question arises: what did men and women find appealing about this way of organizing their families? On its face, polyandry does not sound particularly liberating for either men (who would have limited time with their spouse) or women (who would be overwhelmed with household duties and the competing expectations of multiple husbands). Why did Mazdakites structure their households in this way?

To address this question, it is necessary to discuss sexual violence. Rape culture was a major component of antiquity. In the ancient world, women were commonly objectified, treated as ornaments of masculine honor, and reduced to outlets for male pleasure. People respond in compelling ways to the worst parts of their culture, developing new values in the service of a more equitable society. Mazdakite gender norms should probably be understood in this way, although it took quite some time for them to get there.

* * *

Although Mazdakism takes its name from Mazdak, a Zoroastrian priest who lived in the sixth century CE (this is because Mazdak popularized the religion and became its public face), it originated during the third century CE in the Persian town of Fasa with a Zoroastrian prophet named Zaradusht.[2] According to the Byzantine historian Joshua the Stylite, Zaradusht taught that private property should be abolished and that all goods should be shared within a community. More radically, he taught that spouses "belong in common and everyone may have intercourse with anyone they please."[3] To say that his

ZOROASTRIAN POLYGAMISTS

teaching went against the grain would be an understatement: at the time, Persian elites practiced polygyny (i.e., one man with multiple wives) through the institution of the harem, whereas common folk practiced monogamy. Zaradusht encouraged his followers to try something else—though what exactly he suggested isn't entirely clear. He may have encouraged followers to reject marriage, denounced sexual exclusivity within marriage, or advocated something else entirely.

Zaradusht drew upon Zoroastrian theology, using symbols of cosmic light and darkness to advocate brotherly love and pacifism. According to Zaradusht and later Mazdakites, the Light was a source of wisdom that permitted free choice, whereas the Darkness operated blindly and arbitrarily.[4] The Wise Lord (i.e., god of the Light) was served by seven viziers and twelve spiritual beings, corresponding to the seven astrological planets and twelve signs of the zodiac. Together, these powers ruled the universe. Zaradusht's theology was certainly sophisticated, but the central ideas were standard fare among the religions of late antiquity, fitting comfortably within cosmological and astrological speculations of the time. Ancient sources have little to say about Zaradusht, his theology, or the extent to which people adopted his teachings. It's hard to know what to make of Zaradusht: his communitarian approach to property sounds exciting, but his sexual policies could have either been liberating or oppressive for women—we simply don't know. The sources are too vague, biased, and unreliable for us to extrapolate conclusions with much confidence.

We know next to nothing about Mazdakism during the two centuries after Zaradusht's death, but things become clearer at the end of the fifth century CE, when Zaradusht's ideas underwent a resurgence during the Sasanian Empire. This

Mazdakism was a significant deviation from any of Zaradusht's subversive teachings, especially because Kavad I, the Sasanian King of Kings, promoted the religion in his empire.[5] Kavad rose to the throne in 488 CE at the young age of 15 and ruled from the Sasanian capital of Ctesiphon. Under Kavad, the sect's sexual politics took a turn for the worse before its radical potential blossomed, as we will see later. Kavad expressed profound interest in the religion, but focused mostly on its sexual practices. Essentially, Kavad was enthusiastic about doctrines that allowed him to sleep around. He implemented a law that opened up all marriages to extra-marital intercourse—any man could now sleep with any woman.[6] These reforms were countercultural in obvious ways and they also soured his relationship with the Sasanian aristocracy.

There are several reasons nobility disliked this policy. First, the polygyny of Persian nobility permitted men to amass large harems, and this was undermined by Kavad's reforms.[7] In addition to marrying wealthy women, aristocrats took young women from poor families to become their concubines. These women were expected to remain sexually exclusive to their husband because they served as symbols of his status and wealth: the resources required to provide food and gifts for the women were considerable. This system also necessitated a large cohort of other slaves to wait upon and monitor these women, ensuring they remained loyal (read: sexually pure). These harems led to an uneven sexual economy: most women were trapped with the wealthy, such that poor men had little opportunity to marry. Kings and aristocrats distributed descriptions of their "type" of woman and expected the poor to inform them of suitable relatives.[8] Many people concealed their loved ones when they received such letters. This

ZOROASTRIAN POLYGAMISTS

system fostered resentment among common men and women, as this de facto form of slavery licensed an aristocrat to rape any woman within his own harem; her consent was a non-factor. Kavad's policies completely undermined the harem as a status symbol within the Sasanian Empire, by allowing men to sleep with any woman they pleased—married or not! From the perspective of the aristocrats, Kavad's laws undermined the sexual economy, such that poor men could sleep with women whose sexual exclusivity signified a rich man's status.

The second reason Sasanian nobility resented Kavad's sexual legislation is that they maintained their power in part by cultivating a mystique around their ancestry. As we saw with the Cynics, one's bloodline acted as a marker of honor or shame, so Sasanian nobles often claimed illustrious ancestors to further distinguish themselves from the peasantry. These bloodlines were essential for determining lines of inheritance to transmit wealth from one generation to the next. Kavad's sexual policies muddied the genealogical waters, which is the single most widespread complaint about his reign. One Zoroastrian writer expressed alarm that Mazdakites were guilty of "obscuring the descent of every individual by promiscuous marriage, accompanied by the mixture of sperm."[9] That is to say, when a nobleman's wife gave birth, it was no longer clear whether the child's father was her husband, one of her lovers, or an unknown rapist. It was impossible to ascertain which children were legitimate heirs during this period.

Kavad's policy made him politically vulnerable, since the Sasanian King of Kings held relatively little power over the aristocracy at the time. If anything, the aristocracy provided him with the resources required for political stability. For instance, Kavad's standing army was small, since he relied on the feudal armies of these very elites whenever warfare or unrest broke out. Accounts varied, but they agreed that Sasanian elites schemed against Kavad to ensure there was no way it was going to end well for him. The Islamic historian Muhammad ibn Jarir al-Tabari (839–923 CE) claimed that there was a conspiracy to burn the king alive.[10] Kavad took Mazdakite pacifism seriously and did not attack the dissident aristocrats.[11] The assassination plot failed, but these scheming elites did manage to successfully depose and imprison Kavad in 496 CE. The deposed king escaped and found refuge in the Hephthalite Kingdom to the east of the Sasanian Empire, returning and reclaiming the Sasanian throne in 498 CE. Kavad indicated no interest in Mazdakite religion the second time around, abandoning his earlier policies about non-monogamy, as well as his pacifism. The latter period of his rule is most noteworthy for the destructive wars he waged against the Byzantine Empire and his consolidation of power, no doubt learning particular lessons from his first reign. He ruled without significant controversy until his death in 531 CE.

Nothing about Kavad's reign was particularly anarchistic, let alone democratic. Kavad was king over a powerful empire. In the first period of his rule, he imposed laws with horrific implications for women, whose sexual autonomy, already limited by patriarchy, was eliminated. Though the aristocracy hated him, the earliest accounts of Kavad's reign indicate that common people disliked his policies too, perhaps because Kavad had little interest in Zaradusht's most radical idea—the communal ownership of property.[12] Up through Kavad's reign, Mazdakism at best had some good to go with the bad and at worst was an abusive sex cult that found its way to the seat of imperial power. This would soon change, with the religion's emancipatory potential coming to the fore shortly after Kavad's death.

* * *

Mazdakism turned revolutionary a few years after Kavad's death, thanks to Mazdak, a Zoroastrian priest from the city of Madharaya. Mazdak rose to prominence during the reign of Kavad's son and successor, Khosrow I (reigned 531–579 CE). He preached a full return to the teachings of Zaradusht, with two particular teachings deserving our attention. First was Mazdak's adoption of Zaradusht's idea that monogamy was untenable in a context where wealthy men had dozens of wives and concubines. Mazdak modified Zaradusht's ideas about relationships to more clearly emphasize women's consent and to structure families via polyandrous marriage (i.e., one woman marrying multiple men). Second, Mazdak advocated a return to Zaradusht's teachings on the abolition of private property. Kavad had dispensed with the more egalitarian aspects of Mazdakite doctrine, but Mazdak led the poor to revolt against the Sasanian state, on the grounds that "God has established daily sustenance in the earth for His servants to divide out among themselves with equal shares, but men have oppressed each other regarding it."[13] He taught that while the Wise Lord (god of the Light) created enough for everyone to live comfortably, a handful of people were hoarding life's necessities while the rest of the population starved.

Given the massive inequalities in Sasanian society, Mazdak's message found a receptive audience.[14] In rural parts of the empire, a single nobleman might own an entire village, or several if he was particularly wealthy.[15] These aristocrats contracted peasants as sharecroppers to farm in return for less than a quarter of the harvest. As if that was not bad enough, life was even more precarious than this implies: a capricious landlord could cancel a lease to render the farmer homeless. Landlords could sell entire villages—along with the tenants working their farms—to other wealthy men whenever they pleased. Sasanian laws secured ample income for the rich, which entailed the opposite for everyone else.

The landlords also comprised the local aristocracy, who accumulated many women within their personal harems. Such aristocrats would take the daughters and sisters of the farmers into their harems, who they kept as concubines, of lesser legal status than wives. Of course, this was a society in which marriage entailed the exchange of money (e.g., paying a pre-marital bride price, resource sharing between the two families), so by restricting lower-class women to concubinage, these aristocrats limited any wealth that might transfer to the families of peasant women. This approach to marriage ensured that "legitimate" heirs descended from aristocratic lines, so wealth continued circulating among a small coterie of wealthy families; it was not uncommon for aristocrats to marry their own relatives to ensure money remained within the bloodline.[16] Peasant men were unlikely to marry, given the simple absence of available women—most of whom were taken into the harems. The Sasanian class system thus created an "insuperable barrier" between aristocrats and peasants.[17] This is not to mention how the system also limited population growth among rural peasants; with fewer villagers having children, the population was presumably on an exponential decline.

Khosrow, the new king, imposed a tax proving to be the straw that broke the camel's back.[18] Traditionally, the Sasanians collected taxes in-kind, but Khosrow exacted this new tax via coinage, which presented significant problems for sharecropping peasants. Rural peasants usually had little cash on hand, so sharecroppers needed to sell their harvest at the market to acquire the necessary coinage. Hauling large quantities of crop to a market was difficult, and tenant farmers were hit with a further problem: they were likely cash-cropping—that is, producing crops that were most valuable on the market, rather than most practical for independent subsistence. Everyone in the village had the same landlord, which meant they were probably all growing the same crops and harvesting at the same time. This situation rendered their harvest nearly worthless: a single market was flooded with identical produce, all of which desperately needed to be sold to pay Khosrow's new tax. Precarity became poverty, poverty became destitution, destitution became debt, and debt became default.

There was no pretense of taxation serving the public interest in antiquity. Everyone knew that ancient taxes subsidized vanity projects, underwrote *quid pro quo* gifts to political allies, paid the wages of occupying soldiers, and contributed to the administration's personal coffers. This led to a wildly different conception of taxation than we have today, where if we live in a welfare state, we expect that our taxes will pay for schools, roads, healthcare, and so on. Consider Patricia Crone's vivid description:

> Though we still complain of the tax burden, [a modern government] does not normally have to call upon the army to make us pay, nor do we normally engage in prolonged haggling with the tax-collectors, weeping, crying, tearing our clothes or grovelling in the dust to convince them that

we have not got a penny left, or calling upon every influential friend we have to ensure that no tax-collector would dare to approach us. Such procedures were however commonplace in most pre-industrial societies. For the peasants, tax-collectors were like swarms of locusts descending to strip them of everything they possessed; for the tax-collectors, peasants were like recalcitrant cattle which had to be milked however much they might protest.[19]

Crone's portrait hints at why taxation prompted such strong reactions: taxes were regressive by design and so the poor and the foreigner bore the burden, while aristocrats were basically exempt. This policy applied across antiquity. If anything, taxes were another way to funnel as much wealth as possible from those in poverty into the pockets of the rich. To be clear, much of this could be said about taxation today, which tends to fund military budgets, corporate subsidies, and the like. Moreover, one could rightly argue that the aristocracy continues to pay little or no taxes, while the poor bear a disproportionate burden with taxes and de facto taxes (e.g., late fees, interest payments). The point here is not that we have moved beyond the injustices of ancient taxation, but rather that today we deploy rhetoric about taxation serving the public good (e.g., infrastructure, education, healthcare) that was generally absent during antiquity.

Mazdak's partisans were destitute and Mazdak himself became a sort of Robin Hood figure, encouraging the peasants to take property from the nobility and redistribute it among themselves—going further than Zaradusht ever did.[20] Although many stories about Mazdak are considered apocryphal, they can still give us glimpses into how Mazdak's supporters talked about injustice. For instance, one ancient historian attributed two short poems to Mazdak, the second one building upon the first. The first poem related a story about a man who refused to give an antidote to another man suffering from a poisonous snake bite. The poem concerned the immoral, even criminal, behavior of the man who refused to help. After telling this poem, Mazdak recounted another one and encouraged his listeners to connect the two:

> Picture a man in chains; for want of bread
> He wastes away and soon he will be dead:
> Now he's denied bread by a passerby
> Who lets the miserable captive die.
> Should this man suffer punishment? Or would
> You say that what he did was just and good?[21]

Mazdak's poem posed a pair of questions, to which Mazdakites responded by declaring that the man who refuses to help the starving man commits a crime just as callous as the man in the first poem; anyone who lets another person starve has blood on their hands. This reasoning gave the Mazdakites the justification they needed to loot granaries and redistribute the produce they contained. "Young and old, the poor flocked to him; he confiscated wealth from this man and gave it to that."[22] Mazdakites allotted food according to a person's hunger, quite different from how priestly privilege and wealth usually dictated these things.[23] Mazdak's supporters engaged in direct action to redistribute resources, such that the vulnerable might flourish.

Mazdak himself played a significant role in this popular rebellion, which spread throughout the western part of the

Sasanian Empire. Sources agree that Mazdakites were pacifists, but their doctrines explicitly permitted exceptions for revolts.[24] After thousands of Mazdakites raided grain stores and distributed their contents among themselves, they demanded more of a say in their governance. Less reliable accounts claim that Mazdak attempted to usurp the Sasanian throne. Some mystery surrounds the insurrection, but surviving accounts agree that the emperor executed Mazdak and thousands of his followers in the 530s CE (see Figure 4). Many survived the persecution and continued to practice their religion, but they put even more effort into avoiding urban centers to create communities elsewhere.

Historian Patricia Crone characterizes Mazdakites as "Zoroastrian communists," whereas Peter Marshall suggests an anarchistic undercurrent.[25] But the difference between Crone and Marshall is mostly a matter of phrasing: Crone

Figure 4 The execution of Mazdak and his followers (1330 CE). One account of the mass execution of Mazdakites claimed that the Sasanian king Khosrow buried Mazdakites with their heads in the ground in his garden like seeds. Khosrow and his attendant stand at the right, observing as Mazdak hangs upside down, forced to gaze upon the fruits of his supposedly evil seeds. This illustration is from a medieval manuscript of an epic poem titled *Shahnameh* (known in English as "The Book of Kings"), composed by the Persian historian Ferdowsi (940–1015 CE). (Photograph by the Metropolitan Museum of Art)

concludes that "in modern legal terminology, [Mazdakites] abolished private ownership."[26] Crone and Marshall agree that Mazdakites experimented with a classless society, devoid of coercive power. This certainly sounds like communitarian anarchism, even if Crone and Marshall emphasize different aspects of Mazdakite social life. Ancient writers might have agreed with this assessment, but hardly found it cause for celebration, going so far as to claim that the religion was illegitimate precisely because it demolished social hierarchies. Thus, one Zoroastrian priest confronted Mazdak and tried to ridicule him in front of political leaders:

> If men are to be equal in the world, social distinctions will be unclear; who will want to be a commoner, and how will nobility be recognized? If a laboring slave and the king are the same, when a man dies, who is to inherit his goods?[27]

When Zoroastrian writers and priests condemned Mazdakites, they objected more to their dissolution of social classes than any doctrinal deviation.[28]

* * *

Khosrow was aware that Mazdakism's popularity was symptomatic of widespread discontent. And so, after violently suppressing Mazdak's revolt, he initiated reforms to prevent further unrest, but ceded as little ground as possible to the peasantry. He developed a system of provincial officers termed "Protectors of the Poor," who served as advocates for the poor in court, sending these officers to regions where Mazdakism was still flourishing.[29] Recognizing the Zoroastrian character of the revolt, Khosrow did not appoint political administrators to this role, but instead chose prestigious Zoroastrian priests of the same rank that Mazdak himself had been. Each Protector of the Poor was responsible for huge areas, and was only able to offer sporadic help. Moreover, because these priests were advocates in court, they dealt with issues on a case-by-case basis: these reforms were part of a concerted effort to undermine solidarity among peasants by reducing systemic injustice to personal problems that could be resolved on the basis of individual legal merits.

In short, Khosrow attempted to mitigate unrest by appropriating and watering down Mazdakites' populist solidarity. Khosrow succeeded to the extent that people perceived him as an emperor willing to address the frustrations of his subjects. Khosrow offered little more than lip-service to Sasanian peasants, however. His reforms further subjugated sharecroppers and other poor folk to their landlords. The Mazdakites imagined and implemented another social and economic order. In doing so, they revealed how the aristocracy was more vulnerable than they wanted the populace to know, leading to centuries of unrest in Persia. Historian Touraj Daryaee contends that Mazdak's revolt facilitated "fundamental changes in Iranian societal structure, and furthered egalitarian and anti-state movements in the early Islamic world."[30]

Mazdakites did not disappear, even if the Sasanians and eventually the Muslim caliphs suppressed their religion. Islamic texts give brief glimpses into their life in the following centuries. Particularly noteworthy was a Mazdakite resurgence beginning around 740 CE. Ancient authors termed this form of Mazdakism *Khurramiyya* ("joyous religion") and it found prominence in the Jebal region of what is now western Iran. Khurrami Mazdakites were known for their pacifism, shared wives, vegetarianism, communal property, and idiosyncratic form of Zoroastrianism.[31] It appears that the Khurramis practiced a more hybrid form of Mazdakism, as ancient writers sometimes identified them as engaging in a strange form of Shi'ite Islam, Manichaeism, or Zoroastrianism. It is hard to know how much the Khurramis identified with any of these traditions; it is quite possible that they playfully experimented and drew upon several religions to create something new. One source explicitly notes their tolerance of theological diversity, since "every religious man, according to them, is on the right path."[32] Of course, it is also possible that ancient writers had difficulty understanding the Khurramis and just described them as practicing an odd version of a more familiar religion. Khurrami communities lasted for centuries in rural Iran, thriving under the Umayyad and Abbasid Caliphates.

From this overview, it is clear that Mazdakites varied in their politics. Zaradusht taught that wealth should be shared but the specifics of his views on marriage have been lost to time. Centuries later, Kavad stripped the religion of its radicalism and implemented a regime of terror during his time as a Mazdakite. All accounts indicate that Mazdak himself represented a return to the communitarian ideals of Zaradusht, particularly focusing his energies on the insurrectionary implications of Zaradusht's teachings. Finally, the Khurramis settled down, adapting the religion for long-term collective life. They sought to live out Mazdakism as a matter of daily routine, with entire villages adhering to the religion and its values.

* * *

The rest of this chapter will examine how Mazdakites developed a system of fraternal polyandry (i.e., one woman marrying multiple men who were related to each other) and how this allowed women considerable agency.[33] They created this system in response to the patriarchal institutions that prevailed in Sasanian and Umayyad Persia. Ancient sources purport to tell how both early and contemporary (i.e., Khurrami) Mazdakites organized their families. But since these texts were written in the Islamic era, we should probably regard them as more reliable on Umayyad-era Mazdakism and remain skeptical about their claims regarding earlier Mazdakites, as they probably projected contemporary practices onto their descriptions of Mazdak and other early adherents of the religion. The idea that Mazdakite sexual norms empowered women is a minority view within scholarship, but one that deserves consideration.[34]

At first glance, Mazdakism, despite its claims of egalitarianism, further entrenched patriarchy because Mazdakite polyandry centered masculine concerns, including men's access to heterosexual intercourse in a social context where men comprised the majority of the population. This may conjure a scenario that was unpleasant for women: several men constantly pestering their wife for sex while also expecting her to fulfill her child-rearing and household duties, but for an even larger family than in a monogamous household. It may evoke even worse conditions: sex-trafficking or marital rape. Such a religion sounds horribly opposed to feminist values. After all, no reasonable person can defend Kavad's variety of Mazdakism, within which women were reduced to objects of male sexual pleasure with little regard for their humanity. Under Kavad's regime, even the modest protections offered by the

ZOROASTRIAN POLYGAMISTS

harem system—which valued a patriarch's ability to shield "his" women from any men who might take them as sexual partners—were no longer safeguards from sexual violence.[35] Kavad's reign must have been a nightmare for Persian women.

But Kavad was also not a typical Mazdakite. Kavad, whatever the sincerity of his devotion to Mazdakite religion, was opportunistic in his use of its doctrines: he was more interested in sleeping with married women and undermining his rivals than adapting a populist form of Zoroastrianism for the Sasanian Empire. Every religion has its extremists with ambitions of power, who appeal to sacred doctrines and texts to justify their abuses. That does not mean that they are representative. There is no reason we should suppose that Kavad spoke for most Mazdakites. It is often deeply unpleasant situations—in this case, ancient patriarchy and Kavad's misogynistic variety of Mazdakism—that lead people to innovate radical new ways of living. It may be productive to think about Mazdakite sexual norms outside of cultural prejudices about polyandry and attempt to understand how this system ascribed Persian women agency, reconsidered gender norms, and permitted a freer life than most were accustomed to. There are four reasons to arrive at this conclusion:

1) contrary testimonies are unreliable and largely written to disparage the religion;
2) societies organized similarly today ascribe considerable agency to women;
3) the only surviving eyewitness account of Mazdakite life gives cause to do so; and
4) the absence of a state to reinforce patriarchal power.

Let us consider these in turn.

* * *

First, when ancient writers discussed how Mazdakite men treated women, they were either preoccupied with Kavad opening wealthy men's harems to the public, or they complained about Mazdakites not respecting the sanctity of marriage. In either case, Mazdakism's detractors were men who wanted to keep the firm hierarchies of Persian society in place—especially patriarchy and social class. For instance, al-Tabari described Mazdakites under Kavad as perverts who "were able to indulge their lusts and get their hands on highborn women to whom they would never have been able to aspire."[36] He also claimed that Mazdakites "would burst in on a man in his own house" and kidnap all of the women to claim them as Mazdakite wives.[37] This narrative indicated no concern for the well-being of these women, but rather expressed alarm that the peasant mobs were able to sleep with any women they liked. Al-Tabari and others hoped to horrify their male readership, largely reducing the role of women to props in their historical dramas. Neither al-Tabari nor most other writers took any interest in how women experienced Mazdakism.[38]

Most of these accounts can be safely dismissed as unreliable. Ancient writers deployed a handful of stock polemical tropes to discredit people they didn't like. The sex-crazed cultist was one such character, often used against those with different sexual or gender norms. In deploying this identifiable trope, they wanted to demonstrate that this heresy led to self-indulgent behavior which culminated in the breakdown of society, so they freely invented tales of horror that used this stereotype. We have no reason to take al-Tabari's comments in the previous paragraph seriously and the same goes for most other accounts. The tales of violence within these stories combine wild imagination, literary fiction, and baseless speculation. These trends were quite common in antiquity and remain so today; for instance, in Chapter One we saw how ancient writers made similar claims about the Third Servile War, despite all evidence to the contrary.

Although ancient texts attribute objectifying ideas to Mazdakite men, this misogyny seems to be the authors' understanding of a religion they hated. Disparaging accounts of the Mazdakites were often self-contradictory: the same authors who accused them of rampant sexual violence also described them as pacifist ascetics.[39] It is clear that, with a single exception, no ancient author ever actually met a Mazdakite.[40] Moreover, we will see that the only writer offering eyewitness testimony painted a far less scandalous portrait.[41]

* * *

The second reason to consider the Mazdakite experience of polyandry as radical in relation to gender norms is that societies organized similarly today ascribe considerable agency to women, notably the Lele in the Democratic Republic of Congo. It is helpful to look at similar societies of our own day not least because biases are present in ancient literature, and often the people studying these texts today as well. Scholars of antiquity overwhelmingly live in countries where monogamy not only prevails but remains the normative form of long-term relationships. This leads many scholars to be suspicious of polygamy. The word may, for many people, evoke the patriarchal households of Mormon fundamentalists or an abusive husband who pimps his wife.

Historians have rarely considered how practitioners of polyandry perceive their distinctive form of marriage.[42] It may help to seek a better understanding of polyandrous marriage from a cross-cultural perspective and the Lele, an ethnic group currently living in the Democratic Republic of Congo, provide a useful point of comparison. The Lele practice both polygyny and polyandry in a manner structurally similar to the Mazdakites and Persian elites.[43] Before the 1940s, the Lele faced comparable conditions to Sasanian peasants, as a few influential and powerful Lele men married several women, and the unmarried villagers were disproportionately male. Given that only 40 to 100 people inhabited villages, the remaining men became jealous of the local aristocrats who "hoarded" multiple wives in harem-like marriages. To address the unrest, the Lele developed a system of polyandry in the 1940s to co-exist alongside polygyny, centering around the "village-wife," a woman who marries all of the men around her age in a given village. This system is pervasive among the Lele, with roughly one in ten women being a village-wife. A village-wife does not marry the men of her hometown, but typically arrives at her betrothed village as a young adult with the explicit purpose of becoming a village-wife. There are many reasons women become village-wives, ranging from the enticing (e.g., seduction) to the despairing (e.g., asylum). The woman herself exercises considerable agency in this process, negotiating her status as its prospective village-wife and serving as an intermediary between her hometown and the village she marries.

Following any negotiations, there is little doubt about her position within the community. Mary Douglas observes that the village-wife is "treated with much honour" in all circumstances.[44] A honeymoon period begins once she marries the village, lasting roughly one year, during which time her life is comparable to that of minor royalty. She is free to engage in whatever leisure activities she wants, claim ownership of any merchandise that her husbands produce, eat the village's finest food and delicacies, and is not permitted to do anything even vaguely resembling physical labor: she never cooks, never chops firewood, nor does she ever perform any other work. Instead, her husbands compete for her affection by eagerly taking upon themselves any labor she might consider. If a husband sees the village-wife leaving to collect water at the well, for instance, he intervenes and insists that he does so. Indeed, Lele commonly joke about how demanding a village-wife can be, but no man ever declines any of her requests. She has only three responsibilities while in the honeymoon phase: sweeping out weaving centers (such that she might spend time there and choose what tapestries she wants to keep for herself), anointing her husbands with camwood paste, and having a considerable amount of sex. She invites one of her husbands to spend two nights at her home, another husband spends a couple nights in her home a few days after that, and so on; during the daytime, she might have sex with other husbands. There is no sense of obligation; intercourse, competition, and flirtation are part and parcel of a playful, post-marital courtship with her many husbands. All of this flips the script on traditional gender roles.

After about a year, the honeymoon period concludes, whereupon the village-wife cooks a communal meal for her husbands and selects a handful of those men to form a more permanent relationship: she chooses five or so men to become "house-husbands" who are permitted to visit her home for sex and for whom she might cook meals. Over time, even these five men narrow down to just one or two, as her house-husbands find someone else to marry or forfeit their status as house-husband because they feel jealous of her other house-husbands. At this point, her marriage approximates monogamy and her duties resemble those of other Lele wives, with one major exception: she is free to have sex with any man in the village she wants, so long as she does not do so inside her home.

Village-wives play a significant role in Lele society. They often serve as ambassadors when conflict breaks out between villages—negotiating men might be attacked, but the village wife holds an inviolable status across Lele culture, so no one would consider harming another village's village-wife, even when things are tense. She can also serve as a unifying force within the community, since her children are raised communally, meaning they have a much more robust support network than kids born from a monogamous marriage. Typically, one or two men undertake greater responsibility for raising the village-wife's children, but someone's social father is not necessarily their biological father.

The elevated status of the village-wife and her children is particularly clear when they pass away: their funerals must be observed with the same rituals as the local aristocrats; Lele believe that if they fail to do so, much of the edible wildlife will disappear. Once the government of Belgium—the colonial power governing Congo until 1960—found out about Lele polyandry, they banned it, but failed to eradicate the practice. Both polyandry and polygyny are illegal in the Democratic Republic of Congo today and the practice of polyandry has dwindled, as more Lele move to urban centers and participate

ZOROASTRIAN POLYGAMISTS

in mainstream Congolese society. Even so, some continue to practice non-monogamy today.

The Lele and Mazdakites bear important similarities: the practice of polygyny among the wealthy and polyandry among the poor, a powerful empire condemning their marital practices, communal rearing of children, a non-monetized economy, the rural context, entire villages practicing this way of life, etc. Even the impetus for experimenting with polyandry is the same. There is thus reason to suppose that Mazdakite polyandry functioned in ways that resemble that of the Lele. This is not to deny the various differences between their cultures.[45] But in discussing the Lele, suffice it to say that polyandry can make the lives of women easier, thanks in large part to ongoing processes of communal courtship. Polyandry can afford women a considerable amount of agency in their daily lives and in their sexuality, creating a space to reevaluate oppressive gender norms. We will see that there is reason to suppose that this was also the case within Mazdakite culture.

* * *

Third in our consideration of Mazdakite gender relations is that although we have limited knowledge of Mazdakite marriage, what we do know is similar to that of the Lele. For this, we can rely upon the early medieval traveler al-Maqdisi, who spent time with Khurrami Mazdakites in the tenth century CE. He traversed the Near and Middle East, visiting several Mazdakite villages on his journeys. In fact, al-Maqdisi, himself a Muslim, offered the only surviving account of someone who actually met them; all other accounts of Mazdakites were filtered through multiple intermediaries and colored by questions of heresy and orthodoxy. Al-Maqdisi was curious about how other people lived, and offered a strikingly non-judgmental account. He observed how their men can sleep with a woman "on the condition that she consents to it," further observing that men took care "not to harm anyone."[46] Al-Maqdisi's testimony is supported by the testimony of the Islamic historian Ibn al-Nadim (tenth century CE), who did not personally witness these things, but offered the only surviving account of a Mazdakite wedding. Al-Nadim also emphasized the woman's ongoing consent leading up to and during the ceremony itself.[47] The wedding involved a woman and her new husband sitting on a mattress in front of other men, whereupon the woman gave the witnesses cups. The men ritually sipped three times before the wife handed her new husband a sprig of basil. At this point, their wedding ceremony was complete and the celebration began. This all sounds very symbolic, though it is difficult to parse what exactly each element might mean. Why basil? Why three sips? Much remains obscure.

If similar societies are any indication, the mechanics of Mazdakite marriages must have been complex. In fact, one source relates how they dealt with the obvious issues of who gets to sleep with a shared wife on a given night:

> Their custom was that whenever a man went into a room to have commerce with a woman, he put his hat on the door and then went inside. If another person was seized with the same desire, on seeing the hat hanging on the door he turned back, knowing that somebody was already engaged in that business within.[48]

Similar rituals are attested within other ancient polyandrous societies.[49] Like the Lele, Mazdakites raised children communally and observed matrilineal descent.[50] Both systems account for the uncertainty of biological paternity in such relationships. It also speaks to the way Mazdakites conceptualized and practiced gender in ways that radically differed from prevailing Persian norms, creating communities of care that extended beyond the traditional, patriarchal household. Even though Mazdakites were overwhelmingly men, they created room for women's agency.

As a caveat, one observes that even these more neutral accounts were nevertheless written by men. They cannot substitute for words written directly by Mazdakite women. Unfortunately, no such texts survive. And even in the rare instances when ancient writers claim to quote Mazdakite women, they are reduced to the trope of scheming and adulterous women—another stock character that ancient historians used to discredit groups they did not like.[51]

* * *

Fourth and finally in our reasoning for considering Mazdakite marriage practices liberating for women is the question of the state. The Lele and the Mazdakites both evaded imperial power and refused to implement a state of their own. To be sure, Belgium ruled Congo as the colonial power when the Lele first developed their systems of polygyny and polyandry, but Belgian laws were nearly impossible to enforce in the rural areas that the Lele inhabited. Although the Lele had their own rules, rituals, and customs, there was no legislature to dictate laws, no police to enforce these rules, no judges to mete out rulings, and no penal system to punish offenders.[52] Fights occasionally broke out among the Lele, but dispute mediators handled most of the grievances. Moreover, the wealthy Lele could not convert their economic and social power into legislative or judicial power: they may have been influential within their village, but this did not translate into anything that could be enforced through the "legitimate" violence of the state.

Islamic writers described Mazdakite society similarly. Writers commented on Mazdakites' propensity for *ibaha*.[53] This Arabic word generally means something like "permissive" and was often applied to people with a reputation for libertinism.[54] The Shi'ite theologian Hasan bin Musa Nawbakhti (ninth century CE) regarded Mazdakites' freedom-loving *ibaha* as something dangerous, whereas al-Maqdisi characterized them this way without prejudice. It is easy to see why these writers considered Mazdakites permissive. Even beyond their sexual and marital norms, Muslim writers were offended by the Mazdakite abolition of private property, which they regarded as a threat to the social order of the same magnitude as their non-monogamy. Mazdakite liberality extended to matters of belief, as multiple texts suggested that Mazdakites had no real sense of "heresy." Al-Maqdisi described how Mazdakites welcomed religious diversity, so much so that they prohibited insults arising from theological disagreement.[55] There isn't much evidence of authority figures in their communities either. Again, al-Maqdisi reported his firsthand observations that their "imams" merely served as dispute mediators.

Contrast the freedom and leaderlessness of Mazdakism with another polyandrous society from antiquity—that of Sparta in the fifth and fourth centuries BCE.[56] Spartan brothers commonly shared a wife and raised their children communally, so as to foster cooperation between their families. This system benefited the half-siblings along with the rest of the family: everyone was more deeply invested in their family's well-being and a larger family meant a larger support network.

There were numerous similarities between the Spartans and Mazdakites. Multiple, related men married a single woman with the goal of sharing resources, with both populations concerned about the equitable distribution of property. Rather than inheriting property via primogeniture (i.e., the eldest son inheriting his father's property and titles), Spartans implemented a system of partible inheritance, which divided property equally among a family's children, including the daughters.[57] This, of course, differed from the Mazdakites' communal ownership, but Spartan polyandry ensured large families did not shut anyone out of inheritance. Aristotle expressed skepticism about the Spartan system, noting that "if many are born and the land divided equally, then many will inevitably become poor."[58] Spartans anticipated this potential problem of ever-shrinking inheritances by limiting the number of children a man could have. Each man might have one or two children, but he could nevertheless build a family of significant size with the children his wife bore from other men. By limiting the number of children each man had, they were ensured a reasonable inheritance, while these children benefited from the support of a larger nuclear family that included their half-siblings from their shared mother. The Spartan system even allowed for marriage between half-siblings born of the same woman but with different fathers, so as to permit reunification of property.

Structural differences between Spartans and Mazdakites become apparent around the question of whose interests their polyandry served. In Sparta, it helped only a small portion of the city's inhabitants: citizens and, to a lesser extent, their wives—about 20 percent of the city's population. Spartan polyandry was built around the system of citizenship that animated the city-state's civic life and consolidated property among its small class of citizens.[59] These citizens held immense privilege and the Spartan laws ensured it remained this way, imposing restrictions on anyone who did not have citizenship and ensuring that citizens were deeply loyal to the government. The result was a strong state that encouraged citizens to identify with the Spartan *polis*. Children, helots (i.e., enslaved serfs), and immigrants were all excluded from its benefits. The Spartan system ensured that valuable land, property, and wealth continued to circulate among the city's powerful.[60]

Economically, legally, and socially, the Mazdakites had more in common with Sparta's helots than its citizens. Ancient historians characterized Mazdakites as people who lived below subsistence, and evidence suggests they mainly comprised the sharecroppers discussed above. Mazdakite polyandry served precisely the opposite purpose from Spartan polyandry: to share limited resources among a subjugated population who had no allies within a powerful state. Their system produced *communal* heirs who could benefit from pooled resources. The Sasanian aristocracy was already practicing polygyny through the institution of the harem, which commodified women's bodies such that they were mere ornaments of masculine honor and vehicles for male pleasure. Mazdakite peasant men had nothing to lose in flipping things around and trying out polyandry. In fact, this system offered tangible benefits: the situation in Sasanian Persia resembled that of rural Tibet today, where people practice polyandry both because the region's population is disproportionately male and endemic poverty requires the labor of multiple sources of income to support a single family.⁶¹ If multiple (poor) men marry the same woman, they can alleviate some of their social disadvantages.

Apart from Kavad's unpopular reforms, the state never supported Mazdakism or its marital system. One ancient historian depicted a Zoroastrian priest's objections to Mazdak's radical teachings:

> If a man is poor, he is out of necessity compelled to enter the service and hire of a rich man; thus, high and low rank are manifested. When all property is shared, differences of rank will disappear from the world; the meanest wretch will be equal to the king; in fact, kingship will be nullified. You have come to annihilate the wealth and sovereignty of the royal family of Persia.⁶²

To advocate a classless society was to oppose the Sasanian Empire. Laws that protected the wealthy at the expense of the destitute were illegitimate for Mazdak and his followers. Instead, equity was achieved beyond the state. For all the disparaging comments of anti-Mazdakite historians, we must admit that they were correct in one regard: Mazdakite polyandry and communalism presented a threat to Sasanian authority.

* * *

None of this sounds like the sexual free-for-all that ancient anti-Mazdakite writers depicted. Patriarchy takes different forms from one culture to another. In ancient Persia, patriarchy involved the commodification of women, treating their bodies as resources for Sasanian elites: they marked an aristocrat's status, bore his heirs (but not if they were concubines), and served his sexual desires. Mazdakites experimented with a different marital system in an effort to address the needs of everyone who wasn't an aristocratic man. Women found a community where their consent was valued, while poor men were able to establish families that otherwise would have been impossible. No doubt other ancient Persians undertook different approaches, perhaps trying celibacy and solitude to address the commodification of women and the objectification of their bodies. For the Mazdakites, however, the communal life—shared property, children, spouses, and worship—bore radical potential.

This experimental attitude is evident in other parts of their religion. Mazdakite culture was malleable and welcomed diversity. Nevertheless, Mazdakism largely remained a populist and democratic religion, flouting the laws and customs of the Sasanian and eventually Muslim states. The Mazdakites organized their society in novel ways, by sharing resources, collaborating, and experimenting with alternate models of marriage and kinship—a longstanding tradition among anarchists.[63] Mazdakite men gave up many of the de facto privileges of patriarchy (e.g., claiming exclusive sexual rights over women, patriarchal inheritance systems) in service of more egalitarian gender norms. This was a significant part of their leaderless society. They had no head of state, nor any religious leaders allowed to exert power over them. They created a classless society, wherein all were equals and shared their property, helping each other through an ongoing system of mutual aid. As with other groups discussed in this book, the surviving evidence is limited, and such evidence as we do have often comes in the form of heresiology, identifying, describing, and decrying Mazdakites' deviation from one or another social convention. But perhaps one day, an archaeologist will recover some of their own texts, and it will be possible to see what they had to say about themselves.

Further Reading

Crone, Patricia. 1994. "Zoroastrian Communism." *Comparative Studies in Society and History* 36: 447–62.

Crone, Patricia. 2012. *The Nativist Prophets of Early Islamic Iran: Rural Revolt and Local Zoroastrianism*. Cambridge: Cambridge University Press.

Daryaee, Touraj. 2023. "Mazdak and Late Antique 'Socialism'." Pages 39–55 in *The Cambridge History of Socialism: Volume 1*. Edited by Marcel van der Linden. Cambridge: Cambridge University Press.

Yarshater, Ehsan. 1983. "Mazdakism." Pages 991–1024 in *The Cambridge History of Iran. Volume 3, Part 2: The Seleucid, Parthian and Sasanian Periods*. Edited by Ehsan Yarshater. Cambridge: Cambridge University Press.

Patricia Crone's article "Zoroastrian Communism" and Touraj Daryaee's entry in *The Cambridge History of Socialism* provide excellent introductions to the Mazdakites, while also addressing questions of democracy and economic egalitarianism. Crone's studies have been particularly important for the present chapter, but scholars dispute her interpretations, so readers would benefit from Daryaee's alternate account. Readers might also seek out Ehsan Yarshater's entry in *The Cambridge History of Iran*, which offers another counterpoint to Crone's analysis, though it is now a bit old. Patricia Crone's monograph on native revolts provides outstanding comparative work on Mazdakite doctrines and social practices, though it focuses mainly on Islamic-era iterations of Mazdakism, particularly the Khurramis. Unfortunately, there is no convenient collection of primary sources, for anyone looking to see what ancient writers had to say about Mazdakites. Rather, these are spread across a vast number of ancient and medieval texts, most of which have little to say about the group.

Second Interlude.
Life in the Northern Periphery:
The Sámi People

A handful of Roman writers mentioned the Fenni, an Indigenous population in the far north of Scandinavia.[1] Ancient writers described the Fenni as people who hunted and foraged for food rather than domesticating livestock or farming. Both women and men joined in the hunt. They also wrote that the Fenni clothed themselves in animal furs, did not have permanent houses, and that they placed their infants in slings that hung from trees. Roman writers thus concluded that the Fenni were a backward and uncivilized population. Procopius (sixth century CE) claimed they "live a kind life akin to that of the beasts." Tacitus (56–120 CE) thought the Fenni were downright feral, even in comparison with the unruliness of the Germanic warrior tribes.[2] But ancient authors also noted how content and egalitarian their lives were, since "they do everything communally."[3] Even Tacitus, who described the Fenni as "disgustingly poor," conceded that they had "attained the most difficult thing of all: to need nothing, not even prayers."[4]

These accounts were uncharitable and derived from limited knowledge. The Fenni lived in a region called Scandia (or sometimes Thule), a land Greeks and Romans barely knew. Although anyone who has glanced at a map today knows that this area consists of several peninsulas, Roman geographers were convinced that Scandia was an island. None of these authors ever met the Fenni, let alone traveled to Scandinavia, relying instead on the word of travelers, merchants, and other ethnographers. Ancient writers couldn't even agree on this population's name, with each one assigning them a slightly different ethnonym: Fenni (Tacitus), Phinnoi (Ptolemy), Skrithiphinoi (Procopius), Screrefennae (Jordanes), and Sirdifeni (Aithanarit). Similar terms designated the population in the languages of Old Norse (*Finnar*) and Old English (*Finnas*).[5]

Ancient descriptions of Fenni life, however biased, are largely vindicated by the archaeological evidence. Tacitus' claim that they used bone arrowheads rather than metal weapons has been verified.[6] He correctly described their shelter as well (the *lavvu* and the *goáhti*).[7] Paulus Diaconus (720–797 CE) offered accurate descriptions of skis, reindeer, and the midnight sun of the Arctic summer.[8] Procopius (sixth century CE) seemed to be aware of their use of skis as well.[9] Ancient accounts were infected with prejudice, but they provide valuable glimpses into Fenni life.

The Fenni have not disappeared. Today they are known as the Sámi, an Indigenous population that continues to inhabit the most northeastern portion of Europe.[10] Sápmi, their homeland, stretches across northern Norway, Sweden, Finland, and Russia—much of this land is within the Arctic Circle (see Figure 1). Roughly 100,000 Sámi inhabit Sápmi today.

* * *

The Sámi simultaneously fascinated and repulsed Roman writers. We can attribute this in part to the way Romans conceptualized the relationship between geography and culture. They saw Rome as the center of the inhabited—and thus, civilized—world. The Roman engineer Vitruvius (70

BCE–18 CE) commented that "divine wisdom placed the city of Rome in a unique and temperate region, such that it would rightfully command the whole world."[11] Vitruvius articulated the common understanding that geography determined how a given ethnic group lived. He and others believed that higher and lower gradations of civilization corresponded not only to a population's proximity to Rome, but also to their regional climate. Of course, Rome's supposed location at the world's center rendered its environment perfectly temperate and thus its people were perfectly suited to rule others. But the civilizing power of Rome grew weaker the further one traveled from the capital city. If Rome's climate rendered its people the most civilized, the wilderness made the Germans rustic but intelligent, and the extreme cold of Scandia rendered the Fenni barbarian.[12]

Roman geographers and ethnographers produced and relied upon maps that imagined the world this way, most famously the *Orbis Terrarum* ("The Lands of the World"), completed in 20 CE. Numerous copies of this map were produced, supposedly taken to the empire's great cities. No originals survive, but scholars have attempted to reconstruct the *Orbis Terrarum* based on medieval evidence (see Figure 5). From these reconstructions, we can see that Romans thought that their empire comprised three-quarters of the inhabited world, with massive empires like that of Parthia reduced to an afterthought. This was even more so with Scandia/Thule, which were depicted as tiny islands at the periphery of the world.[13]

Romans believed this geography rendered their empire a civilizing force upon barbarian peoples. Many Romans thought they had an ethical obligation to bring their culture to those they believed were savages. The Stoic philosopher

LIFE IN THE NORTHERN PERIPHERY

Seneca the Younger (4 BCE–65 CE) claimed that it was a gesture of magnanimity that Romans did not keep to themselves, but instead chose to "go out in exchange with the whole earth, claiming the entire world as our country."[14] Of course, what Romans called "exchange," others called "imperial exploitation." This was not too different from more recent rhetoric of imperial benevolence—whether early modern European colonialism or contemporary American and European neo-colonialism—framed in terms of altruism and benefit to the people of Africa, Asia, or elsewhere. But even those who thought that Rome's conquests were benevolent believed this imperial generosity should have its limits. Romans agreed that their culture was great, powerful, and civilized, but conceded that it couldn't exert much influence upon the periphery of the world—not that these areas were worth conquering, anyway. The Roman historian Appian (95–165 CE) praised Rome's approach to expansion, observing that they already controlled the most valuable parts of the planet, rather than "extending it forever, over poor and unprofitable barbarian tribes."[15] The geographer Strabo (63 BCE–24 CE) expressed pride in Rome's conquests, but said there was no point in conquering nomadic peoples beyond Germania: they were isolated and would require constant surveillance.[16] Romans agreed that their empire should only conquer and incorporate profitable territories.

The Sámi way of life was not one that the Romans could easily integrate into their empire. It wasn't a life that the Romans could domesticate, either: the Sámi did not farm, their land was not arable, they did not use money, and they had few trading partners. Rome could not profit from the Sámi, so imperial agents never really considered conquering

Figure 5 A reconstruction of the *Orbis Terrarum* (20 CE). This image reconstructs a Roman map commissioned by the emperor Augustus. It was widely copied during antiquity. This reconstruction was drafted by Erwin Raisz in the twentieth century, based on ancient and medieval descriptions of the original and its copies. The Sámi lived in or near the region of Thule, located at the map's far left—Thule was variously identified with what we today call the Shetland Islands, Greenland, Iceland, and Scandinavia, depending on the geographer. (Image by Universal Art Archive, Alamy)

them. Evidence of Roman presence in Scandia is sparse, but archaeologists have uncovered some Roman coin hoards on the Swedish island of Gotland—evidence of trade with some Scandinavian tribes.[17] Gotland was inhabited by Germanic peoples and not the Sámi, however. When we limit our scope to Sápmi, we find virtually no evidence of Roman interaction, whether with soldiers or merchants—only a handful of Roman coins have been discovered in Sápmi. It seems that the Romans deliberately avoided interactions with the Sámi, even though they traded with others in Scandia.

Throughout antiquity, the Sámi lived in a manner that ensured their freedom. They remained free in that Rome had no desire to expend the resources necessary to conquer them, their culture was egalitarian, they lived without money or debt, and it was difficult to coerce them to do anything. It is not surprising that some scholars describe traditional Sámi society as "anarchist" in its structure.[18] This way of life endured past the fall of the Roman Empire, with little evidence of surrounding chiefdoms and principalities exerting control of Sápmi until centuries later. Indeed, this did not occur until the Viking Age (800–1050 CE). The earliest evidence of any foreign power encroaching upon Sámi freedoms comes from around 890 CE, when the Norwegian chieftain Ohthere reported on his trade with and taxation of the Sámi.[19] The obvious question arises: how did someone tax a society without money and without a class structure? Ohthere claimed that he determined how much to take from one or another person based on their lineage: he deemed some families wealthier and others poorer, taking furs from them accordingly. But there was little evidence of a significant social hierarchy before Ohthere—it seems just as likely that he imposed a hierarchy upon the Sámi than exploited an existing one. Ohthere seems to be the first person who thought it was worth the trouble of conquering the Sámi, seizing their furs and reindeer. What, if any, resistance the Sámi exerted against Ohthere and other Norwegian powers remains unclear.

* * *

When confronted with the power of neighboring states, people such as the Sámi found ways to adapt. For the purposes of this book, the important point is that the absence of currency and trade ensured the Sámi were of little interest to imperial powers, and so remained free. Some radical tendencies survive to this day. Niilas Helander says that identifying as Sámi "is just another way of saying that we are anarchists," pointing to the influence of Indigenous cultures upon anarchist movements.[20] Many scholars arrive at a similar conclusion.[21]

Today, the Sámi resist the continued colonization of their homeland by Norway, Sweden, Finland, and Russia. Colonial governments have subjected Sámi to boarding schools in an effort to impose settler culture upon them, claiming—like the Romans—that this was a benevolent move designed to bring the benefits of imperial civilization to Indigenous peoples.[22] Yet many Sámi continue to seek greater autonomy from the occupying powers and maintain distance from the centers of Oslo, Stockholm, Helsinki, and Moscow as their ancestors did of Rome thousands of years earlier. This, of course, has become considerably more difficult, with geography and climate having become less effective ways of evading state power than they used to be.

5
"Forgive Us Our Debts": The Circumcellions

Within late antiquity, few men loomed larger than Augustine of Hippo (354–430 CE). More of Augustine's writings survive than all classical Latin authors *combined*—Virgil, Cicero, Ovid, Juvenal, Livy, Seneca, and everyone else. Immensely influential even in his own time, Augustine remains one of the most widely read theologians today. Augustine was a Catholic bishop in North Africa and he used this position to denounce popular heresies, including Pelagianism (which taught that humans can achieve perfection on earth), Manichaeism (which promoted an elaborate dualism involving cosmic forces of good and evil), and Donatism (which disqualified priests that denied their faith during persecution). Donatists were prevalent in the century before Augustine and had even rivaled the mainstream Catholic Church in popularity. They had fallen from prominence by the time that Augustine was writing, but their churches were still scattered across the North African landscape.

Augustine expressed particular outrage against a subset of Donatists known as the Circumcellions. He offered a vivid description of how these heretics terrorized men of prestige decades earlier (albeit with dramatic exaggeration):

> What master was not driven to fear his own slave, if that slave sought the protection of the Circumcellions? Who even dared to threaten a destructive servant or someone who instigated conflict? Who could fire a wasteful warehouse worker or demand payment from a debtor, if those people sought protection from the Circumcellions? Owners tossed out the papers of the worst slaves and let them go free, for fear of beatings, arson, and death. Circumcellions even stole debt records and handed them over to the debtors![1]

The Circumcellions had flipped the world upside down. Escaped slaves were now free, lazy laborers could not be punished, and the accounts of debtors were erased. But Augustine wasn't the type to sit back and passively watch this sort of thing happen. Augustine pressed his close friend Bonifatius, the governor of North Africa at the time, to discipline the Donatists in hopes that they might repent and join the Catholic Church.

Augustine's account is full of embellishment, but it might prompt further inquiry. Who were the "Circumcellions"? To what extent did Augustine accurately describe them? Why did they revolt against slave owners, debt collectors, landlords, and other men of affairs? And what do we know about their distinct form of Christianity?

* * *

It would be an understatement to say that Christianity has had a varied history on questions of social liberation. For every emancipatory Christian movement, such as Latin American liberation theology or the Christianity practiced by the Indigenous Atayal people in the Taiwanese village of Smangus, one can easily find its inverse in patriarchal, authoritarian, and white supremacist churches, all of which cite Christian creeds to justify their politics.[2] Which, if either, of these divergent strains more authentically manifests Christian theology is a matter for theologians, rather than historians. But it may be helpful to trace the development of Christianity from Jesus to the Circumcellions to see how people in these different currents laid claim to the same foundational elements of Christianity.

There is no real doubt among historians that a man named Jesus traveled throughout northern Palestine during the 20s and 30s of the Common Era, teaching among his fellow Jews.[3] The precise content of Jesus' teachings remains debated, but scholars agree that he focused foremost on the Kingdom of God. As its name implies, this Kingdom was not a democracy, but a monarchy with the Jewish deity reigning as its sovereign. Scholars agree that Jesus welcomed the poor and dispossessed into this kingdom, but not the wealthy: "It is easier for a camel to pass through the eye of a needle than for a rich man to enter the Kingdom of God."[4] Jesus' preaching bore an apocalyptic edge, as he believed that this kingdom would arrive soon. And when it did, God would flip the world on its head: "The first will be last and the last will be first."[5] When the Kingdom of God arrived, debts would be forgiven, hunger would be satisfied, and the mighty would be brought low. Scholars refer to this apocalyptic transformation of society as the "eschatological reversal." It is not too difficult to see why Jesus' preaching antagonized political leadership, especially the Romans, who ultimately executed him. Before too long, his followers claimed that he had risen from the dead and the new Christian religion spread throughout the Mediterranean.

In the decades after the death of Jesus and his purported resurrection, early theologians debated Christianity's most important ideas, disagreeing about the significance of Jesus' life, death, divinity, and teachings.[6] Archaeologists and historians have discovered hundreds of Christian texts from the first few centuries CE, bearing witness to the astonishing range of ways people practiced the religion. Christianity in this period was so diverse that its adherents had little in common beyond some vague reverence for Jesus—some Christians did not even believe he was the Messiah! As time passed, Christians attributed more and more of their own opinions to Jesus, concocting stories and writing new gospels so they could address one or another disagreement within the church. Although historians agree that Jesus said something like "Blessed are you who are poor, because the Kingdom of God is yours," the author of the Gospel of Matthew (written around 90 CE) adjusted the phrasing to undermine its relevance for peasants: "Blessed are the poor in spirit, because the Kingdom of Heaven is theirs."[7] The differences are small, but significant. First, Matthew added a few, seemingly innocuous, words that completely changed the message: "Blessed are the poor *in spirit*." This reduced poverty to a mere metaphor, deflecting attention away from material deprivation and redirecting it toward matters of "spiritual" humility. Second, Jesus' own phrasing spoke directly to the poor, "Blessed are *you* who are poor," not *about* them, as with Matthew's phrasing ("Blessed are *the* poor"). The differences were subtle, but their effect was significant: Jesus' message to those who experienced material deprivation was reconstrued as something essentially "spiritual." There are countless other ways people modified

Jesus' words to claim the Lord was on their side of this or that debate.

A tug-of-war over the issue of wealth quickly developed. On the one hand, many Christians tried to make their religion more appealing to affluent converts. For instance, the theologian Lactantius (250–325 CE) taught that God did not really mind if you were rich, so long as you were humble and pious.[8] Although Lactantius directly contradicted Jesus' own words, his approach appealed to the sort of people who might fund the construction of churches or serve as patrons to bishops. But other Christians resisted this assimilationist trend, adopting a more countercultural approach. The Desert Mothers and Fathers were a group of Christian ascetics who moved to the Egyptian desert in relative isolation over the course of the third to fifth centuries CE. They believed that the only way they could practice their religion authentically was to move as far away as possible from the corrupting force of wealth and material indulgence. This ascetic approach proved demanding, and few Christians chose this unconventional way of life, especially as the religion became an increasingly mainstream part of the Roman Empire.

Although many Christians were eager to show they weren't doing anything subversive, Romans nevertheless declared their religion a "superstition" and punished anyone who promoted it. The emperor Trajan (reigned 98–117 CE) addressed the matter in a letter to a governor in Asia Minor:

> You have followed the right course of procedure ... in your examination of the cases of persons charged with being Christians, for it is impossible to lay down a general rule to a fixed formula. These people must not be hunted out;

if they are brought before you and the charge against them is proved, they must be punished, but in the case of anyone who denies that he is a Christian, and makes it clear that he is not by offering prayers to our gods, he is to be pardoned as a result of his repentance however suspect his past conduct may be.[9]

Trajan declared that anyone accused of practicing Christianity should have a chance to renounce the religion by offering a sacrifice demonstrating their loyalty to the Roman gods. If the accused complied, they could go free; if they refused, execution followed. Christianity remained illegal for its first few centuries, with the Romans killing many Christians and confiscating church property along the way. Tales of martyrs abound—people who were fed to the beasts, decapitated, burned alive, among other horrific deaths.

Persecution presented a profound theological question concerning apostasy: what happened if someone denied their faith under the threat of death? Certainly, Trajan and subsequent emperors encouraged Christians to do this, allowing apostates to go home free of punishment, and executing anyone who remained steadfast. Was it really that wrong to lie and pretend you weren't Christian to preserve your life? After all, didn't God forgive all kinds of sin? The matter was particularly acute when a priest or a bishop renounced his faith. Did it invalidate the bishop's vows and ministry? The Bible was clear on the matter. According to the Gospels, Jesus had warned: "Whoever denies me before others, I will deny before my Father in heaven," but Christians were divided on what this meant here and now.[10] The debate continued as informal Christian factions coalesced into more formal sectarian identities in the second through the fourth centuries, leading to the emergence of the Catholic Church alongside "heretical" Christian groups. The view that won out was that of the Catholic Church, which argued that all people sin and are nevertheless accepted into the church, meaning that even apostate priests remained welcome. Opposing this view was an African bishop named Donatus (fourth century CE), who became a figurehead for a caucus of North African bishops insisting that anyone who had denied their faith must be excommunicated. Donatus went further when it came to apostate priests, claiming that their prayers and sacraments were invalid in the eyes of God. Donatus expected Christian clergy to practice their faith with rigor. We do not know what he and his allies called this form of Christianity, but Catholics derisively referred to it as "Donatism," nicknaming the sect after its most famous advocate.

The Donatist-versus-Catholic debate was initially limited to Christian bishops quibbling over doctrinal minutiae concerning a handful of apostate priests. But things changed when the Roman/Byzantine[11] emperor Constantine (reigned 306–337 CE) legalized Christianity in 313 CE and began sponsoring church activities. Constantine restored the property that the empire had seized from Christians and he convened church councils wherein bishops debated the doctrine of the Holy Trinity and other issues. While reparations and assistance were no doubt welcome, it also meant that Christianity lost much of its radical edge. Decades earlier, Christians were writing tales commemorating the martyrdom of soldiers who converted to Christianity and were executed for refusing to kill others in battle.[12] But starting with Constantine, the military paraded Christian symbols during warfare, insisting God was on their side of the slaughter. Moreover, Constantine's support of Christianity led to fierce competition within the religion—which among the rival sects should Rome support? Each sect insisted that they alone represented authentic Christianity. Augustine, for instance, leveraged his relationship with various politicians to marginalize other Christian sects and secure the future of the Catholic Church. The Donatists and other once-popular sects of Christianity suffered a steep decline in membership in the two centuries after Constantine legalized the religion: the emperor aligned himself with the Catholic Church, whereas the Donatist Church still had a rather countercultural distaste for the use of state violence in service of Christian doctrine. What began as a subversive religion in a rural corner of the empire had reached the nexus of state power. By the mid-fourth century CE, Christianity had become institutionalized, and the radical doctrines of the Gospels had become submerged within the power machinations of Church and State.

* * *

Donatism was declared a heresy at the First Council of Arles in 314 CE. In subsequent decades, Constantine and his successors seized Donatist property and gave it to the Catholic Church. Our interest lies in the Circumcellions, a sect that had a complicated relationship with the Donatist Church. The particulars of this relationship aren't entirely clear, but ancient texts give the sense that the Circumcellions were either an organization within the Donatist Church or an informal group of enthusiastic Donatists.[13] We don't know what the Circumcellions called themselves, but it may have been *agonistici* (the fighters) or *milites Christi* (the soldiers of Christ).[14]

The limited evidence suggests that the Circumcellions were Amazigh people native to North Africa who resented Rome's presence in the region. Most did not know any Latin, but spoke the local language of Punic.[15] These were people who had little love for the Roman Empire.

"Circumcellion" was a pejorative name for this group of people. The term meant something like "the people who roam around the storehouses," probably a reference to the Circumcellions' predominantly lower-class demographic. One Catholic writer said that the Circumcellions spent much of their time in rural markets, seeking work as day laborers.[16] This is consistent with other testimonies indicating the Circumcellions were malcontent peasants. Augustine called them "vagrants" and another Catholic writer bemoaned how they flipped the social hierarchy on its head: "Journeys became unsafe, since owners were thrown out of their carriages and were forced to run alongside like slaves, while their slaves rode in the carriage's front seat!"[17] You can easily imagine how Circumcellions framed this theologically. The scene looked a lot like the eschatological reversal that Jesus had described as the Kingdom of God![18]

A Roman/Byzantine law from 412 CE further reveals the extent of the Circumcellions' poverty.[19] This law imposed harsh fines on everyone still aligned with the Donatist Church. The penalties were proportionate to social rank, beginning with the few wealthy Donatists of the "Illustrious" rank, who were obliged to pay 50 librae of gold (roughly 36 lb), to the plebians, who owed five librae of gold each. In most situations, a plebian was the lowest-ranking person around. But this law indicates that the Circumcellions were in greater poverty than the plebians, and their fine was far less than the penalty imposed on the plebians who were the next-poorest population on the list. Circumcellions were expected to pay ten librae of *silver* each, which was worth a fraction of the price of gold. The emperors knew that the Circumcellions came from the poorest parts of society—slaves, freedpeople, and day laborers—and set their fines accordingly.

Women were integral to the Circumcellion sect. Circumcellions did not relegate women to the home, forced to watch from afar while men performed heroic deeds in revolt. Rather, they were among those that Augustine called the "awful people of both genders" who partook in the action.[20] But this was not the end of Augustine's vitriol against Circumcellion women. He also chafed that these were "homeless women who refused to marry in order to avoid discipline," implicitly connecting orthodoxy, patriarchy, and chastity.[21] We might recall the discussion in Chapter Two: women found freedom and agency in singleness, a stark contrast to the life of marriage that rendered a woman subject to her husband's disciplinary power. Augustine, who was quite the misogynist even for his own day, claimed that unmarried Circumcellion women could have spent all night reveling in orgies if they wanted to![22] Martine De Marre observes that Augustine regarded these orgies as *hypothetical* acts of debauchery: Circumcellion women *could* do such things, but he never said they actually did.[23] Augustine's speculations on the topic were odd, since sources otherwise indicated Circumcellions' preference for celibacy.[24]

Although many ancient Christians wrote about the Circumcellions, their testimonies are often worthless for historical research. Historian Brent Shaw has shown that most of them merely copied Augustine's hostile account, adding their own fanciful details.[25] They had not met any Circumcel-

"FORGIVE US OUR DEBTS"

lions, lived nowhere near them, and merely speculated about their activities. Historians can safely discard most ancient texts that discuss the Circumcellions, as they are more likely to mislead than to inform. Shaw instead suggests that we look to the earliest texts written by people living in North Africa, including the Catholic bishop Augustine of Hippo, a Catholic bishop named Optatus of Milev (fourth century CE), and yet another Catholic bishop named Possidius (fifth century CE). As the reader has probably guessed, these men were unsparing in their condemnation of the Circumcellions and other Donatists. Their accounts are hardly objective, but these bishops actually had firsthand experience with the sect. Only a few Donatist writings survive, and these can provide further insights, even if we need to account for their distinctive biases.[26] Donatist texts tended to focus on the Catholic persecution of Donatists, celebrating martyrs' commitment to their faith. Upon sifting through these Catholic and Donatist testimonies, we can cobble together a portrait of an unusual Christian sect.

* * *

The Circumcellions were highly opinionated. Circumcellions were Donatists and thus were very rigorous with their standards, as the Donatist Church defrocked any priest who buckled during Roman persecution. Moreover, the Circumcellions enjoyed creating havoc at pagan festivals. Catholics said they did this because they hoped to be lynched by pagans, such that they might die as martyrs.[27] But this claim is not credible. We should probably suppose that this disruptive behavior was a pious, if misguided, effort to destroy false idols or convert pagans to Christianity. The claim that they sought out martyrdom was almost certainly a Catholic effort to discredit Donatism. Catholics implied that Donatists preached a heretical understanding of martyrdom and Christian salvation, further implying that they rejected apostates because they were masochists who thought all true Christians should die for their faith—even seek out death proactively. For instance, Isidore of Seville (560–636 CE; a Catholic bishop), who wrote long after the Circumcellions had disappeared, attested that "in the midst of prayers, they kill themselves by sword or fire, so that they might acquire the name of martyrs by dying violent deaths."[28] Isidore thus implausibly claimed that even the act of prayer could prove lethal when those fanatical Circumcellions were doing it.

As aggravating as the Circumcellions may have been for their non-Christian and Catholic neighbors, they organized around anarchistic principles. For instance, they participated in direct action, that is, the effort to achieve collective goals without recourse to the state.[29] Historical examples of direct action are numerous: rather than waiting for the U.S. government to end slavery, some people developed the Underground Railroad to facilitate the freedom of people who were enslaved, for instance. The Circumcellions did not wait for the emperor or governor to address widespread problems of debt in the province of Numidia. They had a simpler solution: destroy the debt records, loot the houses of the rich, and share the plunder with the people.

And this is exactly what they did around 347 CE, in a revolt against the wealthy in the town of Bagai led by Axido and Fasir. These two men were not ordained clergy, nor were they political leaders, but simply ordinary Circumcellions who put their principles into action. Any lenders attempting to collect were threatened with violence. "Soon everyone lost what was owed to him," Optatus recalled, "often massive amounts."[30] These actions predictably antagonized the local aristocracy, including the Catholic and Donatist leadership. At the time, two imperial commissioners, Paul and Macarius, were traveling around northern Africa distributing alms to the poor and encouraging Donatists to join the Catholic Church. Catholic writers described this as a benevolent gesture, but when Paul and Macarius reached the African city of Bagai, things became violent. Bagai's Circumcellion population refused their gifts and, against the wishes of their own Donatist bishops, attacked Paul, Macarius, and their men. Unable to assert any authority, Donatist bishops resorted to military intervention, requesting support from a Roman military officer (and devoted Catholic) named Taurinus to suppress the Circumcellion revolt. A bloodbath ensued, with the violence spreading beyond the city of Bagai throughout North Africa, where the Catholic Church played a significant role in suppressing the Circumcellions with the goal of eliminating the sect entirely. Neither Catholics nor Donatists wanted to take the blame for the resulting bloodbath: later Donatists admitted that Circumcellions had engaged in violence, but claimed Paul and Macarius instigated it and insisted this was the only time that Donatists had ever shed Catholic blood. Catholics claimed that Donatist bishops had initiated the violence but quickly lost control. Both sides agreed that even though the Circumcellions were Donatists, their own clergy were powerless to stop them.

This massacre became a point of contention for Donatists, despite the fact they called in Roman troops against their own people. Their bishops angrily confronted Catholics at a

411 CE conference that was intended to reunite Christians across Africa: "Let us not forget how much Christian blood was shed by Macarius, Paul, Taurinus, and the rest of the executioners, who slaughtered our saints!"[31] They also accused Catholics of stealing from the poor and raping women during Taurinus' assault on Bagai. Optatus observed how the bones of martyrs were still strewn around Donatist churches several decades later. Even Augustine, the writer most contemptuous of Donatism, had to admit that Catholic attacks on the Circumcellions were brutal and excessive.[32]

Circumcellions' propensity for anarchistic self-organization extended to leaderlessness. Neither Axido nor Fasir held any meaningful authority over the other Circumcellions. Although other people called these two men the "chiefs of the saints," this phrase was not a title of authority. Rather, it was a theological designation for liberators among North African Christians, a reference to Christ's embrace of those who fled to him seeking refuge.[33] Augustine also observed their leaderlessness, commenting that "they show no respect for laws or authority."[34] The Circumcellions' suspicion of authority was further evident in their relationship with the Donatist Church. They refused to heed the orders of their bishops, who had condemned Circumcellions' direct action and called in Taurinus to suppress their rebellion. The Donatist bishops represented the interests of the landholding class, whom the Circumcellions resented. The only Donatist leaders who supported the Circumcellions were low-ranking clergy in rural areas.[35] Augustine mentions Donatist nuns, priests, and deacons—all humble figures, a good portion of whom had taken vows of poverty—among those engaging in Circumcellion action alongside day laborers and slaves.[36] Donatist bishops, however, insisted that their leadership had no hand in, nor any prior knowledge of, the Circumcellion violence against Paul and Macarius.[37]

* * *

Circumcellions' anarchistic principles were also evident in their insistence upon mutual aid. Particularly important in this regard was their destruction of debt records and their refusal of Paul and Macarius' offer of gifts. The details of both matters are disputed, but one might reasonably ask why Circumcellions assaulted the people who brought them money, food, and other gifts.

The attack on Paul and Macarius is best understood at the intersection of Circumcellions' mutual aid, direct action, and leaderlessness. Activist Dean Spade describes mutual aid as "collective coordination to meet each other's needs" or the act of helping each other in an organized fashion.[38] People worldwide engage in mutual aid because existing systems fail to satisfy basic needs. Mutual aid is thus a volunteer-coordinated form of collective effort. Mutual aid takes various forms today, such as transgender people helping other trans folk facing eviction and skill-sharing groups among recent immigrants. These programs are not sponsored by the state. They arise from communities that have identified gaps in "official" systems and that work together to satisfy needs. Mutual aid has been particularly important for marginalized Indigenous, racialized, immigrant, disabled, and other populations. The connection between disenfranchisement (here, referring to people denied the right to participate in governance) and state neglect is important. The state abandons those it disenfranchises, locking life's necessities behind bureaucratic hurdles such as paperwork, waiting times, proof of hardship, or evidence that they're seeking employment. In this way, the state impedes people's flourishing, rendering it incumbent upon communities to satisfy their collective needs. We might think of how diaspora populations commonly develop programs to help fellow immigrants with food, language, and other essentials.

Mutual aid differs from charity in its community-driven origin and its emphasis on accessibility, usually being free of eligibility requirements or means-testing. Whereas "charity" tends to involve affluent individuals who offer modest portions of their wealth either as donations to nonprofit organizations or as taxes to the state, this is not the case with mutual aid. Mutual aid instead arises from the needs of a given community and tends toward democratic distribution: one does not need a teaching degree to impart knowledge to recent immigrants; one does not need to be a medical doctor to teach activists the basics of first aid; one does not need to be a chef to cook food for a community breakfast. Mutual aid efforts are peer-run and peer-served. Mutual aid, moreover, is available to everyone; contrast this with charity, which often requires beneficiaries to maintain sobriety, undergo psychiatric treatment, profess a certain religion, or actively seek work. Mutual aid, of course, has its various weaknesses, including the fact that it depends upon a reservoir of unpaid labor and a deep sense of solidarity—neither of which can be taken as a given.

The state often appropriates mutual aid to undermine solidarity movements. The Black Panthers drew upon research that showed the importance of breakfast for children and recognized that the U.S. government had little interest in addressing these needs within Black communities, so they created a free breakfast program of their own in 1969.[39] The program was an immense success, feeding thousands of kids across America who would otherwise go hungry. But the U.S. government feared such mutual aid might generate public support for the Black liberation movement; J. Edgar Hoover, the erstwhile director of the Federal Bureau of Investigation, thus sabotaged the free breakfast program. Police officers urinated on the food the night before the launch of the Chicago program, for instance. In the end, the U.S. Department of Agriculture appropriated the Black Panthers' mutual aid by expanding its own School Breakfast Program in order to undercut the group's popularity.

Paul and Macarius offered the people of Bagai monetary gifts on the model of "charity," following the direction of emperor Constans (reigned 337–350 CE). The idea was to distribute alms to the poor throughout northern Africa and use the opportunity to convince Donatists to join the Catholic Church.[40] But the Circumcellions refused this charity. This refusal, together with their destruction of debt records, suggests that they regarded charity as an effort on the part of the rich to maintain power over the peasantry by creating a relationship of dependence. Paul and Macarius had no interest in creating a more sustainable life for the people of Bagai. Their gifts would fall into the hands of the local aristocracy anyway, since economic power structures ensured that coinage drifted toward the wealthy. Landlords, debt collectors, tax collectors, and others would make sure the money ended up with the rich before too long, though Paul and Macarius were probably oblivious to this. Thus, their gifts were not particularly useful to the people of Bagai.

This speaks to another problem with "charitable" approaches to inequality: even when well-intentioned, the efforts of outsiders are often uninformed and disconnected from local realities. Because mutual aid arises from the affected community, its participants are better attuned to institutional limitations and the actual needs of the local population. Circumcellion mutual aid was more responsive to the needs of Bagai's peasants. Not only were they aware that the gifts of Paul and Macarius would have ultimately fallen into the hands of the wealthy, but that it came with strings attached: personal debts remained on record and their collection was viable. And so the Circumcellions engaged in direct action to prevent debt collection.

Economically speaking, North Africa was doing better than most Roman provinces around this time. This success, however, was relative. Aristocratic prosperity led to the monetization of the countryside, which in turn led to cash-crop farming, furthering agricultural dependence upon the market and creating the cycles of debt we have seen elsewhere in this book.[41] One of the biggest differences between North Africa and other regions of the Roman Empire was its volatile climate, which rendered its population even more vulnerable to food shortages and unemployment. In any seven-year period, North African farmers expected crops to fail two or three of those years.[42] The frequent barren seasons engendered economic uncertainty for farmers and agricultural laborers, and made them even more reliant on profitable crops. Cash-cropping entailed a shift away from the drought-resistant produce that had been foundational to subsistence farming and toward the crops that could be sold for the most money, to save cash for years of desolation. There was little aid for the rural poor during these barren years, not helped by the fact that debt collectors found it far easier to exploit the destitute in the countryside: agents of the rich frequently (and illegally) seized any harvest that poor farmers had brought to the markets as a payment against any loans. It is difficult to overstate how bad this became, with farmers often compelled by poverty to sell their children as slaves at the market. Rome knew this was a problem. Just a few decades before the revolt spearheaded by Axido and Fasir, people complained to the emperor Constantine about this injustice and he responded by banning such illegal seizures and the sale of children into slavery.[43] But this hardly solved the problem, as Constantine's solution was merely to encourage the provincial governors to show generosity to people in desperate situations. The Roman state was either unwilling or unable to prevent such predatory behavior, and the exploitation continued unabated.[44]

It was bad enough that these markets were the places where people sold their children into slavery and debt collectors illegally seized the harvest of poor farmers. Day laborers also sought work there, no doubt in massive numbers during the years when harvests were meager and many people were desperate for food and income. Every visit to the market was a reminder of a loved one sold into slavery, of hungry stomachs at home, of desperate need for employment. Both Optatus and Augustine indicated that these markets were precisely where Circumcellions met to organize. This was where people's resentments against the rich manifested, both symbolically and materially.

These resentments included suspicion of Catholic charity. Optatus reported that the Circumcellions transformed the Donatist cathedral in Bagai into a public granary after the city began its rebellion in 347 CE, where peasants could obtain food for free.[45] How they got their hands on such staples is unclear. It seems likely that it involved direct action, expropriating the landlords' own grain stores for public benefit. The fact that Circumcellions chose the Donatist cathedral as the place for their public granary is significant, as it contained the throne of the bishop—the very man who would condemn them and call on Taurinus to quell the unrest. The fact that this church was now full of grain meant this bishop was unable to take his seat, directly undermining his authority. The building became a symbolic center for the activity of the Circumcellions, who were ostensibly under the bishop's authority, despite their open defiance. The Circumcellions controlled the granary, which allowed them to distribute resources according to need. Similar to how the Black Panthers distributed food centuries later, the Circumcellions thought it best to address the needs of the community directly, rather than hoping the aristocracy's charity would suffice. And it was clearly successful enough to elicit sympathies well beyond the town of Bagai, as the Circumcellion revolt spread throughout North Africa.

What, then, was Circumcellion life like during this rebellion? Sources are fragmentary and generally hostile, but we can imagine the people of Bagai stopping by the cathedral-turned-granary to collect food after heading to the Donatist Church on Sunday sometime during the year of the revolt (347 CE). With landlords too afraid to demand rent, their bellies were fuller and they could grow the crops they preferred: rather than focusing on olives (which sold for the most money), they were free to grow figs, dates, grains, and legumes that contributed to a more varied diet. After a few festivals that celebrated the Donatist martyrs, the peasantry resumed work and contributed what they could to the cathedral-granary. A patrol of Roman legionaries responded to rumors that Circumcellions had run the Catholic decurions (i.e., the aristocratic municipal council) out of town. The Romans had little success in restoring the town's Catholic regime, as the local Circumcellion faction overwhelmed the soldiers with little more than clubs and shovels. The Circumcellions were eager to show off their bruises to their friends and neighbors. An enthusiastic, but eccentric priest offered a prayer in the Punic language on behalf of injured Circumcellions, praising their devotion before rambling about Bagai as a "fortress of faith." The successful repulsion of the soldiers proved a reasonable excuse for another celebration—four in the last week, given the uptick in everyone's leisure time and an increase in the number of days for rest and socializing. Whether widow, farmer, or shopkeeper, everyone was able to live with a bit more comfort than they were accustomed to. After all, the debt collectors and landlords knew they would regret any attempt to collect outstanding payments.

* * *

The Roman state and Catholic Church collaborated to suppress the Circumcellions' direct action to the extent that even they had to admit that the violence was disproportionate. But Taurinus' suppression of the North African rebellion of 347 CE hardly marked the end of the Circumcellions. Though we know little about Circumcellions in the following decades, they were still active during the time of Augustine in the early fifth century. He complained that the sect consisted of "frenzied groups of drunken youths ... who roam and rampage throughout all Africa."[46] Augustine once again resorted to hyperbole: clearly, they did not rampage throughout the *entire* region of North Africa. We need not take the rest of Augustine's characterization too seriously, since he wrote this in a treatise criticizing the writings of a Donatist bishop named Parmenian who had died a decade earlier. Augustine hoped to demonstrate the extent and horror of Donatist violence, focusing on the Circumcellions—a group that certainly had a connection with Donatism, but as we have seen, hardly accepted the authority of its bishops. There is little reason to think that Parmenian would have had much positive to say about the Circumcellions in the first place. Augustine thought that the ridiculous Circumcellions could discredit Donatism and Parmenian could not respond since he was dead. Augustine's depiction of the Circumcellions rose to absurdity later in this treatise, claiming that they consisted of moneylenders and misers.[47] The suggestion that Circumcellions were loan sharks and hoarded sums of money stretches credulity beyond its limit. Not only did Augustine expect his readers to believe that Circumcellions had reversed their values, but somehow came into immense wealth despite their abject poverty. None of this really makes sense. It seems likely that Augustine was just trying to see what kind of accusations would stick.

A Roman/Byzantine law enacted in 412 CE compelled Donatists to join the Catholic Church.[48] This law had its intended effect and, in 418 CE, Augustine remarked that Catholics continued to deal with "what is left of" the Circumcellion resistance.[49] Few members of the sect remained and, by 438 CE, Catholics wrote about them in the past tense: "There was a new type of corrupt and violent people ... known as the Circumcellions."[50] Less than a century after Axido and Fasir initiated the revolt at Bagai, the Circumcellions were reduced to a memory of heretics-past.

Even after they were gone, Catholic writers enjoyed ridiculing the Circumcellions. They seized upon small details in Augustine's already-questionable depiction to compose tales of their madness. For instance, Augustine recounted an incident where Circumcellions ambushed a Roman judge, but the judge refused to execute them once he captured them, probably aware that, as Donatists, they found the prospect of martyrdom appealing.[51] The judge thus shackled the Circumcellions as if to be executed and abandoned them without harming them. A happy enough ending, it would seem, if a bit humiliating for the Circumcellions. A different writer, Theodoret of Cyrrhus (393–466 CE; you guessed it, another Catholic bishop), read Augustine's one-sentence summary and concocted an elaborate tale, presenting it to his readers as though factual:

> Out of a great multitude of [Circumcellions], some of them, having driven themselves to a deranged state of mind, encountered a strong young man. But when he drew out a bare sword, they ordered him to inflict wounds on them. Indeed, they threatened to cut him up if he did not do what they ordered. The young man then said he was afraid that once some of them had been killed, the others who survived would change their mind and would then take him to court and exact a penalty from him. He said that they would have to tie themselves up first and only then would he strike them with his sword. When they obeyed and had been tied up with bonds, he did indeed strike all of them,

but with lashes of a cane. Then, leaving them tied up, he simply walked away from them.[52]

The differences between the two accounts are vast: whereas Augustine presents a group of potentially violent malcontents expecting execution from a Roman judge, here we have a gang of buffoons seeking martyrdom from a random passerby.

The Circumcellions' direct action—destroying debt records and using the granary for mutual aid—was remarkable. Suspicious of both state and church authorities, they developed a democratic way of life that interrupted major sources of their oppression and addressed their collective needs on their own terms. Similar groups have emerged over the course of Christian history, insisting on direct action and mutual aid: the Lollards of the fourteenth century and the Diggers in the seventeenth century, or more recently, the Catholic Worker Movement and the Zapatistas in Chiapas, Mexico. The lesson from antiquity is that Christianity need not favor the powerful, nor remain incompatible with radical ways of life.

Further Reading

De Marre, Martine. 2020. "'Bad Girls'?: Collective Violence by Women and the Case of the Circumcellions in Roman North Africa." Pages 145–69 in *Piracy, Pillage and Plunder in Antiquity: Appropriation and the Ancient World*. Edited by Richard Evans and Martine De Marre. London: Routledge.

Dossey, Leslie. 2010. *Peasant and Empire in Christian North Africa*. Berkeley: University of California Press.

Shaw, Brent D. 2004. "Who Were the Circumcellions?" Pages 227–58 in *Vandals, Romans and Berbers: New Perspectives on Late Antique North Africa*. Edited by A. H. Merrills. London: Ashgate.

Shaw, Brent D. 2011. *Sacred Violence: African Christians and Sectarian Hatred in the Age of Augustine*. Cambridge: Cambridge University Press.

Optatus' account of the Circumcellions was reasonably concise, whereas Augustine tended toward incidental comments throughout his massive corpus of writings. There is no convenient collection of primary sources discussing the Circumcellions. In terms of scholarly discussion, the work of Leslie Dossey is particularly valuable, especially pages 173–94 of her book. Also worthwhile is Martine De Marre's analysis of women's involvement in the Circumcellion community. Brent Shaw, whose skepticism of the ancient sources runs deeper than most other historians, has published extensively on the Circumcellions, though he doubts that they were a distinct movement or community. Nonetheless, his work on Catholic mythologization and exaggeration of the Circumcellions dispels many longstanding misconceptions. His book has multiple chapters relevant to the study of the Circumcellions.[53]

6

Self-Governance on the Open Sea: Cilician Pirates

Around 580 BCE, a group of pirates from the Greek islands of Cindus and Rhodes sought refuge in unfamiliar terrain, landing on the islands of Lipara (see Figure 1).[1] Once settled, they instituted a new democracy. They elected three of their peers to serve as captains of their ships and lived peacefully among the island's existing residents, forming a united Liparan community. The unified community divided their labor so that some people worked as farmers while others served as a makeshift navy to defend the island from hostile forces. This navy doubled as a fleet of pirates that also looted any unsuspecting merchant ships which happened to be in the vicinity. Their life was built around communitarian ideals, and so this plunder, as well as all agricultural goods, were distributed equitably among the entire population: "They made their possessions common property and shared meals, living in a communal fashion for some time."[2] Since depending on the plunder of banditry tended toward streaks of feast-or-famine, this way of life addressed the economic uncertainties inherent to piracy.

The unified Liparan community flourished, their system lasting more than 200 years, with adaptations along the way. Within a few years, they started cultivating uninhabited islands nearby, eventually deciding that families should rotate plots of land every 20 years—it was unfair that some families could farm on the main island, whereas others needed to sail to their plots. Liparans, being devout people, even tithed ten percent of their goods to the temple of Apollo at Delphi back in Greece.[3] In 393 BCE, Liparan pirates captured a boat full of Roman ambassadors.[4] Normally, a boat of prominent men like this would fetch a considerable ransom for a pirate crew. The Liparans gathered to discuss what to do. When one pirate captain noticed the embassy was transporting an offering to Delphi, the residents took a poll and voted to free the Romans. How fortunate a coincidence for the Romans, that these pirates were devoted to the same temple! Archaeological discoveries have borne out much of this information: we have evidence of the peaceful integration of Cnidian and Rhodian (possibly also Egyptian) seafarers into Lipara's local population, their dedication to the sanctuary at Delphi, and egalitarian burial customs.[5]

The community at Lipara incorporated elements of the surrounding governments into their system, while developing and practicing a distinct form of governance. Shortly after arrival, they built a tower to keep watch over the surrounding waters, probably to fend off Etruscan raids.[6] Around the time they captured the Roman embassy, they started minting coins, most of which depicted some combination of grapes, a cup of wine, dolphins, ships, or King Aeolus (the mythical founder of Lipara).[7] The coins reveal their points of pride: seamanship and the cultivation of wine grapes. The excavation of a large number of theatre masks suggests Liparans also enjoyed the dramatic arts.[8] The island's population was never large, yet it thrived until it was overrun in 396 BCE by the forces of the Carthaginian Empire, which demanded the Liparans' loyalty and tribute. As a result, the island soon served as a base for the Carthaginian navy. When the Romans defeated Carthage during the First Punic War (264–241 BCE), they destroyed the city of Lipara and annexed the island to their republic.

Liparan democracy all sounds very Greek: electing leaders, forming a Popular Assembly, arriving at a consensus when making decisions, and instituting a communal meal system. One might reasonably guess that the pirates imported the democratic processes in their Greek hometowns of Cnidus and Rhodes to their new community at Lipara. But this supposition would be mistaken. Cnidus did not institute democracy until the fourth century BCE and Rhodes did not exist as a distinct city-state until 408 BCE.[9] The pirates were not simply continuing familiar systems from their Greek homeland, but were experimenting with something altogether new. We will see that it is far more likely that they drew upon the radical, *piratical* democracy that they had developed at sea. And, as time went on, other pirate crews would further develop the practice of maritime democracy, drawing influence from a range of Mediterranean institutions.

Pirates, whether from Cnidus, Rhodes, or elsewhere, consistently operated with democratic institutions. To understand why, we must consider the conditions that drove people to give up legitimate employment in favor of seaborne banditry. Merchants physically abused, financially exploited, and emotionally isolated the sailors who manned their ships. Sailors grew to resent their bosses, so many abandoned ship and chose a life where they could use their maritime skills for their own gain. They set themselves against the world and its social institutions, becoming a significant problem for the Hellenistic kingdoms and the Roman Republic. In doing so, they developed radical democracies that suited their criminal lives. This chapter will discuss pirate democracy in Graeco-Roman antiquity, focusing especially on Cilician piracy in the centuries after the pirates at Lipara thrived. The Cilician pirates flourished 146–67 BCE—a period when Hellenistic empires were declining and the Roman Republic was rapidly expanding.

* * *

The Hellenistic period gave rise to several empires in competition for economic supremacy through maritime trade: the Roman Republic in Italy, the Carthaginian Empire in North Africa and Spain, the Ptolemaic Kingdom in Egypt, the Seleucid Kingdom in the Levant and Turkey, the Antigonid Kingdom in Macedonia, and a handful of smaller states.[10] These empires sought to control the trade of the greatest sources of wealth: Egyptian grain, Greek wine, Spanish metals, Syrian dyed textiles, and captives to be sold as slaves. It was cheapest and fastest to transport these goods (and people) by sea, since land routes were slow and increasingly expensive as distances traveled increased (see Chapter One).

As maritime trade developed, a select few became immensely wealthy. Investors developed systems that protected both their assets and reputations, since commerce was regarded as sordid within elite circles. Hoping to keep their honor beyond reproach, the wealthy hired commercial agents to manage their investments (business deals, loans, contracts, etc.).[11] These agents typically worked with a ship owner (*navicularius*) to contract a boat to transport goods. Ship owners had nowhere near the status of their aristocratic clients, but *navicularii* could accumulate enough wealth to engage in some investing themselves; "It is not quite seven years since I gave up voyaging and, having moderate capital, I try to put it to work by making loans on ventures overseas," boasted one.[12] Ship owners sometimes accompanied their boats, but more often they delegated that responsibility. The ship owner assigned all sailing duties to the captain, who contracted the crew and ensured safe travel, having absolute authority over the ship once it was at sea. The captain oversaw the ship's lesser officers, including the sailing master and the first mate. The rest of the crew consisted of a combination of sailors with highly specialized roles (e.g., the ship's carpenter) and more generalist seamen whose roles varied as required.

The aristocracy generated immense wealth through such merchant ships, but they felt no love for the sailors who performed the labor that made them rich.[13] Cicero derided seamen as "men of low status, born in obscure places, traveling to regions they have never seen before, where they are neither known to the strangers whom they visit, nor can they be with acquaintances who can vouch for them."[14] People competed for honor in a very public game, requiring others to speak to their reputation. Most sailors had no one to do this for them, rendering them questionable figures. Ancient writers sometimes commented that most sailors must have an unsavory reputation back home; why else would they seek out such a rough and disreputable life on the seas? Merchant crews typically consisted of society's most destitute—an assortment of castoffs, runaways, fugitives, and slaves.[15] A writer named Synesius (373–414 CE) expressed alarm at how the crewmen transporting him never referred to each other by name, but instead used nicknames based on physical anomalies: "Hey, Cripple!" "Yo, Hernia!" "Listen up, Lefty! "Over

SELF-GOVERNANCE ON THE OPEN SEA

here, Squinty!"[16] Many others shared this feeling of disgust for seamen; one Roman law even referred to merchant crews as "men of the worst quality."[17] We can get a sense of sailors' poverty by turning to ancient artwork, where they are consistently depicted naked or nearly so, indicating their enslaved or slave-like status (see Figure 6; contrast Figure 7). At the harbor, sailors could be identified by their cheap tunics, the only thing they could afford to wear among decent company.[18]

Figure 6 Roman coffin depicting an enslaved ship crew (third century CE). This marble relief depicts enslaved crew members raising the sails on two cargo ships. Notably, the crew is naked. (Photograph by Carole Raddato)

Merchant ships operated with a rigid hierarchy, where insubordination was met with corporal punishment. One Roman novel depicted a captain subjecting his entire crew to 40 lashes for violating an old superstition about getting a haircut the night before their voyage.[19] Given their low status, sailors had little choice but to endure such beatings. One Hellenistic law mentions "the brand" as a distinguishing mark on sailors' bodies, referring to a literal cattle brand that was typically reserved for farm animals.[20] Considering all of this, we should not be surprised that aristocrats like Plato and Aristotle disparaged the maritime mob as a boorish force capable of contaminating society: coastal cities needed to remain vigilant to prevent these louts from corrupting the civilized land-dwellers they encountered.[21]

Sailors' lives were defined by exploitation. Everyone below the captain bore all the physical risk, while the owners and their agents reaped all the rewards. An average crewman might spend shore leave drowning his sorrows in alcohol and sleeping with sex workers—more permanent relationships were difficult to maintain at sea.[22] The Roman poet Horace (65–8 BCE) lamented that it was impossible to sleep during one voyage from Rome down the Italian coastline because a "sailor and passenger, soused with flat wine, rivaled one another in singing to their absent mistresses."[23] It was an authoritarian system that bred resentment. Sailing required a rare combination of immense skill, brute strength, and a willingness to risk one's life regularly. Yet, the few people capable of such work were treated like livestock.

Many sailors abandoned "legitimate" work on merchant vessels to use their unique skillsets in more lucrative and less oppressive ventures. Most pirates were disaffected seamen,[24] and many were mutineers who had commandeered the vessels of abusive ship owners.[25] One 242 BCE law from Hellenistic Egypt gives a sense of how sailors turned rogue.[26] The law concerned enslaved sailors aboard the royal Ptolemaic barges who went absent without leave. What is striking is how this law nearly equates "fugitive sailors" with "bandits," indicating these men turned to piracy. Not only were these sailors subject to harsh punishment, but so were any police who did not detain them if found. This law implied that AWOL sailors were so common (or so dangerous) that many police did not bother to arrest them. In any case, given the expanse of the Mediterranean and their unique skillset, many fugitive sailors managed to elude punishment.

A complex range of economic and social factors pushed desperate people to live on the seas in the first place. Piracy took this a step further. Vincent Gabrielsen characterizes ancient piracy as a form of "alternative employment" for the poorest inhabitants of the Mediterranean.[27] The people who abandoned the lawful ways of merchant sailors in favor of piracy did so as a form of direct action, seizing the means of production away from the wealthy and ensuring it remained in the hands of those who risked life and limb on the seas.

* * *

Many sailors abandoned the merchant ships that had regimented their lives in favor of piratical freedom. Ancient writers describe pirates as fearsome figures. They noted how pirates operated small, agile vessels capable of capturing more cumbersome merchant ships. Once they seized another vessel, they plundered any valuables, took wealthy people on board as hostages, and sold the poor into slavery.[28] Ancient writers described how pirates raided coastal cities, giving residents an allotted period to assemble a ransom—if the civilians met their quota, they left without harming anyone, but failure to do so had grave consequences, such as mass kidnapping or execution.[29] Successful pirates had two options for selling their loot: unscrupulous merchants were always willing to make a quick buck or some cities would buy it (usually as part of a treaty that the pirates avoid pillaging that very town).[30] The key to the pirates' success was their capacity for criminal violence; they had no regard for Roman or Hellenistic laws and were willing to kill anyone who rebuffed their demands.

Or perhaps not.

This may have been the story that ancient politicians and historians told, but a closer look suggests that not only was this depiction of pirates inaccurate, but that something far more interesting was happening. To start, studies have shown that pirate self-mythologization was essential to their success: their reputation as men capable of violence was more important than whether they ever actually engaged in such acts. A civilian who believed that pirates might wound him was just as likely to accede to their demands as any civilians they actually did harm. But even that's not entirely accurate: it required much less effort for a pirate to threaten someone than to shed their blood. Indeed, deception was a defining feature of piracy, with almost every aspect of pirates' self-presentation crafted to elicit a submissive response from potential targets. Pirates showcased their ill-gained wealth with exquisite purple awnings, gilded sails, and silvered oars.[31] Pirate captains also took on the names of great warriors: Agamemnon, Seleucus, Hercules, among others.[32] During face-to-face encounters, many pirates engaged in outright intimidation, such as the captains who presented themselves as autocratic "tyrants" and "kings" to instill fear in civilian populations.[33] However, at other times pirates pretended to be legitimate merchants in hopes of gaining land-dwellers' trust, only to take advantage of them later.[34] This ruse required pirates to spend time on the docks to eavesdrop, and once a pirate overheard which anchored ship had the most valuable cargo, he alerted his crewmates, and they promptly made off with the goods.[35] Ancient authors told variations of this deception so frequently that it must have been a standard con. Taking all of this together, we might doubt that pirates were as cruel as their reputations would have us believe.

Even more striking is pirates' collaboration with each other. We saw above how the community at Lipara took a radical approach to self-governance.[36] Often, when sailors deserted the authoritarian regimes of merchant ships, they organized in profoundly egalitarian ways. In fact, we can get a tentative sense of the democratic processes of pirates and bandits (Greeks and Romans didn't distinguish between the two) through a handful of ancient novels.[37] Although these were works of fiction, they nevertheless drew upon the authors' familiarity with institutions around them and so presented a fairly accurate portrait of Graeco-Roman society, aside from plot contrivances.[38] As a result, we can tentatively speak about pirates' democratic processes with greater specificity than almost any other group discussed in this book.

Pirates preferred non-hierarchical decision-making processes—what is nowadays called "horizontal leadership." We have already seen how pirates elected their captains at Lipara, and elections are well attested across ancient pirate ships.[39] This may not sound particularly anarchistic—the fact that they had a captain might imply that this was not a leaderless society. But piratical democracy extended far beyond intermittent votes concerning leadership. Although the captain was the only officer aboard a pirate ship, he held very little authority.[40] Indeed, the captain was afforded few special privileges and only held the power to command the ship and issue orders *in battle*—in nearly all other respects, he was equal to the crew. The reasoning was simple. Often, battles require split-second decisions. Deliberation can slow things down, so it is most efficient to invest authority in one specific individual who has gained the crew's trust.

This meant that pirates implemented democratic decisions in non-emergency contexts. Many texts depict the seriousness with which pirates took their governance; in one we read: "When the pirates arrived and the rest of the crowd gathered, captain Thyamis seated himself on a mound and declared the island a Popular Assembly."[41] Thyamis then addressed the other bandits as "comrades" and reminded them that his share of the loot was no more than anyone else's. The scene has legal formality and uses technical terms from Classical Greek democracies. And there is good reason for this overlapping vocabulary: we will see that pirate ships had constitutions similar to those of Greek democracies, though pirates drew upon other influences as well. Pirate constitutions limited the captain's power, ensured equitable distribution of goods, and guaranteed the rights of the crew.

Pirates, as they appear in both novels and historical accounts, were particularly insistent about their egalitarian ideals. One novel claims that after pirates looted a ship, they divided spoils into equal shares—the first man to shed blood had the first pick of the shares, meaning that the captain had to wait his turn.[42] Cicero noted that if any pirate captain "failed to distribute booty equitably among his crew, he would be abandoned or even killed by his comrades."[43] Even mild abuse of authority was sufficient for pirates to mutiny against their captain.[44] Whenever a captain acted in self-interest rather than serving the needs of his crew, his execution was likely to soon follow. Since the captain was the only officer aboard a pirate ship, everyone else had equal stations. Incidental duties were chosen by lot. This ensured that every crew member, regardless of seniority or popularity, was as likely to clean the latrines as anyone else.[45]

Outside of battle, important decisions required the deliberation of the entire crew in the Popular Assemblies.[46] These assemblies were ad hoc councils, contemplating a single—possibly divisive—issue, ranging from what to do with captives to where the ship might pursue its next conquest. Sources agree that Popular Assemblies welcomed proposals from the crew, which were then debated—the crewmen addressing one another as "comrade" (Greek: *systratiotes*), regardless of role or office. The captain had the opportunity to offer proposals first, but he was the crew's equal in all other regards. After the proposals were considered, they took a vote. Unanimity was preferable and, when achieved, was grounds for celebration, but a majority vote was sufficient to resolve the issue. If no majority emerged, one of two things happened: either action was deferred pending further development or a brawl ensued.

Pirates' reputation for misanthropy is flatly contradicted by how they extended their egalitarian principles to their friends and family who were not aboard the ship itself. Pirate constitutions codified protections for the women, children, and disabled comrades who lived on land, but remained under their care. They even kept a common fund for those in need.[47] Evidence suggests that the piratical Popular Assembly was mostly concerned with matters on board the ship, such as what to do with any captives on board and the election of the captain. Since members of this broader pirate community were not on the ship, they did not participate in the crew's Popular Assemblies. But if the Liparans were representative of broader trends among pirates, it is reasonable to suppose that these more expansive communities on land (i.e., elderly and injured comrades) took part in larger decision-making assemblies that affected them more directly.

Historian Nicholas Rauh concludes that Hellenistic piracy was "a movement in social reform, with thousands of armed seamen organizing themselves into anarchic, yet highly motivated democracies, more stable communities, and a fair and more equitable social system."[48] All of this was a far cry from the authoritarian abuse at the hands of ship owners that the pirates had experienced when they were sailors on merchant ships. Any pirate captain who tended toward merchant-style autocracy risked his crew's sedition. After all, many pirates had already engaged in mutiny when they took over merchant ships, so there was every reason to think they would do so again if they became too unhappy.[49]

* * *

Crewmen were free to do as they pleased within the bounds of the ship's articles.[50] Although no pirate constitution from antiquity survives in full, a few fragments give us a sense of their contents. One example, though fictional, can give us a sense of the contents and operations of such constitutions. An ancient novel depicts a pirate who objected to his captain having first pick of the loot because "pirate law allows whoever is first aboard an enemy vessel and first to brave the danger of combat on behalf of all his comrades to choose whatever he pleases from the spoils."[51] After hearing this, the captain appealed to another pirate law, which dictated that the crew obey their captain's orders. Of course, the captain conveniently omitted the provision that this measure only applied during battle. The captain's retort did not convince the crew, leading to a riot.

SELF-GOVERNANCE ON THE OPEN SEA

The systems of self-governance adopted by Hellenistic pirates shared many characteristics with those used in the Atlantic during the so-called "Golden Age of Piracy," nearly 2,000 years later (1690–1730 CE). Within both contexts, pirates codified a "share" system to distribute plunder, pensions for injured crewmen, communal decision-making by vote, punishment for taking more loot than allotted, limits on the captain's authority, and so on. In some ways, Hellenistic pirates were even more egalitarian than their "Golden Age" counterparts. The only officer aboard a Hellenistic pirate ship, for instance, was the captain. Booty shares were entirely equitable in antiquity, with no additional portion for captains or other officers. And Hellenistic pirates were more liberal in their sexual policies, since their crews accommodated the presence of lovers and sex workers.[52]

How did these remarkably sophisticated democracies come to be? Constitutions, consensus, voting, and equitable shares are hardly the type of thing that most people would expect from illiterate outlaws living thousands of years ago. This section will argue that these factors were *precisely* what put the pirates of antiquity in an excellent position to devise anarchistic ways of organizing their communities. Their democracies not only comprised escaped slaves, outlaws, and bankrupt peasants, but empowered them in ways that were unimaginable in their previous lives. Let us consider three specific ingredients in their recipe for radical self-organization.

First, Hellenistic pirates were extremely diverse in their origins. The Roman historian Appian wrote that pirates in this period comprised destitute seamen from "Cilicia, Syria, Cyprus, Pamphylia, and Pontus, and those of all the eastern nations."[53] Various other texts mentioned pirates from Liguria,

Illyria, Crete, Judaea, and Arabia, among other coastal lands.[54] Such diversity no doubt presented significant problems aboard pirate ships: the mix of languages, habits, and cultures would have made it difficult for crewmen to get along with, let alone understand, each other.

That said, such diversity also meant that pirate crews brought together people familiar with a wide range of democratic processes. Although Alexander the Great's conquest ended Athenian democracy (recall the story of Erotis in this book's Introduction), other Greek city-states maintained some independence as the Roman and Hellenistic empires encroached. Let us consider a handful of island Greek city-states off the coast of Asia Minor—the sorts of places that Appian mentioned above. Iasos worked on a model of civic consensus for ratifying legislation and paid all who attended the Popular Assembly to encourage democratic participation.[55] Nearby Rhodes had implemented extensive measures to care for the disabled and poor.[56] Not too far from that, Kalymna employed a system that reduced the number of civic officials to the practical minimum.[57] Beyond Asia Minor, Judaeans participated in a system where an advisory council curtailed the symbolic leader's powers.[58] Any Romans who turned piratical brought their experience electing military officers and voting in referenda. And some democratic systems were already found in maritime contexts; freelance sailors had long maintained a system of equitable "shares" for distributing wealth, for instance.[59] This is not to mention sailors' shared displeasure with the rigid authoritarianism aboard merchant vessels. The abundant diversity of the Mediterranean was visible within any given pirate crew, with individual members hailing from various different places and bringing distinctive political experiences with them.

A second ingredient in pirate democracy was their combat proficiency and experience. As Aristotle observed, any given city-state's military dictated its form of government.[60] States that relied foremost on cavalries tended to be aristocratic, since horses required substantial wealth to purchase and maintain. Thus, the interests of aristocratic soldiers tended to be prioritized in their constitutions. If a city-state relied upon heavy infantry, then those soldiers could vote too—not just the aristocrats, but men of moderate wealth. But Aristotle noted that if a city-state relied upon a navy or slingers, then the constitution enfranchised the entire citizenry, since any able-bodied man could row or sling. David Graeber explains why this was the case:

> Underlying the institution [of majoritarian voting] was the rather commonsensical idea that if a man was armed, his opinions had to be taken into account. Ancient military units often elected their own officers. It's also easy to see why majority voting would make sense in a military unit: even if a vote was 60–40, both sides are armed; if it did come down to a fight, one could see immediately who was most likely to win. And this pattern applies, broadly, more or less across the historical record: ... pirate ships, which were military operations, used majority vote.[61]

Collective decision-making is never easy, but disagreement can escalate to bloodshed when debate gets heated among armed populations. There is also the risk that some people might attempt to impose their will through force. Majoritarian voting has historically served to prevent such violence, particularly when these groups consist of social equals who are armed. And certainly, pirates were defined by their willingness to use armed force in defiance of the law and contempt for authority. Pirates valued the contributions of individual crew members and this factored into their governance. Of course, voting was hardly a perfect system, as people sometimes violated protocol and tempers flared. One Hellenistic novel depicted the precise situation Graeber imagines: a disagreement over a proposal led to a violent mutiny setting the captain's supporters against those who opposed his suggestion, culminating in mass slaughter.[62] This also explains why pirates celebrated any consensus emerging from the Popular Assembly: this way it was less likely that anyone would harbor hard feelings that might linger and grow into something violent. The very nature of piracy lent itself to voting on potentially divisive issues, if simply to avert bloodshed among comrades.

The final ingredient was the shared experience of isolation and exploitation at sea. Sailors working for merchants were a uniquely alienated group of people: they could not separate daily life from work, they lived without autonomy or privacy, they experienced immense emotional strain and physical abuse, they were deprived of meaningful social ties, and they had nowhere to call home.[63] Despite these awful conditions, their work required specialized skillsets and immense trust in their crewmates to perform maneuvers under the stress of inclement weather, unfamiliar waters, and fatigue. Being at sea, a sailor's closest friends were his crewmates—one can only imagine the countless conversations, games, and dire situations any ship's crew experienced together. The resulting

SELF-GOVERNANCE ON THE OPEN SEA

seclusion pitted sailors against the respectable world, which in turn contributed to a sense of solidarity rarely seen in the ancient world: pirates regarded each other as comrades in a way that was rare within any given occupation. Socrates observed that pirates "could hardly succeed if they began committing injustices against one another" and Cicero later declared that they "could not survive without some canons of justice among themselves. ... Hence the rule 'honor among thieves' which they are all obliged to observe."[64] There are numerous accounts of pirate crews assisting other pirate ships for no reason other than comradery. Shared experiences aboard the vessel culminated in a desire for an alternative social order, and pirates created this new order in "defiant contradistinction to the world they left behind."[65] Although they were slandered as miscreant criminals, they formalized processes for dispute-resolution, decision-making, division of spoils, and so on—doing so in ways that served their needs, rather than those of anyone who might claim to be their master.

This combination of demographic diversity, armed resistance, and crew solidarity were powerful contributors to pirates' democratic impulses. Graeber makes a profound observation about Golden Age pirates during the early eighteenth century, which applies equally to those of the Hellenistic period:

> We are dealing with a collection of people in which there was likely to be at least some firsthand knowledge of a very wide range of directly democratic institutions, ... suddenly finding themselves forced to improvise some mode of self-government in the complete absence of any state. It was the perfect intercultural space of experiment. There was

likely to be no more conducive ground for the development of new democratic institutions.⁶⁶

In other words, the motley crews manning these ships were not impediments to democracy, but assets to radical governance. Invested in their own survival, they developed participatory forms of governance that were custom-made for their situation.

Figure 7 Pirates in a Roman mosaic (third century CE). This mosaic was made in the Roman colony of Dougga in the province of Africa. The entire mosaic depicts the god Dionysus repelling Tyrrhenian pirates—a myth recounted in the seventh *Homeric Hymn* and by Philostratus the Elder (*Images* 1.19). Here, we see detail of the pirates assaulting the deity's ship. (Detail from a photograph by Larry Koester)

SELF-GOVERNANCE ON THE OPEN SEA

There were, however, limits to the egalitarian tendencies of Hellenistic pirates. Though ancient texts show considerable bias against ancient pirates, we can nevertheless be confident that some crews ransomed and even enslaved their captives.[67] Pirate ships were also masculine spaces that excluded women from their crews and presumably from their Popular Assemblies; if there were any women pirates in antiquity, all evidence of them has been lost. The prospect of violent retribution lingered over every disagreement among the crew. Despite this, pirates of the Hellenistic period expressed remarkable contempt for the state as an institution, particularly the growing Roman Republic—they weren't just democratic, but anarchistic as well. The most famous pirates of antiquity were those from Cilicia, who flourished in the period 146–67 BCE. The final section of this chapter will explore how these pirates marauded the coasts of the Roman Republic.

* * *

Late Hellenistic Cilicia, in what is now the southeastern coast of Turkey, had a reputation for piracy.[68] As the Carthaginian, Seleucid, Antigonid, and Ptolemaic empires declined, the Roman Republic tightened its grip on the Mediterranean. But Rome's navy was the weakest branch of their military; the catastrophic defeats its recently established fleet were well known, such as the Battle of Drepana (near Sicily) in 249 BCE or the Battle of Lipara in 260 BCE. Whenever possible, Romans preferred to fight on land. Given that Rome was not a major player in the maritime merchant game, around 146 BCE they realized they had nothing to lose and everything to gain by aiding these pirates. Consequently, Roman politicians were initially happy to collaborate with the Cilician pirates. The more the pirates disrupted sea-trade, the more they weakened Rome's rivals, and so the Roman Republic eagerly provided markets where pirates could sell their plunder. These pirates harbored in Cilicia, though we have seen that their crews were drawn from all corners of the Mediterranean. Cilicia was particularly appealing as a home base for pirates: brigandage was largely accepted among land-based Cilicians, its terrain concealed their ships, and the coasts consisted of treacherous rocky terrain navigable only by small vessels with a skilled crew.[69]

But after about 40 years of allowing piracy throughout the Eastern Mediterranean, Rome had established itself as the region's dominant power on land and now sought control of the sea too. Roman politicians and merchants began to assert a claim to the seas that their rivals had long controlled. The pirates they once saw as allies now presented an obstacle. Like the preceding empires, Rome bore much responsibility for the rise of piracy. Rome's conquests of the eastern Mediterranean drove people into hardship, turning peasants toward a life of banditry, whether on land or sea. Even ancient historians who hated pirates, such as Appian, Florus, Plutarch, and Cassius Dio, agreed that people were driven to piracy on account of the Mithridatic Wars (88–63 BCE), in which Rome defeated the Seleucid Empire.[70] In the process, Rome destroyed existing institutions and installing their own governors to exploit recently conquered people for the benefit of far-off aristocrats. Rauh argues that Cilician piracy was "a political act—a protest against the obvious use of state institutions to defend property and discipline labour."[71] Rauh's observation calls to mind a famous anecdote about Alexander

SELF-GOVERNANCE ON THE OPEN SEA

the Great. When Alexander captured a pirate ship, he asked the captain why he used warfare to seize possession of the sea. The captain responded with a question of his own, "Why, rather, do *you* use warfare to seize the whole earth? I am called a criminal because I do it with a little ship, but you are called the emperor because you do so with a massive fleet."[72] In other words, the biggest difference between pirate ships and an imperial navy was their perceived legitimacy. Pirates consisted of the shameful and the destitute. A crew of slaves and malcontents would never find legitimacy in the eyes of Greek or Roman aristocrats.

Pirates felt contempt for the Romans, whose conquests drove them from their homelands, and who now occupied those lands, enslaving many of their kinfolk. Cilician pirates mocked Roman values by adopting outlandish dress that emphasized their shameless lives—big hats, eyepatches, rust-colored cloaks.[73] Pirates enjoyed annoying Romans with their obnoxious songs.[74] Particularly comical, if cruel, was how Cilician pirates treated aristocratic Roman hostages. Plutarch said that when someone objected to being held captive on the grounds that he was Roman nobility, pirates pretended to regret the error and begged the man's forgiveness. Then, they outfitted the prisoner in a toga (the tuxedo of the time) and other luxury gear, claiming they did not want to repeat the mistake. The pirates would continue this charade for some time to amuse themselves, but once they were out at sea, they invited the Roman prisoner to go free, dropping a ladder into the Mediterranean. If the hostage refused, they simply threw him overboard.[75]

The geographer Strabo thought piracy came down not only to the land and who controlled it, but also the level of civilization. Weak governments enabled piracy to take root, he claimed; but more importantly, regions far from Rome could not benefit from the republic's civilizing influence and thus were prone to piracy.[76] Roman writers engaged in a propaganda campaign to convince the public that they had a moral responsibility to suppress the Cilician pirates, exaggerating their supposed terrors and debauchery.[77] The more the public hated and feared pirates, the easier it was to justify Roman imperial expansion.

Rome began its campaign against pirates in 103 BCE. Numerous generals claimed they defeated the Cilician pirates once and for all, but the pirates were like a hydra—if you cut off one head, then two more would emerge. Marcus Antonius declared definitive victory over them in 102 BCE when he was governor of Cilicia. The Roman government awarded him with a triumphal parade to celebrate his victory.[78] This was a bit premature, since Pompey the Great claimed the same success in 67 BCE, with a more plausible case for bringing an end to Cilician piracy. But the emperor Augustus was also eager to take credit a few decades after that. Augustus, after all, inaugurated the great *pax Romana* of the early Empire. As far as Roman politicians were concerned, this Roman peace also applied to the seas: cities erected monuments that declared Augustus emperor over "land and sea."[79] Supposedly, he had destroyed the remaining pirates in 36 BCE. Obviously, three men cannot all lay claim to conclusive victory over Mediterranean pirates, but to the extent that Roman historians discussed piracy after Augustus, they depicted it as something happening in foreign lands whose wilds Rome had yet to fully subdue.[80]

Though this may have been the official story, there are hints that pirates continued to harass aristocrats in the following decades. One horoscope from the first century CE predicted that pirates would steal someone's possessions, for instance.[81] The widespread depiction of pirates in popular novels of the Roman Empire continued. They remained figures of fascination for centuries afterward.

* * *

Although sailors aboard merchant ships were subject to slavery and misery, many sailors found opportunities through piracy. This was a new life in which a shared contempt for maritime exploitation fostered radical democracy. These incongruous gangs of malcontents from different corners of the Mediterranean were in a position to adapt the flawed systems with which they were familiar into something far more responsive to their situation. This life incurred many costs: habitual violence, the constant threat of punishment by the state, and the ongoing dangers of the sea. Pirates could expect to end their time on the seas either as a casualty in battle or by crucifixion after capture—it was only a matter of time.[82] Their ships were temporary communities, in which new rules and modes of behavior prevailed. It was commonly accepted that each crew had an expiration date, but that temporariness invited exciting new forms of social experimentation, wherein people could slip through the nets of the surrounding empires. Hellenistic pirates played with non-hierarchical ways of organizing themselves while developing reputations for carnage.

Further Reading

De Souza, Philip. 1999. *Piracy in the Graeco-Roman World*. Cambridge: Cambridge University Press.

Gabrielsen, Vincent. 2001. "Economic Activity, Maritime Trade and Piracy in the Hellenistic Aegean." *Revue des Études Anciennes* 103: 219–40.

Knapp, Robert C. 2011. *Invisible Romans: Prostitutes, Outlaws, Slaves, Gladiators and Others*. London: Profile. Pages 290–314.

Rauh, Nicholas K. 2003. *Merchants, Sailors and Pirates in the Roman World*. Charleston: Tempus.

Few books have been published on Hellenistic and Roman piracy. The work of Nicholas Rauh has been vital for understanding Cilician pirate ships as democratic institutions and Philip De Souza has published an excellent study of the historical development of Mediterranean piracy. These books are the two best starting points. Vincent Gabrielsen's article concerns the demographics of pirates and their relationship to the "legitimate" violence of Hellenistic navies, which is productively read in conversation with Rauh's research. Finally, Robert Knapp has an insightful chapter on bandits and pirates in the Roman world.

Third Interlude.
Living in the Ruins:
The Fall of Rome in Britannia

The Western Roman Empire fell in 476 CE, but ancient writers had been taking note of its waning power for decades. Consider the only two surviving eyewitness accounts of Roman abandonment of the province Britannia. The Christian monk Gildas (sixth century CE) catalogued the famines, slaughter, and illnesses that the Britons faced after Rome abandoned the region in 407 CE.[1] By 420 CE, many Roman institutions—the legions, the bathhouses, the villa, and so on—had either fallen out of use or vanished altogether. The other writer, Saint Patrick (fifth century CE), described how he was kidnapped and taken to Ireland as a prisoner in the last days of Roman presence.[2] Patrick was a Roman citizen, the son of a wealthy British landowner who served on the city council. As Rome's power rapidly diminished, not even influential families could count on imperial protection.

Britannia was about as far from the city of Rome as one could get while still remaining in the Empire. It is no surprise Rome's decline affected the empire's outskirts like this, but what was true of the periphery was also true of Rome. Pope Gregory I (540–604 CE) wrote about great families that had fallen destitute within Italy itself. Gregory donated to the widows of noblemen and former governors who had fallen on hard times. The once-robust aristocracy could no longer rely upon the Roman state for security or the provision of pensions.³ The fragmentation of the empire took many forms. Another ancient historian wrote about how, upon invasion of the empire's interior, the Germanic Lombards killed "many noble subjects of the empire" in order to plunder their estates during the late sixth century CE.⁴ The accounts of Roman nobles and their historians suggest that the gradual collapse of the empire entailed suffering and discomfort: barbarian raiders, mass poverty, pandemics, loss of Roman technological conveniences, not to mention grand Roman monuments and buildings falling into disrepair. They contend that the quality of life *must* have declined as Rome lost its grip.

This understanding of Rome's fall draws its conclusions from the experience of its most wealthy inhabitants, who were a small minority of the population. When Romans abandoned Britannia, it certainly affected the lives of peasants and other ordinary folk. If anything, Rome's loss was their gain.

* * *

How did Rome's decline affect the majority of the population in Britannia? How did common people—peasants, townsfolk, beggars, etc.—emerge from the ashes of the Roman Empire? Literary accounts are unreliable and focus on the most affluent. The wealthy were more likely to leave recoverable archaeological remains than the poor—archaeologists might find a stone inscription honoring a local aristocrat or his massive estate, while any small wooden crosses marking peasants' graves or the humble shack where they lived would have long decomposed, for example. Whereas in other areas of the empire, papyri record the correspondence that ordinary folks sent to one another, Britannia's damp climate hastened the deterioration of such texts, so they have been lost to time. But archaeologists have devised ways of answering these questions from the data that survives. Let us consider the changes in Britannia across the pre-Roman (500 BCE–43 CE), Roman (43–407 CE), and post-Roman periods (407–700 CE).

With few textual records from pre-Roman Britannia, historians have largely depended on archaeology and there is general agreement that although inequality was certainly present, it was not a significant part of social life.[5] The Britons experienced a great deal of warfare between rival chieftains during this period, but the chieftains' power over daily life was weak. Throughout these difficulties, the communities of pre-Roman Britannia remained strong.

This way of life ended with Rome's conquest of Britannia in 43 CE. Earlier in the book, we saw a statue that depicted the emperor Claudius preparing to rape the personification of the British people (see Figure 3). This was Rome's way of commemorating their own conquest, but anti-Roman propaganda would probably have depicted the scene identically! Romans started to reframe the relationship as a friendly fusion of two cultures, but there is plenty of evidence that Rome continued to exact violence upon locals.[6] Roman rule concentrated wealth in the hands of its favored aristocrats, leading to a sharp increase in inequality. This is evident in the massive discrepancy between the largest and smallest homes throughout the province.[7] The wealthy became much wealthier, such that their average house sizes more than doubled. Those of the poor remained about the same.

Rome's control of Britannia came to a permanent end in 407 CE, following a series of battles against the Scots and Picts. This period is often called the "post-Roman" period of Britannia, since several centuries passed before any centralized state took control of the region. Although later writers tended to talk about the post-Roman period as little more than a series of battles between kings and warlords, archaeological evidence paints a very different picture. Subsistence, not warfare, was the primary concern for denizens of post-Roman Britannia.[8] Without Roman governors and powerful landlords, farmers were no longer beholden to the extensive system of property rights that determined who held the legal right to farm in what location. The lawcourts, military, and bureaucrats who had been responsible for enforcing tax evasion, punishing people who defaulted on their loans, or enforcing strict lines of property ownership came to have little sway. Rather, people discarded Roman-era institutions concerning property ownership and farmed where it made the most sense to them.

The loss of Roman power also led to the collapse of Britannia's cities. Rome had required significant surpluses to feed its massive urban populations in Britannia, where specialists of all sorts labored, ranging from craftspeople to soldiers to administrators. These people did not produce food, so Rome exacted significant taxes from farmers to ensure the urban population was fed and the urban markets could function. Urban sites nearly vanished in the post-Roman period and so did the comforts that came with their markets. Robin Fleming observes that "skills related to iron and copper smelting, wooden board and plank making, stone quarrying, commercial butchery, horticulture, and tanning were disappearing."[9] Knowledge of how to produce Roman pottery, build in stone, and engineer sophisticated structures also declined. Social classes flattened in this period. Archaeologists observe that as urban economies faded, large estates were abandoned, and social inequality diminished. During the post-Roman period, people were rarely buried alongside expensive goods.[10]

This post-Roman flattening of the social hierarchy, far from simply reducing the quality of life for everyone to a lower level, led to healthier lives. This is evident in skeletons found throughout Western Europe, which show fewer bone lesions and are taller in the post-Roman period than during the Roman occupation.[11] Height is a valuable index of general health. Average height is particularly informative when it is possible to compare a large number of skeletons from a single ethnic group over different periods of time. Consider the factors that can lead to shorter height within large populations; malnutrition, slavery, gender discrimination, cash-cropping, poverty, and exploitation all contribute to the inequitable distribution of nutritious food. Widespread deficiencies can have significant effects on average heights, since these factors apply not only to the person under question, but also to their mother, as her health plays a significant role in that of her unborn and nursing child.

The absence of urban markets meant that farmers had to produce fewer luxury foods for the sake of aristocrats, instead cultivating staples for their own consumption—something amply evidenced in post-Roman Britannia.[12] In a similar vein, the decentralization of power meant that even the aristocrats and landlords who still had some power over farmers did not take as much: the amount of work required for a post-Roman farmer to feed an absentee landlord and a few of his thugs was considerably less than the farmer who was expected to feed an entire city under Roman occupation. Archaeologist Robert Perry Stephan demonstrates how inequality diminished after the collapse of Roman Britannia.[13] Stephan compares the size of hundreds of remains of ancient British homes across antiquity. He attributes the change in house sizes not only to wealth differentials between homeowners, but also to the fact that the poorest people in Roman Britannia did not own a house at all. Many people lived as slaves and dependents in the largest estates, their lodging dependent on landowners and without any property to call their own. Large estates were far less common in the post-Roman period and more poor people owned their own homes, rather than renting them or living in estates as dependents.

Roman rule had facilitated exploitation and its absence allowed more egalitarian social structures to flourish. This suggests something very different from the conventional view of life as idyllic under the *pax Romana*, in which Rome's protection was said to have contributed to a high quality of life within the empire's provinces. Instead, Roman conquest and administration entailed significant inequality. And when the Romans abandoned Britannia, the people who benefited most from the exploitation of the region's commoners either left the region as well or saw their social status diminish to one approximating a commoner.

* * *

Of course, much was lost in the post-Roman period. Particularly visible was the slow dilapidation of the once-flourishing Roman scenery. The city of Bath (which the Romans called Aquae Sulis), for instance, had once been a symbol of Roman values within Britannia, with luxurious facilities for public bathing, a temple to the goddess Sulis Minerva, and city walls to prevent the incursion of any hostile outsiders. Less than a century after Rome left the region, these impressive structures had fallen into ruin and disrepair. An eighth-century poet described Roman ruins in the city of Bath, reflecting on its lost glory:

> Bright were the castle buildings, many the bathing-halls,
> high the abundance of gables, great the noise of the multitude,
> many a mead-hall full of festivity,
> until Fate the mighty changed that.
> Far and wide the slain perished, days of pestilence came,
> death took all the brave men away;
> their places of war became deserted places,
> the city decayed.[14]

Written in Old English, this poem offered a moody reflection on the city's former grandeur, contrasting Roman opulence with its subsequent decline. Bath had once evoked colonial greatness and imperial power that stretched far beyond its capital city in Rome over a thousand miles away. The wealthy donors who helped fund the construction and maintenance of these facilities were fading memories. For some, as this poem indicates, this was cause for melancholy.

But Rome's absence also meant that people were free of many constraints the Romans had imposed: less time required for farming, no requirements of what crops to grow, fewer restrictions on how to build homes, and so on. Now at liberty to attend to their own needs, rather than those of the aristocracy, the people of post-Roman Britannia lived freer and healthier lives than their ancestors had under the empire. Rather than imagining the end of Roman rule in Britannia as the empire ceding the land to barbarian marauders, we might instead think of it along the lines of the Byzantine historian Zosimus (fifth and sixth centuries CE):

> The barbarians north of the Rhine, having assaulted everything as they wanted, led both the Britons and some of the Celts to defect from Roman rule and live apart from Roman law. The Britons did not fear danger and took up arms, liberating their own cities from barbarian threat. Armorica and the other Gallic provinces followed the Britons' lead: they freed themselves, ejected the Roman magistrates, and set up home rule at their own discretion.[15]

Although Zosimus was hardly an objective historian, his narrative described common people's experience, ascribing them far more agency than we are accustomed to. Zosimus understood them as capable humans, rejecting Rome and resisting the incursions of the petty tyrants who sought to replace Roman power with their own. For the common folk of Britannia, freedom defined the post-Roman period and this freedom demanded preservation, far more so than the monuments and architecture of urban aristocrats.[16]

Conclusion: The Ghost of Spartacus

Heroes and Ghosts

The Third Servile War concluded in 71 BCE when the Roman legions defeated Spartacus and his army in the Battle of the Silarius River. In the aftermath, the Romans crucified thousands of former slaves who had been living in Thurii. As for Spartacus' own demise, ancient historians disagreed, and most of their accounts were vague. Plutarch claimed that two centurions killed him in battle. Livy and Athenaeus both referred to his defeat at the hands of the general Crassus. Florus simply stated that he died bravely in combat.[1] None of these reports paint a particularly evocative scene. But the historian Appian wrote an account so peculiar that it's worth quoting in full:

> Since so many tens of thousands of desperate men were involved, the result was a protracted battle of epic proportions. Spartacus took a spear wound in his thigh. Collapsing on one knee, he held his shield up in front of him and fought off those who were attacking him, until he and the large number of men around him were finally surrounded and cut down. The rest of his army was thrown into disarray and confusion and was slaughtered in huge numbers. The killing was on such a scale that it was not possible to count the dead. The Romans lost about a thousand men. The body of Spartacus was never found.[2]

The specificity of Appian's narrative diverged from others, but especially strange was his comment about the missing corpse. Ancient historians almost never mentioned the failure to find a single body on a battlefield where thousands died, so why did Appian include this odd detail? This scene prompts further questions. Did Appian imply that Spartacus survived the battle? Or did he mean that Spartacus died, but his body disappeared through supernatural means? Did some people at Thurii believe that he rose from the dead, as Christians later claimed about Jesus?

In trying to trace the democratic and anarchistic impulse, we should bear in mind what those in antiquity thought of life, death, and what happened after that. Aldo Schiavone observes how the disappearance of Spartacus' corpse "consigns the conclusion of the story to the indecipherable, shadowy mysteries, between life and death, the human and the divine, where everything became possible."[3] Spartacus vanished and although Appian hinted at postmortem possibilities, he did not really elaborate on what this entailed. If we pause to consider where Spartacus may have gone, whatever comes to mind blurs the boundary between life and afterlife, inhabiting a murky realm where the dead can be faintly felt but remain unseen. There is something unsettling about the idea that the Roman gods refused Spartacus eternal rest, leaving his spirit to wander among the living.

But Spartacus was hardly the only one whose afterlife was the object of speculation. Some ancient writers claimed that the Cynic philosopher Diogenes achieved immortality and became a star after he died. The Roman poet Ausonius imagined a dialogue between a nameless man and the sculpture of a dog that sat outside Diogenes' tomb:

CONCLUSION

Anonymous: "Tell me, dog, whose grave is this?"

Dog: "A dog's."

Anonymous: "But which dog is that?"

Dog: "Diogenes."

Anonymous: "He's passed away?"

Dog: "He hasn't passed away, but he has gone away."

Anonymous: "Diogenes, whose knapsack was his treasury and who slept in clay pots, has gone away to the shades?"

Dog: "Cerberus prohibits him from that place."

Anonymous: "So where has he gone away to?"

Dog: "Where the bright star of Leo shines, a dog now helps righteous Erigone."[4]

This epigram is dense with allusion and warrants unpacking. Although the anonymous man knew that Diogenes was no longer around, the dog revealed that this was not because the philosopher's soul had been vanquished nor because he joined the collective dead known as the *manes*. Rather, Diogenes lived in the night sky near the constellations Virgo (i.e., Erigone, the daughter of Icarius) and Leo, having been transformed into the star named Sirius. Sirius, appropriately enough, was known as the dog star; it was the brightest star in the night sky at the time and remains so in the twenty-first century. Some believed that Diogenes watched over them and continued to assess their commitment to justice alongside Erigone.

Others terrified people from beyond the grave, but in less supernatural ways. Some Christian writers claimed that the Circumcellions never disappeared but continued as a secret sect that hid among the population by pretending to be Catholics like wolves in sheep's clothing. Others wrote that Cilician pirates were like zombies that kept reviving after catastrophic defeats to attack merchant ships. Mazdakites were said to have adapted their radical ideas to welcome people of different religions in heretical defiance of the caliphs. These anarchists also had afterlives, in the sense that they continued to threaten the social order even after their demise. Whenever someone took up their cause—be it years or even centuries later—their ideas and legacies found new life.

Many ancient authors used the metaphor of ghosts to keep these communities alive, both their ideas and practices, whether as inspiration or warnings. In imagining these people as ghosts, ancient writers acknowledged their deaths, but hoped they might haunt us and compel us to act. Readers are probably familiar with Charles Dickens' tale of the ghosts who terrorized Ebenezer Scrooge into changing his ways on Christmas Eve; the people of Greece and Rome told similar stories.[5] Patroclus' spirit appeared to his beloved Achilles in a dream, insisting that Achilles ensure a proper burial.[6] The ghost of Clytemnestra manifested before the Furies, urging them to pursue and punish her killer.[7] There were ghosts who warned of impending disaster, ghosts who frightened people to stay away from or to visit a significant location, ghosts who sought revenge.[8] Examples pervade ancient literature and the sheer quantity speaks to their cultural importance.[9] In pursuing the metaphor of ghosts and haunting, we do not need to suppose that ghosts literally walk the earth or that there is an afterlife that allows them to communicate with us through supernatural channels.[10] Rather, we might reflect on how people who died long ago continue to rattle and unnerve our psyche.

This line of thinking is preferable to conceptualizing radicals from the past as heroes—figures of adoration and veneration.[11] Heroes are people who lived in a manner that we can only aspire to. We offer gratitude to heroes precisely because they did things that we cannot. The act of veneration means we owe them little more than our gratitude—they do the work for us, lightening our load. Sometimes, we feel like our imagined relationship with heroes can alleviate our responsibility to engage directly with the struggles in the world around us.

This is the ultimate cop-out. To deem someone a hero is too often to admit our own inability to do what they did; heroes intervened on our behalf, since they exceeded any standards that we can realistically achieve. The lives of heroes were precious, to be sure, but too extraordinary for us to replicate. They were exceptional individuals whose bravery and courage exceeded the rest of us. Our reverence toward heroes rarely extends beyond moral agreement: we can continue business as usual, so long as we *believe* things should be another way. If we believe in our hearts that exploitation is wrong and that capitalism is evil, and we revere those who have fought so bravely, then we are free to go about our day.[12] We act as though our appreciation of Spartacus, Diogenes, and others can absolve us from acting. Heroes seek only our veneration and fascination, asking little more of us. If we adopt such a posture, then we become fatalists incapacitated by our own imperfections. If we regard them as heroes, we foreclose the possibility that we can create more democratic societies ourselves. We forget that Spartacus was no more important than any other slave in the Third Servile War, that Diogenes was one among thousands of Cynics, that Axido and Fasir were mere catalysts for a much wider Circumcellion revolt, that we do not know the name of a single Essene or Therapeut, that Cilician pirates were former slaves who rejected the abuse meted upon their bodies, and so on. We forget that anybody can do these things.

Ghosts, by contrast, compel us to behave in particular ways, unlike heroes, who only prompt us to reflect on their unattainable virtue. Ghosts recognize our agency and demand that we act. We often forget that we have this capacity within us and, as a result, become resigned to the status quo: the hurdles required to bring about a better world can seem insurmountable. But ghosts do not allow us to admit defeat. In the same way that they defied the empires of antiquity, they insist that we use our agency to defy the empires of our own day. These reminders are timely, given the widespread tendency to assume there is no alternative to the current system of state-enforced capitalist exploitation. Yet David Graeber reminds us of this capacity:

> The hidden reality of human life is the fact that the world doesn't just happen. It isn't a natural fact, even though we tend to treat it as if it is—it exists because we all collectively produce it. We imagine things we'd like and then we bring them into being. But the moment you think about it in these terms, it's obvious that something has gone terribly wrong. Since who, if they could simply imagine any world that they liked and then bring it into being, would create a world like this one? ... It only exists because we wake up and continue to produce it. If we woke up one morning and all collectively decided to produce something else, then we wouldn't have capitalism anymore.[13]

As a ghost, Spartacus looms in shadowy spaces and liberates us, reminding us that it is possible to do what he did over

CONCLUSION

2,000 years earlier. We can take up his legacy and create societies free of money, sexual violence, and hierarchy. As a ghost, Diogenes urges us to renounce honor and shame, wealth, and nationalism. And so also with the Mazdakites, Circumcellions, Essenes, Cilician pirates, and others.

Ghosts confront us with a simple question: how might the past compel us to think differently about the present? Numerous writers from antiquity claimed they knew how to summon the dead and speak with their souls. One Greek papyrus, for instance, describes an elaborate ritual to summon a ghostly assistant, requiring the favor of various gods, incantations in various languages, a donkey's hide, a recent grave, a flax leaf, among other *materia magica*.[14] Thankfully, our task is much simpler. As students of history, we engage in a kind of necromancy or communing with the dead when we summon the ghosts described throughout this book. Through this act of necromancy—that is, the act of integrating these people into our understanding of human possibilities—their spirits induce us to create another world. When we do so, the people of Thurii, Mazdakites, Cynics, and others no longer rest in their graves. Once resurrected, these people have the potential to remind us of our capacity to engage the world around us.

The Broken Promises of Athenian Democracy

It is clear that ancient democracies were flawed institutions. Athens itself was built upon slavery, patriarchy, xenophobia, and other exploitative systems.[15] Today, we can easily understand how these injustices contributed to the city's various crises, but wealthy Athenians argued that their problems arose from democracy itself. They criticized the common people and claimed democracy allowed such fools to exert power over the wealthy. We saw in the Introduction that Socrates, Plato, and Aristotle had no love for democracy, but these men are just three among the innumerable wealthy critics of Athenian democracy. One anonymous author whom scholars have nicknamed "The Old Oligarch" was a contemporary of Socrates. The Old Oligarch published a screed around 420 BCE that denounced Athenian democracy on the grounds that it empowered the poor, giving "more power to the worthless, the impoverished, and the common people than to the wealthy."[16] Such criticisms were standard fare in ancient literature. The rich had no love for the direct and borderline "radical" democracies of Greek antiquity, as these systems ensured that the poorest citizens had a considerable say in how their society was run. Of course, we should recall that the most destitute in these societies were even worse off than the poorest citizens, such as slaves and immigrants. Democracy, aristocrats argued, was a gateway to chaos. Affluent Athenians tried to rectify the problems supposedly inherent to democracy, offering solutions that advanced their own interests. These were essentially variations on the same suggestion: that the city should be run by men of affairs elected as representatives or an unelected council composed of the city's largest landowners. The reasoning was that these men could afford the best education and had sufficient time to reflect on matters of public interest, not to mention their capacity to contemplate deeper concerns of justice and virtue. They insisted that either option would ensure that political leadership was highly qualified, so they called this system "aristocracy."

Throughout this book, I have used this word in the conventional sense, denoting a class of wealthy individuals who hold

CONCLUSION

considerable political power. But the Greek term had another meaning, as it also referred to a political system that placed power in the hands of society's "best" men: *aristos* (best) + *kratia* (power). This term was a clever marketing ploy, since it was difficult to sound reasonable when arguing against the idea that "the best" people should run society—you might as well declare that you want to put the city's biggest fools in charge of things. The Old Oligarch offered his own reasons for preferring *aristokratia*:

> Throughout the world, the best people oppose democracy. For the best men have little debauchery or injustice within them, but are instead deeply concerned with important things. Contrast this with the common folk (*demos*), who contain the utmost ignorance, disorder, and malice. Poverty leads them into shameful lives; it is precisely because they do not have money that they remain uneducated and ignorant.[17]

Throughout his treatise, the Old Oligarch deployed a range of terms to describe the wealthy men that he hoped would abolish Athens' democratic constitution in favor of an aristocratic government: the noble, the best, the most effective, the capable, the cleverest, etc. He wanted to convince his readers that democracy could not be reformed. Rather, Athens would require the implementation of a completely different system so that folks like himself could run the city without the interference of common people. The Athenian poor only had their own interests in mind, he argued, whereas men like himself contemplated loftier topics such that they could create a better society. The Old Oligarch was one among many wealthy men who thought democracy was irredeemable, preferring a system that involved the election of Athens' most qualified citizens into political office.

Any form of aristocracy would have put considerably more influence in the hands of the wealthy, given that they were the only ones who could fund a political campaign, afford a full education, or satisfy the tremendous property requirements to run for office. We tend to think of fair elections as a pivotal, perhaps even definitive, element of democracy. But ancient writers understood elections as an aristocratic method for selecting public officials: citizens elected their leaders from among a handful of career politicians who were independently wealthy.[18] The argument was that wealthy people had a more detached perspective than the common folk who worked for a living. The poor had to look out for themselves, so they were less concerned about what was best for the city. The viability of democracy remained a contentious issue in Athens. The city's Constitution was regularly revised to formalize or revise class divisions. These changes had significant political implications: Solon's Constitution, introduced around 594 BCE, instituted a distinction of four property-based classes, and undid an earlier system that served old-money Athenians known as the Eupatridae. Cleisthenes reformed the Constitution in 508 BCE, further diluting the powers of the wealthy and instituting the system of sortition (i.e., randomly choosing politicians by lot), such that everyone could participate. Athenian sortition favored the representation of common people by the simple fact of their greater proportion. It would be only a minor overstatement to describe Athenian history as a series of conflicts between these two factions: the

CONCLUSION

defenders of popular democracy and the rich who thought their wealth should grant them political power.

Athens wasn't the only city where democracy and aristocracy were in conflict. The Roman Republic was another famous example. The Greek historian Polybius (208–118 BCE) surveyed different governments of antiquity and expressed a preference for the republic's division of power between three distinct social elements: the monarchic, the aristocratic, and the democratic.[19] The Roman Republic had two consuls serving as head of state, exercising authority in all public matters: military, executive, and punitive. Polybius deemed this monarchic, even though the consulship was not hereditary; rather, it consisted of two men chosen by the Senate to serve annual terms. The Senate comprised a permanent assembly of wealthy property-owners that served in the aristocratic function. They directed the collection and expenditure of funds, and also managed most diplomatic matters. Finally, the democratic aspect was found both in Popular Assemblies that conferred honors and oversaw trials and the power of the plebian tribunes, who could veto the Senate's laws in the interest of the plebs.

Polybius deemed this the best form of governance, conveniently overlooking how it consolidated the power of the aristocracy: the Senate not only chose the consuls, but the consuls were selected from among the senators themselves. The plebian tribunes, who served as a democratic check on the power of the Senate, were not actually permitted to enter the Senate assembly and instead had to listen in from outside its doors. All legislative and executive, as well as most judicial, authority lay with the Senate. Democratic power could do little against this aristocratic aspect of government, despite

Polybius' insistence that they held equal power and kept each other in check. He and others deemed this system "mixed governance."

Mixed governance was political sleight of hand that gave the impression of concessions to the general population, while ensuring the government remained in the hands of the wealthy. This permitted the affluent to acknowledge the population's frustrations without ceding anything of importance. Polybius was hardly alone in praising such arrangements, as Plutarch, Aristotle, Plato, and other ancient writers endorsed constitutions that divided power between monarchic, aristocratic, and democratic entities.[20] Like Polybius, they praised these constitutions in a manner that downplayed the fact that power mostly circulated among the wealthy. They insisted that, at best, democracy could exist as part of a mixed political system. And even then, it should be significantly curtailed by aristocratic elements.

One fact that has lingered throughout this book is that ancient conceptions of democracy bear little resemblance to so-called "democratic" governments today. Presently, the word "democracy" largely refers to systems involving the election of representatives who govern with minimal public involvement. The word "democracy" today denotes any political system involving elections, having nothing to do with the concept of people-power that the Greek word designated: *demos* (population) + *kratia* (power). No one inhabiting Classical or Hellenistic Greece would characterize any national government today as *demokratia*. If anything, purportedly "democratic" governments have implemented the exact decision-making processes that the *anti*-democratic factions of antiquity had advocated—most notably elections. The

CONCLUSION

political class of most countries comprises the wealthy, or at least people with wealthy benefactors. These politicians often implement unpopular policies, with little recourse for the general population, whose involvement was central to ancient conceptions of democracy. How did the meaning of the word change so drastically from antiquity to the present day?

The "Horrors" of American Democracy

The concept of democracy is taken for granted today. Even the wealthiest usually regard it as an obviously "good" thing. And, indeed, it is foundational to the national myths of various countries, especially the United States. Every American schoolchild is taught that King George III was a tyrant and America's Founding Fathers implemented democracy to replace his rule, developing a bicameral legislature to prevent any single person or faction from accumulating too much power. The British king and nobility had done their best to ensure that American colonials had little say in their own governance. In the face of this injustice, the Founders declared that political power should reside in the hands of the people, creating the world's first modern democracy. "No taxation without representation," after all. Or so the story goes.

In truth, no one in the Western world really had anything good to say about democracy before the American Revolution and many people despised it even after the revolution came to an end.[21] Up through the mid-eighteenth century, nearly everybody in Western Europe and colonial America regarded democracy as a threat to the social order, to the point that it was difficult to find anyone with something positive to say about it. America's Founding Fathers loathed the monarchy and expressed frustration with American exclusion from the British Parliament, but they disparaged democracy with nearly equal vigor.

Writers from early America articulated the same criticisms of democracy as ancient aristocrats had done, citing especially its empowerment of common rabble. The Founding Fathers and other wealthy Americans regularly quoted anti-democracy screeds from antiquity, affirming their view that democracy would open the door to chaos. Particularly influential was Thucydides' *History of the Peloponnesian War*. Thucydides wrote this monumental work around 400 BCE, when the once-mighty Athenian Empire had diminished, following its defeat in the war of the book's title. Thucydides detested the city's democracy, though his disdain should not surprise us, since he was very wealthy—so much so that he owned multiple gold mines.[22] Thucydides was opportunistic in his characterization of Athenian history, highlighting some crises and explaining others so as to depict democracy as a threat to peace and freedom.[23] The English philosopher Thomas Hobbes published a popular translation of Thucydides' opus in 1628, so people who did not know Attic Greek could now study Thucydides' anti-democratic chronicle. Hobbes' own philosophical writings touched on similar concerns. He famously argued in his treatise *Leviathan* (1651) that people are naturally inclined to selfish violence and so must relinquish their freedoms to a strong state for the sake of a civilized society.[24] Hobbes opposed radicals in England who advocated such wild ideas as universal male suffrage, a decentralized government, and the abolition of the monarchy.[25] He found an ally in Thucydides, claiming that the Greek historian had convinced him that "democracy was wrong and one man was far wiser than a throng."[26] Both men agreed that the poor were incapable of self-governance and that any systems empowering them risked considerable harm. Democracy, according to Hobbes and Thucydides, was dangerous.

Hobbes' political philosophy proved influential and his translation of Thucydides was read throughout the anglophone world. It had a particular effect on the Founding Fathers, who commonly cited Thucydides alongside Polybius, Plutarch, and other ancient writers when denouncing what John Adams (who would become the second president of the U.S.) called "the horrors of democracy."[27] Early American newspapers regularly published letters to the editor that looked back to antiquity for grounds to reject this system of government: "Let us only view the state of Greece and Rome when under a democratical government. ... Liberty was forced to hide her head and her gentle rays were so eclipsed that nothing but anarchy and confusion were among the people!"[28] Though this kind of fearmongering was common, others offered more thoughtful objections to Greek-style direct democracy, appealing to pragmatic concerns; democracy may have worked for Athens (and Argos, Chios, Erythrai, Megara, Rhodes, Samos, Syracuse, etc., etc.), but it wouldn't work for America for reasons of scale. Thus, one letter to the editor objected to the democratizing factions in his own state: Pennsylvania already contained some 275,000 people, whereas Sparta and Athens only had 20,000 citizens.[29] The letter's author then clarified that his primary objection to democracy was that "the rude, envious, and illiterate spirit of the peasantry will predominate." James Madison, who became the fourth president of the U.S., articulated this same point in the *Federalist Papers*, arguing that even though Athens may have functioned democratically, its political system could not be adapted for the fledgling United States, which spanned a much larger area.[30] The Founding Fathers generally agreed that it was preferable to have an aristocratic system of elected representatives to ensure that only the most educated and thus most qualified (and therefore, the wealthiest) could shepherd the American flock. This American aristocracy, consisting of elected representatives, differed little from the British Parliament. For Madison, Adams, and others, the problem with the British government was not the fact that it was a parliament, but that it was *British*. At this time, only land-owning men could vote in Britain's parliamentary elections, a policy that Adams and Madison also supported for the young United States. Greek and Roman writers remained a strong ally throughout these arguments.[31]

At best, democracy was something that could exist as part of a larger system such as the one Polybius had advocated, where it would be regulated by the moderating forces of the aristocracy and monarchy. Consider one letter to the editor, published under the pseudonym "Cato."[32] Although the letter insisted on a mixed system of government, favorably citing the opinions of Polybius and Plutarch, this was a red herring: the author bemoaned both the British monarchy and the prospect of American democracy, but had nothing negative to say about the aristocracy's power. Perhaps the author's pseudonym should have cued us to his aristocratic sympathies; Cato (95–46 BCE) was a Roman aristocrat famous for his leading role among the *optimates*—a conservative faction of the late Roman Republic that supported the supremacy of the Senate and tried to limit the people's power.[33] Polybius and other ancient aristocrats claimed that democracy consistently

CONCLUSION

devolved into *ochlocracy* (mob rule) and the Founding Fathers (among other affluent men) leveled similar charges against democratic efforts in early America.[34] This reasoning held obvious appeal for affluent Americans, who sought to harness the fervor of anti-British resentments while reining in democratic tendencies among the masses.

This Is What Democracy Looks Like

This is not the whole story, however. Around this time, more radical factions began to reclaim the term "democracy" as part of an egalitarian ideal. Many people addressed the objections of Adams and Madison, hoping to implement a form of direct democracy in the United States. Thomas Jefferson—the most democratic of the Founding Fathers—wanted to divide the country into thousands of "wards" that were governed locally. His reasoning was expressly democratic:

> Divide the counties into wards of such size as that every citizen can attend when called on, and act in person. ... These wards, called townships in New England, are the vital principle of their governments, and have proved themselves the wisest invention ever devised by the wit of man for the perfect exercise of self-government, and for its preservation.[35]

This system would have ensured that every citizen personally played a meaningful role in collective decision-making processes. A network of wards, each a direct and participatory democracy, united in a loose confederation, sounds very Greek.

Jefferson did not just come up with this idea by examining history books. Rather, he was impressed by the town assemblies found throughout America, where democratic tendencies were in full force. Major cities like Boston, Philadelphia, and New York regularly held mass meetings—wealth played no role in who could attend or speak at these events.[36] These were places for radical action to emerge, such as the Boston Tea Party, the Paper Money Riot, and the Whiskey Rebellion. In rural areas, smaller communities developed their own methods of self-governance, often with anarchistic elements. In 1795, a group of 500 Pennsylvanian farmers formed a militia to erect liberty poles (used to indicate an upcoming town assembly) and pressure a certain tax collector to stop seizing money from the poor.[37] When the county's judges heard about this, they raced on horseback to find the militia and prevent them from destroying the tax collector's ledger. Upon arrival, the judges asked to speak with the militia's officer. The farmers responded that they didn't have officers, since "they were all as one." Then, ignoring the judges' demands, the militia erected the liberty poles and destroyed the tax book. Democracy's antagonism to the exploitation of the poor runs through this anecdote. Popular democracy in early America was spontaneous, localized, leaderless, and participatory—just as Jefferson had suggested. It bore a radical edge that aristocrats like James Madison, John Adams, and others did their best to blunt. During this founding period, the character of American politics remained up in the air, as it had not yet ossified into the pseudo-democracy of representative governance.

These farmers, butchers, stonemasons, and other laborers were eager to draw upon ancient legacies to support democracy, just like their oligarchic opponents. One ongoing issue in South Carolina around this time was the question of which

CONCLUSION

citizens should have political rights. Aristocrats wanted to create a minimum property requirement, but many opposed this in favor of Athenian-style popular democracy, as evident in a 1794 letter to the editor: "In the assembly of the people at Athens, the lowest mechanic or labourer had a right to vote. Themistocles, Cimon, or Pericles had no more."[38] The author of this piece went by the penname of Appius, evoking the Roman statesman Appius Claudius Caecus (312–279 BCE), who reformed the law so that the children of former slaves could serve in the Senate and extended voting rights to landless peasants. Even more radical was a 1793 letter to the editor from the Democratic Society of Lexington, Kentucky, which warned that it is impossible to properly vet any elected representatives, since they could make secret promises or engage in unscrupulous behavior. "Had the citizens of Athens been attentive to the conduct of their public men, the pitiful stratagem of Pisistratus [600–527 BCE] would not have imposed upon his country an odious tyranny."[39] Pisistratus advocated for democracy, but rose to power and became a tyrant over the city. The Democratic Society's letter tacitly urged leaderlessness, written under the guise of cautioning against tyrannical leadership. The Lexington Democratic Society also wanted to implement "a new system" of dealing with crime, one that did not rely so heavily on punishment—their letters sought the abolition of corporal punishment, capital punishment, and debt prisons. They advocated for the poor man caught in a web of crime outside his own control, contrasting him with the corrupt politician who walked free and lived comfortably.

Particularly striking was the Pennsylvania Constitution of 1776, which included some radical provisions: it mandated that all proposed laws be printed and made public with adequate time for the population to weigh in, extended voting rights to citizens who did not own land, assigned the executive role to a council of twelve instead of a single governor, eliminated debt prisons, and was the only state to abolish property requirements for elected officials. Early drafts of the Pennsylvania Constitution were even more egalitarian, instituting limits on how much wealth anyone could possess. Historian David Lefer remarks that Pennsylvania's 1776 Constitution "was probably the closest attempt at direct democracy since the days of Pericles."[40] Pericles (495–429 BCE) was a leading Athenian politician, ushering in the city's "golden age," when its arts flourished, participation in the Popular Assembly was robust, and its citizens experienced a period of prolonged peace.

It is hard to overemphasize the significance of antiquity within these debates. American democrats and aristocrats hashed out what became pivotal institutions of the United States by citing analogies and wisdom from the ancient past. "It was a rare newspaper essayist," notes Gordon Wood, "who did not use a Greek or Latin phrase to enhance an argument or embellish a point and who did not employ a classical signature."[41] Antiquity was a useful resource for thinking about the human capacity for self-governance, what might work and what to avoid. Americans agreed that ancient historians offered many lessons on the matter, even if they disagreed on what those lessons were.

In the end, the American Constitution codified Polybius' approach, balancing monarchic, aristocratic, and democratic elements within a single government.[42] But like the Roman Republic, this really meant that power lay primarily with the wealthy. The American Constitution initially ensured that

CONCLUSION

the Senate selected the president (monarchic function), the Senate was selected from among the independently wealthy (aristocratic function), and the House of Representatives was elected by America's general citizenry (democratic function), the latter with a role that did not extend much beyond directing finances.

The U.S. government has changed significantly since the eighteenth century, but not as much as it might seem. As noted earlier, elections are an inherently aristocratic mode of governance, since nearly all candidates are supported by major corporations and private interest groups. We tend to think there is something foolish about trusting any politician at all, given the deals and money that often take place behind closed doors. The aristocratic quality of the U.S. government is further evident in the cycle of politicians becoming lobbyists, the role of a few organizations in shaping elections (e.g., NRA, AIPAC), and the ability of corporation-backed politicians to transform popular discontent into bigotry against vulnerable populations. This is not to mention how public involvement in decision-making basically evaporates the minute that voting concludes. The House of Representatives was a sad consolation prize for those hoping to build upon the participatory democracy of township assemblies. The Constitution rendered these assemblies superfluous, so they quickly disappeared, bringing an end to the important debates and direct action that had been foundational to early American democracy.

The remarkable tradition of direct democracy in American history has been largely forgotten. This is partially attributable to the fact that the meaning of the word rapidly changed just a few decades after the American Revolution. By the early nineteenth century, "democracy" became synonymous with the more innocuous term "republic" (i.e., almost anything that wasn't a monarchy) and it was celebrated across the political spectrum. With democracy now devoid of its radical connotations, the American aristocracy appropriated stories of Athens and other ancient societies for anti-democratic causes, most notably the idea that citizens should determine the legality of slavery.[43] Just as the Athenians owned slaves and the Spartans had their helots, so also should "the people" have the right to choose slavery within American democracy—it's the will of the people! Of course, we might ask the obvious question about *which* people were allowed to make this decision about slavery.

All this is to say that there was nothing inevitable about the U.S. government taking its current form. Presently, the country's inhabitants play little role in their own governance, immensely unpopular laws are implemented regularly, the wealthiest can virtually dictate policy, prominent legislation tends to restrict freedoms, and political involvement rarely extends beyond the act of voting or contacting elected officials. In its founding period, the U.S. was like a volatile isotope that could have become any number of different things, including a loose federation of states whose political motors were local councils built upon principles of participatory democracy. Early efforts to implement radical democracy were popular and initially successful, with ancient concepts of *demokratia* and *anarchia* playing an integral role.

For many on the left, it may seem strange to think of early America as a place brimming with democratic and even anarchistic potential. We instead think of this period in terms of the displacement and genocide of Indigenous people and

CONCLUSION

the mass enslavement of human beings. For this reason, the founding period of the United States sometimes feels tainted, as though we should keep it at arm's length. However radical Lexington Democratic Society and participants of the Pennsylvania Constitutional Convention may have been relative to their contemporaries, their values did not align with what we would today call progressive or radical. They took settler colonialism for granted and many regarded slavery as morally acceptable. Like their aristocratic counterparts, they wanted to confine women to the "domestic sphere" and limit their participation in politics.

Much the same could be said about Graeco-Roman antiquity. One time, an interviewer asked the great classicist Mary Beard which Roman emperor was her favorite. Beard's answer was short and direct: "They were all horrible."[44] They all owned slaves, committed atrocities in war, and exploited countless others, didn't they? And it is difficult to disagree with Beard's assessment—Roman emperors do not deserve our celebration. And even beyond the emperor, many ancient Greeks and Romans created and participated in unjust systems: the soldiers who engaged in mass slaughter, the slaveowners who reduced other people to property, the landlords who exploited and immiserated the masses, and so on.

The legacy of antiquity has hardly fared much better. British politicians of the colonial era looked to Rome's occupation of overseas territories as a blueprint for their own governance of India.[45] Historians under Nazi Germany argued that the Greek and Roman empires collapsed because foreigners contaminated their bloodlines.[46] Recall that the Holy Roman Empire, a government that claimed continuity with the empire of Augustus, only came to a formal end in 1806. More recently, emperors of Russia and Bulgaria took the title of "Tsar" (until 1917 and 1946, respectively), those of Germany and Austria "Kaiser" (until 1918 and 1919, respectively), and those of India "Kaisar-i-Hind" (until 1947), all of which derive from "Caesar." Today, many white nationalists look to classical antiquity as a golden age of the European man and find sympathy with the chauvinism of many ancient writers.[47] Radicals are happy to concede the legacy of Graeco-Roman antiquity to right-wingers and look elsewhere for inspiration. Anarchists, socialists, and other radicals often feel little political connection to early America or antiquity. Indeed, it is simpler to relinquish these legacies than to put in the effort to reclaim them.

But we feel this way in part because we have been taught histories that omit these important tales. Over the course of this book, we have excavated a range of exciting political formations from the historical record. Many people resisted slavery, patriarchy, respectability politics, and economic exploitation. Moreover, people formed groups that treated these concerns as foundational to their social practices and identities. Many ancient communities flirted with forms of social organization that we now identify as anarchist or as having anarchistic tendencies. What these communities did, typically under the pressure of poverty or oppression, was to free themselves by taking direct control of their lives, but by doing so in a manner that stressed democratic participation. They saw that leadership and cultural norms could impede freedom. Instead, they celebrated social forms that prioritized leaderlessness, direct action, classlessness society, and mutual aid. And there is no reason for us to let these ancient people fade from memory. Figures like Diogenes, Spartacus, and

CONCLUSION

Mazdak have the potential to haunt our political imaginations.[48] They can remind us that not only are anarchistic ways of living possible, but that they have been regular features of human history.

Discussion Questions

Introduction

- What are some ways that your communities (religious, social, familial, athletic, etc.) are simultaneously modeled upon and intentionally different from the government? For instance, do you operate with majoritarian or consensus-based decision-making? Or how do you ensure one person does not dictate everything? Did you decide to do things this way intentionally, did it emerge out of group dynamics, or did it come about some other way?
- Although governments claim authority over their territory, it is often clear that they hold little power in many places or under certain circumstances. What were some instances when the government made unjust laws that people simply ignored? How do people exercise agency in the face of such prohibitions?
- Do you feel that your government is responsive to the populace? How do people take matters into their own hands when the government is not responsive?

Chapter One: Slaves at Thurii

- Almost no one in antiquity ever advocated for the abolition of slavery, not even slaves or former slaves. Why do you think this was the case? Are there forms of oppression today that people 2,000 years from now might be

amazed that people of the twenty-first century never seriously questioned?
- Abolishing money and prohibiting valuables ensured an egalitarian democracy for the community at Thurii. What are some ways your own communities try to prevent people from using their wealth to exert power (think also of the !Kung)?

Chapter Two: Essenes and Therapeutae

- The Essenes and the Therapeutae adopted two very different approaches to combating patriarchy. Do you find either of them compelling? Or were they too flawed for modern populations to adapt?
- Does marriage inherently perpetuate patriarchy? Or can we engage in romantic and sexual relationships that actively *undermine* patriarchy—how?

First Interlude: Phrygians

- People often move to rural areas to avoid the state's grasp. What are some benefits and disadvantages, whether in antiquity or today? What might lead people to choose this option?

Chapter Three: Cynics

- Athenian democracy excluded much of the population on the basis of citizenship, enslavement, or gender. In this context, several people became Cynic philosophers, so they could experiment with a different way of living.

How do some excluded people create their own way of living today?
- Cynics distinguished between *nomos* (arbitrary, human-made customs) and *physis* (natural or divine moral principles). Do you make similar distinctions in your own life?

Chapter Four: Mazdakites

- Was Mazdakite polyandry compatible with feminist principles? Why or why not?
- After Khosrow suppressed Mazdak's rebellion, he instituted some changes that were watered-down versions of Mazdakite demands (e.g., the creation of the priestly "Protectors of the Poor"). What are other examples, historically and in our own time, of the government appropriating radical politics or using radical language to continue business as usual?

Second Interlude: Sámi

- Historically, colonial empires have found it more difficult to conquer stateless Indigenous peoples (e.g., Sámi, Haudenosaunee, Navajo) than those governed by a powerful state (e.g., Inca, Aztec). Why might this be? What do you know about the governance of the people who are Indigenous to your current location?

Chapter Five: Circumcellions

- Christianity was initially a radical religion, but within a few centuries it was largely subsumed into the Roman

DISCUSSION QUESTIONS

imperial machine. Was this inevitable or not? Why do some countercultural groups eventually assimilate into the mainstream whereas others successfully maintain a radical edge?
- The Circumcellions refused the charity of the Catholic Church, instead insisting on mutual aid. Were they stubbornly digging their heels in or were they right to reject the charity of Paul and Macarius?

Chapter Six: Pirates

- Pirate democracy was built upon the threat of violence—against powerful empires, against ships they captured, and even against other crew members. How can violence help or hinder democracy, in different situations?
- The demographic diversity aboard ancient ships meant that people brought very different political experiences to the community. What are some instances where you and others adapted your own diverse experiences to improvise or improve decision-making processes?

Third Interlude: Britons

- What do you imagine life would be like if the government abandoned your state or province? What conveniences would disappear? What opportunities would arise?

Conclusion

- America is the most powerful empire on the planet. How might the past 250 years have been different if

proponents of radical democracy had won instead of aristocrats who sought a mixed system of government?
- Thomas Jefferson wanted the United States to consist of thousands of small, autonomous "wards" governed through direct democracy. Does this strike you as feasible? Why or why not?
- Who are some other figures from the past who haunt you, politically speaking?

General Discussion

- Audre Lorde famously said, "The master's tools will never dismantle the master's house. They may allow us temporarily to beat him at his own game, but they will never enable us to bring about genuine change." How did these different communities either use or refuse their masters' tools (honor and shame, violence, slavery, etc.)? Do you think Lorde's assessment bears out in the examples discussed in this book?
- Most of these radical communities were widely condemned. They were denounced as violent, sinful, or just plain weird. To what extent do we see similar rhetoric used against radicals today? How does retrospect negatively color our interpretation of radical groups? Or do we have the opposite tendency: to romanticize radical movements of the recent past (e.g., the Civil Rights, gay rights, and anti-war movements)? Why might this be?
- Women and gender non-conforming people are generally omitted from the historical record of antiquity, as most ancient historians said little about them. How might we read between the lines of ancient texts to

uncover their contributions to radical movements? Are there any clues that hint at their involvement? If ancient anarchist movements sought to disrupt social hierarchies, to what extent did they challenge or reinforce gender roles?
- This book discusses "experiments" in radical democracy, exploring the human capacity for trying new ways of organizing our lives and politics. Do you think that such experiments are more successful *within* mainstream society (e.g., Cynics), *as far as possible* from mainstream society (e.g., pirates), or some combination of both (e.g., Essenes, Thurii)?
- What is the relationship between democracy and anarchy?

Notes

Introduction

1. This portrait is extrapolated from an inscription written around 300 BCE (*IG* 2.2.2347), drawing from its discussion in John S. Kloppenborg and Richard S. Ascough, *Greco-Roman Associations: Texts, Translations, and Commentary. I: Attica, Central Greece, Macedonia, Thrace* (Berlin: De Gruyter, 2011), no. 12. The narrative takes artistic license with the details of Erotis' life, following the method of critical fabulation elaborated in Saidiya Hartman, "Venus in Two Acts," *Small Axe* 12, no. 2 (2008): 1–12; Sarah Levin-Richardson and Deborah Kamen, "Epigraphy and Critical Fabulation: Imagining Narratives of Greco-Roman Sexual Slavery," in *Dynamic Epigraphy: New Approaches to Inscriptions*, ed. Eleri H. Cousins (Oxford: Oxbow, 2022), 201–21.

2. Nicholas F. Jones, *The Associations of Classical Athens: The Response to Democracy* (Oxford: Oxford University Press, 1999); John S. Kloppenborg, *Christ's Associations: Connecting and Belonging in the City* (New Haven: Yale University Press, 2019), 278–305.

    Scholars debate the extent to which ancient governments should be deemed "states." They certainly differed from the modern nation-state, but some scholars follow the ideas of Carl Schmitt to argue that "the state," as a distinct configuration of collective and institutional power, first emerged in sixteenth century Europe. For compelling arguments that the Roman Empire is usefully understood as a state, see Brent Shaw, "Was the Roman State a State?," *Medieval Worlds* 18 (2023): 3–36.

3. We must distinguish between citizens and inhabitants. "Citizens" were the small portion of the population who held citizenship (e.g., roughly 15 percent in Athens, roughly 5

NOTES

percent in the Roman Empire), consisting of arms-bearing men who held the right to vote, whereas "inhabitants" (or denizens, population, etc.) refers to all people living in a state's territory, which included not only citizens, but also women, children, slaves, immigrants, locals with mixed ancestry, etc.

4. Josiah Ober, *Mass and Elite in Democratic Athens: Rhetoric, Ideology, and the Power of the People*, corrected ed. (Princeton: Princeton University Press, 1990); John Ma, *Polis: A New History of the Ancient Greek City-State from the Early Iron Age to the End of Antiquity* (Princeton: Princeton University Press, 2024).

5. See also C. L. R. James, "Every Cook Can Govern," in *A New Notion: Two Works By C. L. R. James*, ed. Noel Ignatiev (Oakland: PM Press, 2010), 129–55.

6. See Mirko Canevaro, "Majority Rule vs. Consensus: The Practice of Democratic Deliberation in the Greek *poleis*," in *Ancient Greek History and Contemporary Social Science*, ed. Mirko Canevaro et al. (Edinburgh: Edinburgh University Press, 2018), 101–56.

7. Thucydides, *History of the Peloponnesian War* 2.40.

8. Demosthenes, *Orations* 23.204; Plutarch, *Themistocles* 22. We know of only 13 citizens who were ostracized across Athenian history.

9. Mabel L. Lang, *The Athenian Agora, Volume 25: Ostraka* (Princeton: Princeton University Press, 1990), no. 1031; Stefan Brenne, "Teil II: Die Ostraka (487–ca. 416 v.Chr.) als Testimonien," [Part II: The Ostraka (487–circa 416 BCE) as Testimonies] in *Ostrakismos-Testimonien I: Die Zeugnisse antiker Autoren der Inschriften und Ostraka über das athenische Scherbengericht aus vorhellenistischer Zeit (487–322 v. Chr.)* [*Ostrakismos* Testimonies I: The Accounts of Ancient Authors, Inscriptions, and Ostraca on Athenian Ostracism from the Pre-Hellenistic Period (487–322 BCE)], ed. Peter Siewert (Stuttgart: Steiner, 2002), T1/149, T1/147.

10. Brenne, "Ostraka," T1/150. This translation is literal; the Greek word here is *katapygon*.

11. Plato, *Republic* 555c–560a. Scholars debate whether Plato's *Republic* is a work of political or ethical philosophy, but this presents a false dichotomy, since it is probably both; see Malcolm Schofield, *Plato: Political Philosophy* (Oxford: Oxford University Press, 2006); C. D. C. Reeves, *Philosopher-Kings: The Argument of Plato's Republic* (Princeton: Princeton University Press, 1988).
12. Plato, *Republic* 369c–541b. Plato's student Aristotle (*Politics* 4.2) also expressed a low opinion of democracy, deeming it preferable to oligarchy and tyranny, but worse than monarchy and aristocracy.
13. We will discuss this further in this book's Conclusion. See Josiah Ober, *Political Dissent in Democratic Athens: Intellectual Critics of Popular Rule* (Princeton: Princeton University Press, 1998); Jennifer Tolbert Roberts, *Athens on Trial: The Antidemocratic Tradition in Western Thought* (Princeton: Princeton University Press, 1994).
14. Aristotle, *Athenian Constitution* 13.1 (referring to 590–589 and 586–585 BCE); Xenophon, *Hellenica* 2.3.1 (referring to 404 BCE). The meaning of the Greek word *anarchia* changed over time; see Jonah F. Radding, "Euripides and the Origins of Democratic 'Anarchia'," *Erga-Logoi* 7 (2019): 58–61.
15. Herodotus, *Histories* 9.23.
16. Plato, *Republic* 560e.
17. Plato, *Laws* 942c; *Republic* 562c–e; see Uri Gordon, "Anarkhia: What Did the Greeks Actually Say?," *Anarchist Studies* 14, no. 1 (2006): 84–91; Melissa Lane, "Antianarchia: Interpreting Political Thought in Plato," *Plato Journal* 16 (2016): 64–69.
18. Mark Fisher, *Capitalist Realism: Is There No Alternative?* (Ropley: Zero Books, 2009), 1.
19. For a summary of these petitions, see John Whitehorne, "Petitions to the Centurion: A Question of Locality?," *Bulletin of the American Society of Papyrologists* 41 (2004): 155–69. To be sure, some of these petitions were written on behalf of marginalized people, but the majority showcased the petitioner's status.
20. Cary M. Barber, "Undermining the Emperor in Late Roman Africa: Corruption, Maladministration, and the View from the

NOTES

Provinces," in *Local Self-Governance in Antiquity and in the Global South: Theoretical and Empirical Insights from an Interdisciplinary Perspective*, ed. Dominique Krüger, Christoph Mohamad-Klotzbach, and Rene Pfeilschifter (Berlin: De Gruyter, 2023), 225–89, citing Augustine, *Epistles* 185.4; Augustine referred to Donatist Christians here, related to the Circumcellion sect discussed in Chapter Five.

21. Barber, "Undermining the Emperor," noting how the Africans' public decree in *CIL* 8.17896 contradicts the imperial edict recorded in *Codex Theodosianus* 1.16.

22. This refers to the Safaitic-writing population that inhabited North Arabia from the first century BCE to the fourth century CE. See Michael C. A. Macdonald, "The Desert and Its Peoples," in *A Companion to the Hellenistic and Roman Near East*, ed. Ted Kaizer (London: Wiley Blackwell, 2022), 327–33; Michael C. A. Macdonald, "Nomads and the Hawrān in the Late Hellenistic and Roman Periods: A Reassessment of the Epigraphic Evidence," *Syria* 70 (1993): 303–413.

23. Ahmad Al-Jallad, *An Outline of the Grammar of the Safaitic Inscriptions* (Leiden: Brill, 2015), 20, 59–60.

24. Pierre Clastres, *Society Against the State: Essays in Political Anthropology*, trans. Robert Hurley and Abe Stein (New York: Zone, 1987).

25. Clastres focuses on Indigenous peoples of South America during the twentieth century, but others have built upon his work to show that defection from the state is a common occurrence. Most famously, James C. Scott, *The Art of Not Being Governed: An Anarchist History of Upland Southeast Asia* (New Haven: Yale University Press, 2009); James C. Scott, *Against the Grain: A Deep History of the Earliest States* (New Haven: Yale University Press, 2017); David Graeber and David Wengrow, *The Dawn of Everything: A New History of Humanity* (London: Farrar, Straus, and Giroux, 2021). Anarchist anthropology has thrived in recent years, with many more writing in this field.

26. Bertolt Brecht composed a wonderful poem titled *Questions from a Worker Who Reads* (1935). To quote one couplet: "Caesar

beat the Gauls. / Did he not even have a cook with him?" Bertolt Brecht, *Poems 1913–1956*, ed. John Willett, Ralph Manheim, and Erich Fried (London: Methuen, 1976), 252–3.

27. For ancient discussions of Zeno, see Doyne Dawson, *Cities of the Gods: Communist Utopias in Greek Thought* (Oxford: Oxford University Press, 1992), 160–97. On Zeno's *Republic*, see Diogenes Laertius, *Zeno* 33, 131.

28. Peter Kropotkin, *Anarchism: A Collection of Revolutionary Writings* (Mineola: Dover, 2002), 288.

29. See the discussion of fascism, totalitarianism, and Plato in Karl R. Popper, *The Open Society and Its Enemies. Vol. 1: The Spell of Plato*, 5th ed. (Princeton: Princeton University Press, 1966).

30. The Epicurean philosopher Philodemus (110–35 BCE) expressed frustration that Zeno's politics "consisted of impossible hypotheses for people who don't exist"; *On the Stoics* (P.Herc. 155). See Malcolm Schofield, "'Impossible Hypotheses': Was Zeno's *Republic* Utopian?," in *The Philosophy of Zeno: Zeno of Citium and His Legacy*, ed. Theodore Scaltas and Andrew S. Mason (Larnaca: Municipality of Larnaca, 2002), 311–22.

31. Ovid, *Metamorphoses* 1.89–96; translation from A. D. Melville, ed. and trans., *Ovid: Metamorphoses* (Oxford: Oxford University Press, 1986), 3–4. Also noteworthy is Aesop's fable known as "The Frogs Who Wanted a King," which extols a sort of primordial anarchy; see Aesop, *Fables* 44 (Perry).

32. Homer, *Odyssey* 9.112–115; translation from Emily Wilson, ed. and trans., *Homer: The Odyssey* (New York: Norton & Company, 2020), 98. Plato (*Laws* 680b–c) discussed this passage, deeming the cyclopes' governance "self-rule" (*autarchia*).

33. See, e.g., John Ferguson, *Utopias of the Classical World* (Ithaca: Cornell University Press, 1975).

34. All communities require at least semi-standard means of resolving disputes and have a few minimal rules governing its constituent members (e.g., prohibiting murder). The questions here are twofold: 1) Do these rules prioritize social equality? 2) Are these rules enforced by a state (or state-like) apparatus? See Gregory S. Kavka, "Why Even Morally Perfect People

NOTES

Would Need Government," *Social Philosophy and Policy* 12, no. 1 (1995): 1–18.

35. Max Weber, "Politics as Vocation," in *From Max Weber: Essays in Sociology*, ed. and trans. H. H. Gerth and C. Wright Mills (Oxford: Oxford University Press, 1946), 78. More recent definitions tend to be similar; see, e.g., Walter Scheidel, *The Great Leveler: Violence and the History of Inequality from the Stone Age to the Twenty-First Century* (Princeton: Princeton University Press, 2017), 43.

Chapter One

1. On Greek and Roman conceptions of freedom, see Kurt A. Raaflaub, *The Discovery of Freedom in Ancient Greece*, trans. Renate Franciscono, revised and updated ed. (Chicago: University of Chicago Press, 2004); Valentina Arena, *Libertas and the Practice of Politics in the Late Roman Republic* (Cambridge: Cambridge University Press, 2013). Admittedly, my characterization does not account for the radical Stoic communities; on Stoics as a threat to the Roman imperial order, see Ramsay MacMullen, *Enemies of the Roman Order: Treason, Unrest, and Alienation in the Empire* (Cambridge: Harvard University Press, 1966), 46–94.
2. Arrian, *Discourses of Epictetus* 1.1, 1.19, 1.26.
3. Arrian, *Discourses of Epictetus* 1.9.
4. *P.Oxy.* 51.3617 (third century CE), which provides the text and the translation, lightly edited.
5. Appian, *Civil Wars* 1.9.
6. Galen, *How to Detect Malingerers* 19.4–5 (Kühn). This was a tale of mundane (and rather sweet) resistance. The slave's owner was about to travel and expected the young slave to go with him. The young man feigned illness as part of his plan to stay home and spend time with his girlfriend while his master was away.
7. *Babylonian Talmud*, tractate *Gittin* 57b.
8. Keith R. Bradley, *Slavery and Society at Rome* (Cambridge: Cambridge University Press, 1994), 72.

9. When ancient writers recounted the abolitionist opinions of others, they resolutely dismissed the idea as absurd: Aristotle, *Politics* 1253b; Xenophon, *Hellenica* 2.3.48.
10. But see Synesius, *On Kingship* 12.3. On the collective organization of slaves during the three Servile Wars, see Sarah E. Bond, *Strike: Labor, Unions, and Resistance in the Roman Empire* (New Haven: Yale University Press, 2025), 44–71.
11. Athenaeus, *Learned Banqueters* 265d–266e.
12. Although the rebel slaves lived in various places during the early stages of the revolt, remnants of the group associated with Spartacus continued to reside near Thurii even after the rebellion was suppressed. "Thurii" thus provides a convenient, if imprecise, designation for that community.
13. Diodorus Siculus, *Historical Library* 34/35.2.4–9.
14. See the discussion in David Engels, "Ein syrisches Sizilien? Seleukidische Aspekte des Ersten Sizilischen Sklavenkriegs und der Herrschaft des Eunus-Antiochos," [A Syrian Sicily? Seleucid Aspects of the First Sicilian Slave War and the Rule of Eunus/Antiochus] *Polifemo* 11 (2011): 231–51.
15. Diodorus Siculus, *Historical Library* 34/35.2.14, 34/35.2.17.
16. Diodorus Siculus, *Historical Library* 34/35.2.48.
17. E. S. G. Robinson, "Antiochus, King of the Slaves," *Numismatic Chronicle* 20 (1920): 176.
18. Interestingly, this Syrian "king" was a Cilician pirate who claimed the Seleucid throne. For more on Cilician piracy, see Chapter Six.
19. Diodorus Siculus, *Historical Library* 36.4.4–36.5.4.
20. Robinson, "Antiochus," 176.
21. See K. M. Coleman, "Fatal Charades: Roman Executions Staged as Mythological Enactments," *Journal of Roman Studies* 80 (1990): 44–73; Erik Gunderson, "The Ideology of the Arena," *Classical Antiquity* 15 (1996): 113–51.
22. Eutropius, *Summary of Roman History* 6.7; Livy, *History of Rome* 97; Appian, *Civil Wars* 1.117; Velleius Paterculus, *Roman History* 2.30.5–6.

NOTES

23. The freeborn people already residing at Thurii functioned reasonably well alongside the former slaves who took over the city and its environs. That said, the slaves at Thurii had little love for Roman legionaries. Roman historians uniformly report the harsh treatment all opposing soldiers received: rebels at Thurii refused admission to deserting legionaries and they may even have offered captured legionaries as human sacrifices.
24. Suetonius, *Augustus* 3, 7.
25. The major exception in this regard is Diodorus Siculus. On Diodorus' sympathy for revolting slaves, see Theresa Urbainczyk, *Slave Revolts in Antiquity* (London: Acumen, 2014), 81–90. Roman fearmongering about Spartacus and the Third Servile War resembled what they had said about Hannibal, Pyrrhus, and other enemies.
26. Orosius, *Histories* 5.24.3.
27. Katharine P. D. Huemoeller, "Sexual Violence in Republican Slave Revolts," in *Slavery and Sexuality in Classical Antiquity*, ed. Deborah Kamen and C. W. Marshall (Madison: University of Wisconsin Press, 2021), 162–4.
28. Diodorus Siculus, *Historical Library* 34/35.12. According to Diodorus, Eunus/Antiochus granted an exception for people who had shown him favor when he was a slave.
29. Appian, *Civil Wars* 1.117; Pliny the Elder, *Natural History* 33.49–50.
30. Appian, *Civil Wars* 1.116–117.
31. Historia Augusti, *Maximinii* 9.6. The Historia Augusta are notoriously unreliable as historical narratives, but the author nevertheless indicates what people thought about Spartacus in his own time, notably that Spartacus refused to permit nobility in his presence.
32. It is unlikely that the people at Thurii bartered with each other, since people tend to barter only in relationships without much trust—strangers, vagabonds, and even potential enemies. Thurii was a marginalized community that unified as part of a rebellion, so the shared goodwill renders this transactional exchange of goods improbable. See Caroline Humphrey, "Barter and

Economic Disintegration," *Man* 20 (1985): 48–72; David Graeber, *Debt: The First 5,000 Years*, new and expanded ed. (Brooklyn: Melville House, 2014), 21–41. For nuancing of this observation, see Patrick Spread, *Economics, Anthropology and the Origin of Money as a Bargaining Counter* (London: Routledge, 2023), 176–90. More likely, they implemented some kind of credit system, an allotment program, or communitarian distribution.

33. Likewise, the Jewish rebels during the Jewish War (66–73 CE) and the Bar Kokhba War (132–136 CE) minted coins celebrating the creation of their state, serving as propaganda to literally put into the hands of the local population. See Michaël Girardin, "The Propaganda of the Jewish Rebels of 66–70 C.E. According to Their Coins," *Scripta Judaica Cracoviensia* 14 (2016): 23–40.

34. Graeber, *Debt*, 434–5 n. 11. These ideas are further developed in John Weisweiler, ed., *Debt in the Ancient Mediterranean and Near East: Credit, Money, and Social Obligation* (Oxford: Oxford University Press, 2023).

35. Graeber, *Debt*, 228–32.

36. See Robert Manuel Cook, "Speculations on the Origins of Coinage," *Historia* 7 (1958): 157–62, which was initially criticized, but has found support in recent years.

37. See Luuk de Ligt, "Demand, Supply, Distribution: The Roman Peasantry between Town and Countryside: Rural Monetization and Peasant Demand," *Münstersche Beiträge zur antiken Handelsgeschichte* 9, no. 2 (1990): 33–43.

38. E.g., *PSI* 4.379 (using pigs; 248 BCE); *P.Amh.* 2.104 (using produce; 125 CE); *Tosefta*, tractate *Bava Metzia* 9.14 (using produce; second century CE).

39. William E. Arnal, *Jesus and the Village Scribes: Galilean Conflicts and the Setting of Q* (Minneapolis: Fortress, 2001), 115–18; Keith Hopkins, *Sociological Studies in Roman History* (Cambridge: Cambridge University Press, 2017), 302.

40. Michael H. Crawford, *Coinage and Money under the Roman Republic* (Berkeley: University of California Press, 1985), 227–30.
41. Athenaeus, *Learned Banqueters* 152d–f. See the discussion of this similar use of money among Gallic aristocrats in Daphne Nash, "The Chronology of Celtic Coinage in Gaul: The Arvernian 'Hegemony' Reconsidered," *Numismatic Chronicle* 15 (1975): 214–15.
42. See Plutarch, *Crassus* 10.3–4.
43. Bill Angelbeck and Colin Grier, "Anarchism and the Archaeology of Anarchic Societies: Resistance to Centralization in the Coast Salish Region of the Pacific Northwest Coast," *Current Anthropology* 53 (2012): 547–52.
44. Richard Borshay Lee, "Eating Christmas in the Kalahari," *Natural History* 78 (1969): 14–22, 60–64.
45. See, e.g., Livy, *History of Rome* 95; Eutropius, *Summary of Roman History* 6.7; Florus, *Epitome* 2.8.3; Lucius Ampelius, *Memorial Book* 41.1. Other Roman authors probably projected their own (hierarchical) understanding of military authority onto the revolting slaves; see Patrick McGushin, *Sallust: The Histories. Volume 2: Books III–V* (Oxford: Oxford University Press, 1994), 113.
46. Plutarch, *Crassus* 8.2.
47. Sallust, *Histories* 3.44b; cf. Plutarch, *Crassus* 9.5–6. Although Sallust implies that Spartacus himself made this decision, we should be suspicious of such claims. As noted above, ancient writers usually used Spartacus' name as shorthand for the rebelling slaves.
48. Tacitus, *Histories* 3.33; translation from LCL.
49. See Craig A. Williams, *Roman Homosexuality*, 2nd ed. (Oxford: Oxford University Press, 2010), 112–16.
50. Seneca the Elder, *Declamations* 4.preface.10.
51. Chariton, *Chaereas and Callirhoe* 2.6.2; translation from LCL.
52. This has been discussed extensively; see Williams, *Roman Homosexuality*, 31–40.

53. Admittedly, Sallust (*Histories* 3.44b) claimed that the rebel army raped free women of all ages, even if he said Spartacus tried to stop such violence. It is hard to know whether or not this happened, since it seems like the type of thing Sallust would have made up, as he explicitly connected slavery with sordid desire throughout his work. On the other hand, it is entirely possible that not everyone respected the ban on sexual violence. Only very late and unreliable sources (like Orosius, *Histories* 5.24.3) depicted routine sexual violence on the rebels' part.
54. On the plausibility of these three features at Thurii, see Christopher B. Zeichmann, "He's No Spartacus: Jesus, Slavery, and the Utopian Imagination," *Journal for the Study of the Historical Jesus* 22 (2024): 17–18.
55. Sacrifice: Appian, *Civil Wars* 1.117. Gender segregation: Sallust, *Histories* 4.29; cf. Plutarch, *Crassus* 11.3.
56. Plutarch, *Crassus* 10.3–4. For more on pirates of this period, see Chapter Six.

Chapter Two

1. For a collection of ancient tales about Beruriah, see David M. Goodblatt, "The Beruriah Traditions," *Journal of Jewish Studies* 26 (1975): 68–85.
2. Rashi, discussing *Babylonian Talmud*, tractate *Avodah Zarah* 18b; translation is based on Goodblatt, "Beruriah Traditions," 78.
3. See the discussions in Tal Ilan, "The Quest for the Historical Beruriah, Rachel, and Imma Shalom," *AJS Review* 22, no. 1 (1997): 1–8; Tova Hartman and Charlie Buckholtz, "'Beruriah Said Well': The Many Lives (and Deaths) of a Talmudic Social Critic," *Prooftexts* 31 (2011): 181–209.
4. A few historians have even suggested that Philo invented this community as a literary fiction, concocting it as an example of how people should live: Troels Engberg-Pedersen, "Philo's *De Vita Contemplativa* as a Philosopher's Dream," *Journal for the Study of Judaism* 30 (1999): 40–64; Ross Shepard Kraemer,

NOTES

Unreliable Witnesses: Religion, Gender, and History in the Greco-Roman Mediterranean (Oxford: Oxford University Press, 2012), 57–116. In response to this skepticism, see Mary Ann Beavis, "Philo's Therapeutai: Philosopher's Dream or Utopian Construction?," *Journal for the Study of the Pseudepigrapha* 14 (2004): 30–42; Joan E. Taylor, *Jewish Women Philosophers of First-Century Alexandria: Philo's 'Therapeutae' Reconsidered* (Oxford: Oxford University Press, 2003), 3–20. This chapter operates with a historical reading of ancient testimonies about the Therapeutae and the Essenes. Many scholars avoid such an approach, instead preferring to analyze these groups as literary constructions of Philo, Josephus, and Pliny in order to avoid claims about how the real, historical Essenes lived. It is difficult, maybe impossible, to entirely separate fact from fiction in the ancient accounts, but this chapter offers one attempt to do so.

5. There is no evidence of special emphasis on medical or miraculous healing among the Therapeutae. Their name was likely metaphorical in meaning.
6. On their allegorical readings of Jewish scripture, see Taylor, *Jewish Women Philosophers*, 126–53.
7. Matthew David Larsen, "Listening with the Body, Seeing Through the Ears: Contextualizing Philo's Lecture Event in *On the Contemplative Life*," *Journal for the Study of Judaism* 47 (2016): 447–74.
8. Philo, *On the Contemplative Life* 70.
9. Lisa Marie Mignone, *The Republican Aventine and Rome's Social Order* (Ann Arbor: University of Michigan Press, 2016).
10. Indeed, the Roman Empire itself was conceptualized as a series of concentric circles: the city of Rome radiated power from the empire's core, surrounded by trustworthy senatorial provinces, with the more rebellious provinces beyond that, and allied kingdoms just outside of Rome's borders. This is a topic to which we will return in the Second Interlude.
11. Josephus implausibly claimed that the Essenes were entirely deferential to governmental authorities (*Jewish War* 2.140), practiced trials and executions (*Jewish War* 2.145), had a hierarchy

of their own (*Jewish War* 2.150), commonly lived to more than 100 years of age (*Jewish War* 2.151), and enjoyed being tortured for martyrdom (*Jewish War* 2.152–153). For more on this, see note 15 below. Even more ridiculous is the account offered by Pseudo-Hippolytus, *Refutation of All Heresies* 9.13–26, which accused Essenes of murdering uncircumcised men.

12. Josephus, *Jewish War* 2.123.
13. Philo, *Apology for the Jews* 11.5.
14. Philo, *Apology for the Jews* 11.10.
15. See, most importantly, Philo, *Every Good Person Is Free* 75–91, *Apology for the Jews* 11.1–18; Pliny the Elder, *Natural History* 5.15; Josephus, *Jewish War* 2.119–161, *Antiquities of the Jews* 18.18–22. Surprisingly, the New Testament and the rabbis never mention the Essenes or the Therapeutae.

    It is worth cautioning that the reports about the Essenes differ in substantial ways, which mandates caution when discussing the "real" Essenes. Steve Mason, "Essenes and Lurking Spartans in Josephus' *Judean War*: From Story to History," in *Making History: Josephus and Historical Method*, ed. Zuleika Rodgers (Leiden: Brill, 2007), 219–61. Josephus' account is largely ignored here, as it contradicts the other two accounts in fundamental ways: his Essenes lived in cities, married, and were mostly happy to partake in business as usual. This cannot be reconciled with the accounts of Pliny and Philo, which are more reliable, despite their biases.
16. Philo, *Every Good Person Is Free* 79; contrast *KhQ* 1, a contract that documented one member of the community at Qumran selling a slave named Chisday to another man who had recently joined the group.
17. For accessible criticism of the hypothesis that Essenes wrote the Dead Sea Scrolls, see Lawrence H. Schiffman, *Reclaiming the Dead Sea Scrolls: The History of Judaism, the Background of Christianity, the Lost Library of Qumran* (New York: Doubleday, 1994). See also Edna Ullmann-Margalit, *Out of the Cave: A Philosophical Inquiry into the Dead Sea Scrolls Research* (Cambridge: Harvard University Press, 2006).

18. Doron Mendels, "Utopia and the Essenes," *Harvard Theological Review* 72 (1979): 207–22.
19. Iambulus' novel has been lost, but see the summary in Diodorus Siculus, *Historical Library* 2.55–60.
20. Philo, *Every Good Person Is Free* 79.
21. Agnès Rocamora, "Pierre Bourdieu: The Field of Fashion," in *Thinking Through Fashion: A Guide to Key Theorists*, ed. Agnès Rocamora and Anneke Smelik (London: Routledge, 2016), 233–50.
22. Many have noted the similarities between the Therapeutae and the Essenes. The "Groningen Hypothesis" offers a particularly compelling explanation for their resemblance, along with their affinities to the Dead Sea Scrolls; see Florentino García Martínez and Adam S. van der Woude, "A 'Groningen' Hypothesis of Qumran Origins and Early History," *Revue de Qumrân* 14 (1990): 521–41; Florentino García Martínez, "The Groningen Hypothesis Revisited," in *The Dead Sea Scrolls and Contemporary Culture*, ed. Adolfo D. Roitman, Lawrence H. Schiffman, and Shani Tzoref (Leiden: Brill, 2011), 17–29.
23. Richard Valantasis, *The Making of the Self: Ancient and Modern Asceticism* (Cambridge: Clarke & Co., 2008), 8, 101–16. It should be noted that asceticism is not inherently subversive. Rather, it is *oppositional* and this oppositionality can prove conservative and even oppressive. For instance, white supremacists adopt ascetic lives because they believe that the purity of their race can only be maintained through a strict diet and rigorous physical training.
24. Michael G. Jarrett, "Decurions and Priests," *American Journal of Philology* 92 (1971): 513–38.
25. See, e.g., Richard Finn, *Asceticism in the Graeco-Roman World* (Cambridge: Cambridge University Press, 2009), 36–39, 47–50; Vincent Desprez, "Jewish Ascetical Groups at the Time of Christ: Qumran and the Therapeuts," *American Benedictine Review* 41 (1990): 291–311.
26. These dates mark the beginning of direct Roman rule. Rome had played a significant role in both Judaean and Egyptian

politics decades earlier, but only through proxy rulers (e.g., Judaea's Herod the Great) and alliances (e.g., Marc Antony and Egypt's Cleopatra).

27. These texts tended to take the form of trial transcripts and dialogues. For a helpful discussion, see Andrew Harker, *Loyalty and Dissidence in Roman Egypt: The Case of the Acta Alexandrinorum* (Cambridge: Cambridge University Press, 2008).

28. For Augustus' monumental stele, see Josephus, *Antiquities of the Jews* 4.188, *Against Apion* 2.37. For one example of later emperors intervening, see *P.Lond.* 1912 (41 CE), which concerns the emperor Claudius. On the topic of Jewish rights within Alexandria under Roman rule, see Sandra Gambetti, *The Alexandrian Riots of 38 C.E. and the Persecution of the Jews: A Historical Reconstruction* (Leiden: Brill, 2009), 57–76.

29. Philo, *Every Good Person Is Free* 76–78, *Apology for the Jews* 11.6–10; Josephus, *Jewish War* 2.129, *Antiquities of the Jews* 18.19.

30. The biblical books of 1 Kings (6:1–9:25) and 1 Chronicles (3:1–7:22) claim that Solomon completed construction of the First Temple around 960 BCE. See the accessible discussion of why scholars doubt this account in Israel Finkelstein and Neil Asher Silberman, *David and Solomon: In Search of the Bible's Sacred Kings and the Roots of the Western Tradition* (New York: Free Press, 2006).

31. See Marty E. Stevens, *Temples, Tithes, and Taxes: The Temple and the Economic Life of Ancient Israel* (Grand Rapids: Baker Academic, 2006).

32. On the diversity of Judaism in this period, see Lester L. Grabbe, *An Introduction to Second Temple Judaism: History and Religion of the Jews in the Time of Nehemiah, the Maccabees, Hillel, and Jesus* (London: Bloomsbury, 2010).

33. See Catherine Hezser, *Jewish Literacy in Roman Palestine* (Tübingen: Mohr Siebeck, 2001).

34. On refusal to participate in sacrifice as a rejection of patriarchy, see Nancy Jay, *Throughout Your Generations Forever: Sacrifice,*

NOTES

Religion, and Paternity (Chicago: University of Chicago Press, 1992).
35. Taylor, *Jewish Women Philosophers*, 59–67.
36. Kabbalistic biblical interpretation differs from those of the Essenes and the Therapeutae, but also centers on esoteric meanings hidden within scripture. On the Essenes rejecting sacrifice, see Philo, *Every Good Person Is Free* 75; Josephus, *Antiquities of the Jews* 18.19. On the Therapeutae rejecting sacrifice, see Taylor, *Jewish Women Philosophers*, 143–5.
37. Philo, *Allegorical Interpretation* 1.2–18.
38. See the discussion of this phenomenon within several ancient religions in Stanley Stowers, "The Religion of Plant and Animal Offerings Versus the Religion of Meanings, Essences, and Textual Mysteries," in *Ancient Mediterranean Sacrifice*, ed. Jennifer Wright Knust and Zsuzsanna Várhelyi (Oxford: Oxford University Press, 2011), 35–56.
39. For an ancient example of such criticism, see Aristophanes, *Peace* 43–49.
40. This presents yet another reason to suspect that the Essenes did not write the Dead Sea Scrolls: there is ample evidence of the presence of women at Qumran, which contradicts the claims of Philo and Pliny; see Tal Ilan, "Women in Qumran and the Dead Sea Scrolls," in *The Oxford Handbook of the Dead Sea Scrolls*, ed. John J. Collins and Timothy H. Lim (Oxford: Oxford University Press, 2010), 123–48.
41. See the accessible discussion of these issues in Marilyn B. Skinner, *Sexuality in Greek and Roman Culture*, 2nd ed. (London: Wiley-Blackwell, 2013).
42. See, e.g., Maud Bernett McInerney, *Eloquent Virgins: From Thecla to Joan of Arc* (New York: Palgrave Macmillan, 2003), 15–45.
43. Gillian Clark, "Women and Asceticism in Late Antiquity: The Refusal of Status and Gender," in *Asceticism*, ed. Vincent L. Wimbush and Richard Valantasis (Oxford: Oxford University Press, 1998), 38–41; Joyce E. Salisbury, *Church Father, Independent Virgins* (London: Verso, 1991).

44. Philo, *Apology for the Jews* 11.14. On Philo's misogynistic depiction of the Therapeutae, see Holger Szesnat, "'Mostly Aged Virgins': Philo and the Presence of the Therapeutrides at Lake Mareotis," *Neotestamentica* 32 (1998): 191–201.
45. M. E. O'Brien, *Family Abolition: Capitalism and the Communizing of Care* (London: Pluto, 2023), 6.

First Interlude

1. Synesius, *Epistles* 148.16.
2. Phaedrus, *Fables* 1.15. A few additional examples come to mind: 1) Gospel of Mark 12:13–17: it certainly seems that no one among Jesus, the Pharisees, or Herodians knew the name of the current emperor; 2) Aristotle (*Politics* 1276a) claimed that even two days after the Achaemenid Persians captured Babylon in 539 BCE, the city was so vast that many inhabitants did not realize they had been conquered; 3) the disconnect between emperor and empire is further evinced in ancient inscriptions, which often misunderstand, invent, or are oblivious to the titles of the current emperor; see the fascinating discussion in Christian Witschel, "Der Kaiser und die Inschriften," [The Emperor and Inscriptions] in *Zwischen Strukturgeschichte und Biographie: Probleme und Perspektiven einer neuen Römischen Kaisergeschichte* [Between Structural History and Biography: Problems and Perspectives of a New History of the Roman Emperors], ed. Aloys Winterling (Munich: Oldenbourg, 2011), 100–6.
3. Peter Thonemann, "Phrygia: An Anarchist History, 950 BC–AD 100," in *Roman Phrygia: Culture and Society*, ed. Peter Thonemann (Cambridge: Cambridge University Press, 2013), 1–40; Peter Thonemann, *The Lives of Ancient Villages: Rural Society in Roman Anatolia* (Cambridge: Cambridge University Press, 2022).
4. Scott, *Art of Not Being Governed*.
5. Clastres, *Society Against the State*, 177.
6. Thonemann cites Mary M. Voigt and T. Cuyler Young, Jr., "From Phrygian Capital to Achaemenid Entrepot: Middle and Late

NOTES

Phrygian Gordion," *Iranica Antiqua* 34 (1999): 220–36; Elspeth R. M. Dusinberre, *Gordion Seals and Sealings: Individuals and Society* (Philadelphia: University of Pennsylvania Museum of Archaeology and Anthropology, 2005), 10–14; Keith DeVries, "Greek Pottery and Gordion Chronology," in *The Archaeology of Midas and the Phrygians: Recent Work at Gordion*, ed. Lisa Kealhofer (Philadelphia: University of Pennsylvania Press, 2005), 53; Lisa Kealhofer, "Settlement and Land Use: The Gordion Regional Survey," in *The Archaeology of Midas and the Phrygians: Recent Work at Gordion*, ed. Lisa Kealhofer (Philadelphia: University of Pennsylvania Press, 2005), 147–8.

7. Pierre Briant, *From Cyrus to Alexander: A History of the Persian Empire*, trans. Peter T. Daniels (Winona Lake: Eisenbrauns, 2002), 413–14.
8. Isaiah 44:28–45:1. See the similar sentiment articulated in Ezra 1:1–8.
9. Thonemann, "Phrygia," 15.
10. See, e.g., *SIG* 3.279.
11. E.g., Paul McKechnie, *Christianizing Asia Minor: Conversion, Communities, and Social Change in the Pre-Constantinian Era* (Cambridge: Cambridge University Press, 2019), 3.
12. Clastres, *Society Against the State*.

Chapter Three

1. Apuleius, *Florida* 14; cf. Diogenes Laertius, *Lives of Eminent Philosophers* 6.87. Diogenes Laertius (the biographer of philosophers) bore no relation to Diogenes of Sinope (the Cynic philosopher).
2. See Peter Liddel, *Civic Obligation and Individual Liberty in Ancient Athens* (Oxford: Oxford University Press, 2007).
3. Diogenes Laertius, *Lives of Eminent Philosophers* 6.72–73.
4. Diogenes Laertius, *Lives of Eminent Philosophers* 6.38.
5. Diogenes Laertius, *Lives of Eminent Philosophers* 6.11.
6. Aristotle, *Rhetoric* 1.9.22; translation from LCL, lightly edited.
7. Xenophon, *Symposium* 3.8.

8. Diogenes Laertius, *Lives of Eminent Philosophers* 6.96–98; Apuleius, *Florida* 14. On Crates' disabilities, see Julian, *Orations* 6.201.
9. Diogenes Laertius, *Lives of Eminent Philosophers* 6.72, 6.98; Apuleius, *Florida* 14. On the marriage of Crates' and Hipparchia's son: Diogenes Laertius, *Lives of Eminent Philosophers* 6.88–89. Diogenes reportedly had sex in public as well: Diogenes Laertius, *Lives of Eminent Philosophers* 6.69.
10. Diogenes Laertius, *Lives of Eminent Philosophers* 6.3.
11. Diogenes Laertius, *Lives of Eminent Philosophers* 6.69.
12. The theologian Augustine (354–430 CE) took particular issue with this aspect of Cynicism, arguing that the shame humans feel about sex is a sign that we should not engage in sexual acts publicly; *City of God* 14.20.
13. Robert Halsall, "Sloterdijk's Theory of Cynicism, Ressentiment and 'Horizontal Communication'," *International Journal of Media & Cultural Politics* 1 (2005): 170.
14. Diogenes Laertius, *Lives of Eminent Philosophers* 4.46–47; translation from Robert Dobbin, ed. and trans., *The Cynic Philosophers: From Diogenes to Julian* (New York: Penguin, 2012), no. 99.
15. Diogenes Laertius, *Lives of Eminent Philosophers* 6.82, 6.99.
16. Diogenes Laertius, *Lives of Eminent Philosophers* 2.86, 3.20; Plutarch, *Dion* 5; Diodorus Siculus, *Historical Library* 15; Philodemus, *History of the Academy* (P.Herc. 164, 1691/1021), occurring either 404 or 399 BCE. Contrast the conspicuous silence in Plato, *Epistles* 7; note also the vitriol later philosophers expressed about Anniceris (e.g., Heraclitus, *Homeric Problems* 78; Gregory Nazianzus, *Against Julian* 1.72). See the discussion in Page DuBois, *Slaves and Other Objects* (Chicago: University of Chicago Press, 2003), 153–69.
17. See, e.g., Plato, *Laws* 720, 773e, 966b.
18. Diogenes Laertius, *Lives of Eminent Philosophers* 6.29, 6.74–75; Arrian, *Discourses of Epictetus* 4.1. This tradition is of questionable reliability, though, as it contradicts Dio Chrysostom, *Discourses* 6.1–3. On the question of Diogenes and slavery, see

NOTES

Seneca the Younger, *Tranquility of Mind* 8.7; Aelian, *Various Histories* 13.28.

19. Barbarians: Diogenes Laertius, *Lives of Eminent Philosophers* 6.73; Pseudo-Anacharsis, *Epistles* 1 (Malherbe). Children: Diogenes Laertius, *Lives of Eminent Philosophers* 6.37. Animals: Diogenes Laertius, *Lives of Eminent Philosophers* 6.22, 6.75; Dio Chrysostom, *Discourses* 6.13, 6.18, 6.21–22, 10.16; and, of course, dogs are mentioned repeatedly. On animals in Cynic philosophy, see Michael-John Turp, "Shameless Dogs: Cynics and Nonhuman Animal Ethics," *Society and Animals* 33 (2025): forthcoming.
20. Diogenes Laertius, *Lives of Eminent Philosophers* 6.35.
21. Diogenes Laertius, *Lives of Eminent Philosophers* 6.20–21.
22. Philodemus, *On the Stoics* (P.Herc. 339).
23. Lucian, *The Fishermen* 35.
24. See the depictions of Diogenes, Antisthenes, and others in the writing exercises from ancient students collected in Ronald F. Hock and Edward N. O'Neil, eds., *The Chreia and Ancient Rhetoric: Classroom Exercises* (Atlanta: Society of Biblical Literature Press, 2002).
25. Lucian, *Demonax* 55. This Epictetus is the same philosopher discussed at the beginning of Chapter One.
26. Simplicius, *Commentary on the Handbook of Epictetus* 46.
27. MacMullen, *Enemies of the Roman Order*, 61.
28. We will see that these *chreiai* sometimes served misogynistic and xenophobic purposes, especially as time went on. Particularly interesting are Byzantine-era school exercises that invented *chreiai* featuring Diogenes. Teresa Morgan suggests that these later interpretations marked a significant change from earlier understandings of Cynics, as they now encouraged students to "identify with powerful high-status Greek or Roman socio-cultural groups." To rephrase, *chreiai* eventually became a handbook for mocking people of lower status. Teresa Morgan, *Literate Education in the Hellenistic and Roman Worlds* (Cambridge: Cambridge University Press, 1998), 150.

29. E.g., Arrian, *Discourses of Epictetus* 3.22. See also Nickolas Pappas, *The Philosopher's New Clothes: The Theaetetus, the Academy, and Philosophy's Turn Against Fashion* (London: Routledge, 2016), 211–13.
30. Pseudo-Diogenes, *Epistles* 26 (Malherbe).
31. *Palatine Anthology* 7.413.
32. Diogenes Laertius, *Lives of Eminent Philosophers* 6.38; translation from LCL, lightly edited. See the longer version of this story in Plutarch, *Alexander the Great* 671d–e.
33. William D. Desmond, *Cynics* (Stocksfield: Acumen, 2008), 185.
34. Marie-Odile Goulet-Cazé, *Cynicism and Christianity in Antiquity*, trans. Christopher Smith (Grand Rapids: Eerdmans, 2019), 213. Cf. Shea, *Cynic Enlightenment*, 83: "The Cynic republic [was] a community of loosely associated individuals without laws or distinction of rank, characterized by sexual freedom and the elimination of taboos."
35. See the discussion in Fouad Kalouche, "The Cynic Way of Living," *Ancient Philosophy* 23 (2003): 181–94.
36. Pseudo-Crates, *Epistles* 5 (Malherbe); translation from Dobbin, *Cynic Philosophers*, no. 93.
37. Cassius Dio, *History of Rome* 65.13. Demetrius was banished first by Nero, then returned under Galba, until Vespasian banished him once more.
38. Suetonius, *Nero* 39. For further examples, see, e.g., Lucian, *Demonax* 50; Plutarch, *How to Tell a Flatterer from a Friend* 69c–d.
39. For this distinction between *nomoi* and *physis* in Cynic teaching, see Diogenes Laertius, *Lives of Eminent Philosophers* 6.11, 6.38, 6.71. This is not to imply that Cynics invented the distinction, as the Sophists had been making much of it in the preceding decades.
40. Plato, *Hippias Major* 282c–d.
41. Lucian, *Runaways* 12.
42. Roman freedpeople were permitted to adopt a proper three-part Roman name (the *tria nomina*) and even vote in elections. That said, they were prohibited from running for office and

there were limits as to the status they could achieve—for instance, they were ineligible from joining the Senate. Roman literature indicates that people continued to look down upon former slaves, reasoning that their enslavement had tainted them morally (they were often depicted as shameless social climbers in Roman fiction), but the point here is that Romans implemented legal mechanisms enabling freedpeople to acquire far more rights than was possible in the Greek city-states. For more, see Henrik Mouritsen, *The Freedman in the Roman World* (Cambridge: Cambridge University Press, 2011).

43. See the excellent discussion in Greg Woolf, *Becoming Roman: The Origins of Provincial Civilization in Gaul* (Cambridge: Cambridge University Press, 1998).

44. See Margarethe Billerbeck, "The Ideal Cynic from Epictetus to Julian," in *The Cynics: The Cynic Movement in Antiquity and Its Legacy*, ed. R. Bracht Branham and Marie-Odile Goulet-Cazé (Berkeley: University of California Press, 2000), 205–21; Goulet-Cazé, *Cynicism and Christianity*, 53–133. The narrative offered here greatly simplifies the evidence. Nearly all surviving sources for Cynicism derive from the Roman period: Diogenes Laertius, for instance, wrote in the third century CE and the Cynic Epistles were mostly composed around the turn of the Common Era. Roman reception of earlier Greek Cynicism surely colored their depiction in historical and philosophical works.

45. *Jerusalem Talmud*, tractate *Gittin* 38b with the insights of Menahem Luz, "A Description of the Greek Cynic in the Jerusalem Talmud," *Journal for the Study of Judaism* 20 (1989): 49–60.

46. Leontius of Neapolis, *Life of Symeon the Fool*. Note also Maximus I of Constantinople (fourth century CE), better known as Maximus the Cynic—an unrecognized archbishop of Constantinople (he claimed the title through surreptitious means not recognized by the Catholic Church). His rival and official archbishop of Constantinople, Gregory of Nazianzus, decried Maximus' adoption of a Cynic lifestyle (*Concerning His Own Life* 750–774).

47. Arrian, *Discourses of Epictetus* 3.22. To be sure, Epictetus held Cynicism in high regard, even if he expressed frustration with people whose practice of Cynicism differed from his own conception of the philosophy.
48. Dio Chrysostom, *Discourses* 32.9.
49. Cicero, *On Duties* 1.148; translation from Dobbin, *Cynic Philosophers*, no. 69, lightly edited.
50. Julian, *Orations* 6, 7.
51. Julian, *Orations* 6.182; translation from Dobbin, *Cynic Philosophers*, no. 136.
52. *P.Bour.* 1.146–153 (fourth century CE).
53. By racist, I mean bigotry on the basis of skin color (for such *chreiai*, see, e.g., *P.Bour.* 1.157–168; *SB* 1.5730). Romans didn't have a concept of race comparable to ours, but see Benjamin Isaac, *The Invention of Racism in Classical Antiquity* (Princeton: Princeton University Press, 2004).
54. Max Stirner, *Der Einzige und sein Eigenthum* [The Ego and Its Own] (Leipzig: Wigand, 1845), 30.
55. See, for instance, Murray Bookchin, *Social Anarchism or Lifestyle Anarchism: An Unbridgeable Chasm* (Edinburgh: AK Press, 1995).
56. Suzanne Husson, "Utopia and the Quest for *autarkeia*," in *Utopias in Ancient Thought*, ed. Pierre Destrée, Jan Opsomer, and Geert Roskam (Berlin: De Gruyter, 2021), 194–7.

Chapter Four

1. This statement requires some nuance. Three ancient texts claimed to quote excerpts from the *Disnad*, a Mazdakite holy text: al-Shahrastani, *Kitab al-milal wa-al-nihal* 1.192–194 (Cureton); al-Jabbar, *Al-Mughni* 5.16 (al-Khudayri); *Dabestan* 1.372–379 (Shea and Troyer). But there are numerous issues, not least of which is the fact that none of them actually quote the *Disnad*, but derive their excerpts from another source; see Patricia Crone, "Kavād's Heresy and Mazdak's Revolt," *Iranica Antiqua* 29 (1991): 39 n. 165.

NOTES

2. Scholars still debate the development of Mazdakism, since ancient sources contradict each other. Most texts even claim that Mazdak allied with the Sasanian king Kavad, but this is hard to believe. Much remains uncertain. This chapter adopts (with modifications) the narrative sequence suggested by Patricia Crone, "Kavād's Heresy," 21–42; Patricia Crone, "Zoroastrian Communism," *Comparative Studies in Society and History* 36 (1994): 447–62; Patricia Crone, *The Nativist Prophets of Early Islamic Iran: Rural Revolt and Local Zoroastrianism* (Cambridge: Cambridge University Press, 2012).
3. Joshua the Stylite, *Chronicle* 20. Cf. al-Tabari, *Tarikh* 893 (Goeje).
4. Al-Shahrastani, *Kitab al-milal wa-al-nihal* 1.192–194 (Cureton). Al-Shahrastani was generally reliable in his representation of others' beliefs. Also valuable are al-Jabbar, *Al-Mughni* 5.16 (al-Khudayri); al-Malahimi, *Kitab al-mutamad* (McDermott and Madelung); note also the less reliable account of *Dabestan* 1.372–379 (Shea and Troyer).
5. See, e.g., John Malalas, *Chronicle* 12.42, 18.30; Joshua the Stylite, *Chronicle* 20; al-Tabari, *Tarikh* 885–887 (Goeje).
6. Al-Biruni (eleventh century CE) made this exact point, claiming that Kavad converted to Mazdakism because he wanted to sleep with his cousin's wife; al-Biruni, *Kitab al-athar al-baqiyah* 209 (Sachau).
7. For a helpful overview of harems in the Sasanian Empire, see A. Shapur Shahbazi, "Harem. I: In Ancient Iran," in *Encyclopædia Iranica*, ed. Ehsan Yarshater (London: Encyclopædia Iranica Foundation, 2003), 11.671–2, 12.1–3. On social class and polygamy in Sasanian Iran, see Jenny Rose, "Three Queens, Two Wives, and a Goddess: The Role and Images of Women in Sasanian Iran," in *Women in the Medieval Islamic World: Power, Patronage, and Piety*, ed. Gavin G. R. Hambly (New York: St. Martin's Press, 1999), 32–34.
8. See the anecdote in al-Tabari, *Tarikh* 1025–1027 (Goeje).

9. *Denkard* 6.18–7.16 (Madan); translation from Mansour Shaki, "The Social Doctrine of Mazdak in the Light of Middle Persian Evidence," *Archiv Orientální* 46 (1978): 292, lightly edited.
10. Al-Tabari, *Tarikh* 866 (Goeje). Fire remains an important symbol within Zoroastrianism, possibly indicating the aristocracy hoped to "cleanse" the empire of Kavad's wrongdoing.
11. On Kavad's early pacifism and vegetarianism, see Crone, "Kavād's Heresy," 26.
12. E.g., Procopius, *History of the Wars* 1.5.1–2.
13. Al-Tabari, *Tarikh* 865–886 (Goeje); translation from al-Tabarī, *The History of al-Tabarī: An Annotated Translation. Volume V: The Sasanians*, ed. and trans. C. E. Bosworth (Albany: State University of New York Press, 1999), 5.132.
14. See Michele Campopiano, "Land Tenure, Land Tax and Social Conflictuality in Iraq from the Late Sasanian to the Early Islamic Period (Fifth to Ninth Centuries CE)," in *Authority and Control in the Countryside: From Antiquity to Islam in the Mediterranean and Near East (Sixth–Tenth Century)*, ed. Alain Delattre, Marie Legendre, and Petra M. Sijpesteijn (Leiden: Brill, 2018), 464–99.
15. Jairus Banaji, "Aristocracies, Peasantries and the Framing of the Early Middle Ages," *Journal of Agrarian Social Change* 9 (2009): 84–86.
16. Paul John Frandsen, *Incestuous and Close-Kin Marriage in Ancient Egypt and Persia: An Examination of the Evidence* (Copenhagen: Museum Tusculanum Press, 2009), 60–119; Rose, "Three Queens."
17. Mansour Shaki, "Citizenship. I: In the Sasanian Period," in *Encyclopædia Iranica*, ed. Ehsan Yarshater (London: Encyclopædia Iranica Foundation, 1992), 633.
18. Crone, "Kavād's Heresy," 33–34.
19. Patricia Crone, *Pre-Industrial Societies: Anatomy of the Pre-Modern World*, 2nd ed. (London: OneWorld, 2013), 46. On Sasanian taxation, see V. G. Lukonin, "Political, Social, and Administrative Institutions: Taxes and Trade," in *The Cambridge History of Iran. Volume 3, Part 2: The Seleucid, Parthian and Sasanian*

NOTES

Periods, ed. Ehsan Yarshater (Cambridge: Cambridge University Press, 1983), 744–6.
20. Banaji, "Aristocracies, Peasantries," 80 n. 56.
21. Translation from Aboloqasem Ferdowsi, *Shahnameh: The Persian Book of Kings*, trans. Dick Davis, expanded ed. (New York: Penguin, 2016), 788.
22. Translation from Ferdowsi, *Shahnameh*, 789 (Davis).
23. *Denkard* 653.10–654.8, 750.12–19 (Madan); see Maria Macuch, "Legal Implications of Mazdakite Teaching According to the *Dēnkard*," in *Husraw Ier: Reconstructions d'un Règne. Sources et Documents*, ed. Christelle Jullien (Paris: Association pour l'avancement des Études Iraniennes, 2015), 159–64.
24. See especially al-Maqdisi, *Kitab al-bad* 4.31 (Huart).
25. Crone, "Zoroastrian Communism"; Peter Marshall, *Demanding the Impossible: A History of Anarchism* (London: Harper Perennial, 1993), 86. Many Soviet writers praised the Mazdakites for engaging in a people's uprising. For Soviet publications about Mazdakism, see Otakar Klíma, *Mazdak: Geschichte einer sozialen Bewegung im sassanidischen Persien* [Mazdak: History of a Social Movement in Sasanian Persia] (Prague: Československa Akademie Věd, 1956), 243–4.
26. Crone, "Zoroastrian Communism," 455, quoting and translating al-Malati, *Kitab al-Tanbih* 72–73 (Dedering).
27. Translation from Ferdowsi, *Shahnameh*, 790–791 (Davis).
28. See, e.g., Shaki, "Social Doctrine," 302–3.
29. Jean de Menasce, "Le protecteur des pauvres dans l'Iran Sassanide," [The Protector of the Poor in Sasanian Iran] in *Mélanges d'Orientalisme offerts à Henri Massé à l'occasion de son 75ème Anniversaire* (Tehran: Imprimerie de l'Université, 1963), 282–87. Note also how Khosrow formalized attachments between the aristocracy and peasantry: Mario Grignaschi, "Quelques spécimens de la littérature sassanide conservés dans les bibliothèques d'Istanbul," [Some Examples of Sasanian Literature Preserved in the Libraries of Istanbul] *Journal Asiatique* 254 (1966): 99, in conversation with Werner Sundermann, "*Commendatio pauperum*: Eine Angabe der sassanidischen

politisch-didaktischen Literatur zur gesellschaftlichen Struktur Irans," [*Commendatio pauperum*: A Statement of Sasanian Political-Didactic Literature on the Social Structure of Iran] *Altorientalische Forschungen* 4 (1976): 175.
30. Touraj Daryaee, "Mazdak and Late Antique 'Socialism'," in *The Cambridge History of Socialism: Volume 1*, ed. Marcel van der Linden (Cambridge: Cambridge University Press, 2023), 40.
31. See Crone, *Nativist Prophets*.
32. Al-Maqdisi, *Kitab al-bad* 4.31 (Huart).
33. On Mazdakite fraternal polyandry, see *Denkard* 653.10–654.8 (Madan), as quoted and discussed in Shaki, "Social Doctrine," 294, 304; cf. Macuch, "Legal Implications," 165–6, 168–9.
34. See, e.g., Leila Ahmed, *Women and Gender in Islam: Historical Roots of a Modern Debate* (New Haven: Yale University Press, 1992), 20–21. Contrast Crone, "Kavād's Heresy," 38 n. 104; Shaki, "Social Doctrine," 301–5.
35. On such protections, Khosrow allegedly remarked, "I kept [the women in my harem] in such ease and prosperity and lavished so much wealth on them that they themselves showed no inclination to leave me for any man. ... If any one of them wished to marry and leave my palace, I would give her a dowry and send her to a husband. None showed any desire." Balami, *Tarikhnama* 1174–1175 (al-Shuara and Gunabadi); translation from Shahbazi, "Harem," 12.2–3.
36. Al-Tabari, *Tarikh* 893 (Goeje); translation from al-Tabarī, *History of al-Tabarī*, 5.148 (Bosworth).
37. Al-Tabari, *Tarikh* 886 (Goeje); translation from al-Tabarī, *History of al-Tabarī*, 5.132 (Bosworth).
38. This was typical of Persian literature of the period, see Rose, "Three Queens."
39. For the various sources and specifics of this way of life, see Ehsan Yarshater, "Mazdakism," in *The Cambridge History of Iran. Volume 3, Part 2: The Seleucid, Parthian and Sasanian Periods*, ed. Ehsan Yarshater (Cambridge: Cambridge University Press, 1983), 1006–18; Moshe Gil, "King Qubādh and

NOTES

Mazdak," *Journal of Near Eastern Studies* 71 (2012): 75–90; Crone, *Nativist Prophets*, 191–450.

40. See the accounts discussed in Crone, "Kavād's Heresy," 24–25; Shaki, "Social Doctrine," 301–5.
41. Referring to al-Maqdisi, *Kitab al-bad* 4.31 (Huart). The author of *Dabestan* 1.372–379 (Shea and Troyer) claimed he conversed with Mazdakites, but this is hard to believe, given that he wrote around 1655 CE.
42. See the helpful overviews in Katherine E. Starkweather, "A Preliminary Survey of Lesser-Known Polyandrous Societies," *Nebraska Anthropologist* 24 (2009): 17–35.
43. This refers to the Lele of the mid-twentieth century. Most Lele live in DRC's capital city of Kinshasa nowadays: Mary Douglas, *Implicit Meanings: Selected Essays in Anthropology*, 2nd ed. (London: Routledge, 1999), 78. The following discussion draws upon Mary Tew, "A Form of Polyandry among the Lele of the Kasai," *Africa: Journal of the International Africa Institute* 21 (1951): 1–12; Mary Douglas, *The Lele of the Kasai*, 2nd ed. (London: Routledge, 2003). Mary Tew is better known as Mary Douglas.
44. Tew, "Form of Polyandry," 3.
45. To wit: the Mazdakites practiced some form of communitarian property sharing, engaged in a specifically fraternal variety of polyandry, and were pacifists. None of this can be said about the Lele. This is not to mention the Lele's intricate system of human-based commerce with "pawns." Pawns, to be clear, are not slaves and there is no comparable status in North American or European culture.
46. Al-Maqdisi, *Kitab al-bad* 4.31 (Huart).
47. Al-Nadim, *Fihrist* 2.820–822 (Dodge). The account is plainly apocryphal, but nevertheless indicates that even people who disliked the Mazdakites knew that women's consent was important within the sect.
48. Al-Mulk, *Siyasatnama* 44.4; translation from Nizam al-Mulk, *The Book of Government or Rules for Kings*, ed. and trans. Hubert Darke, 3rd ed. (London: Routledge, 2002), 192.

49. Herodotus, *Histories* 1.216 (Masagetes, using quivers), 4.172 (Nasamones, using staffs); Strabo, *Geography* 16.4.25 (Arabia Felix, using staffs). I cannot help but mention the heartwarming tombstone of a woman named Allia Potestas, who lived with her two lovers in Roman Italy during the second century CE: Nicholas Horsfall, "CIL VI 37965 = CLE 1988 (Epitaph of Allia Potestas): A Commentary," *Zeitschrift für Papyrologie und Epigraphik* 61 (1985): 251–72.

50. See, e.g., *Bundahishn* 276–277 (Anklesaria): Mazdak taught that "men ought to have wife, children, and wealth in common and in co-partnership." Matrilineal parentage: Macuch, "Legal Implications," 164–5, discussing the testimony of the *Denkard* 653.10–654.8 (Madan).

51. E.g., al-Nadim, *Fihrist* 2.820–822 (Dodge).

52. Graeber, *Debt*, 142–3. He points especially to the discussion in Douglas, *Lele of Kasai*, 168–73.

53. E.g., al-Maqdisi, *Kitab al-bad* 4.31 (Huart); al-Nawbakhti, *Kitab Firaq al-Shia* 86–88 (Kadhim).

54. Hamid Algar, "Ebāhīya," in *Encyclopædia Iranica*, ed. Ehsan Yarshater (London: Encyclopædia Iranica Foundation, 1996), 7.653–4.

55. Al-Maqdisi, *Kitab al-bad* 4.31 (Huart). The notion of "heresy" within Sasanian Zoroastrianism is tricky; see Khodadad Rezakhani, "Mazdakism, Manichaeism and Zoroastrianism: In Search of Orthodoxy and Heterodoxy in Late Antique Iran," *Iranian Studies* 48 (2015): 55–70.

56. On Spartan polyandry, see Xenophon, *Constitution of the Spartans* 1.7–10; Polybius, *Histories* 12.6b.8; Plutarch, *Lycurgus* 15.6–10, *Morals* 242b; Philo, *Special Laws* 3.4.22. On communal raising of Spartan children, see Xenophon, *Constitution of the Spartans* 6.1–2; Plutarch, *Lycurgus* 15.8.

57. See Stephen Hodkinson, *Property and Wealth in Classical Sparta*, paperback ed. (London: Duckworth, 2009). Hodkinson refutes the view popularized by the Roman historian Plutarch, who claimed that Spartans owned no private property but tempo-

NOTES

rarily held property that reverted to the state upon death, which would then apportion it out anew.
58. Aristotle, *Politics* 1270b; cf. Xenophon, *Constitution of the Spartans* 1.9.
59. Andrew G. Scott, "Plural Marriage and the Spartan State," *Historia* 60 (2011): 413–24.
60. Robin Lane Fox, "Aspects of Inheritance in the Greek World," *History of Political Thought* 6 (1985): 222–3.
61. Ben Jiao, *Polyandrous Marital Status in Rural Tibet* (Beijing: China Tibetology Publishing House, 2014), 133–68. Cf. the discussion of gender and poverty in Katherine E. Starkweather and Raymond Hames, "A Survey of Non-Classical Polyandry," *Human Nature* 23 (2012): 149–72.
62. Al-Mulk, *Siyasatnama* 44.13; translation from al-Mulk, *Book of Government*, 197 (Darke), lightly edited.
63. See, e.g., Jenny Alexander, "Alexander Berkman: Sexual Dissidence in the First Wave Anarchist Movement and Its Subsequent Narratives," in *Anarchism & Sexuality: Ethics, Relationships and Power*, ed. Jamie Heckert and Richard Cleminson (London: Routledge, 2011), 25–44.

Second Interlude

1. Tacitus, *Germania* 46.3; Ptolemy, *Geography* 2.11, 3.5; Procopius, *History of the Wars* 6.15.16–25; Jordanes, *Gothic History* 3.20–21. For English translation of these texts, see Carl-Gösta Ojala, *Sámi Prehistories: The Politics of Archaeology and Identity in Northernmost Europe* (Uppsala: Uppsala Universitet, 2009), 83–85. Note also the anonymous eighth century *Cosmographia* 4.12–13, which summarized what an otherwise-unknown Gothic scholar named Aithanarit said about the Fenni; scholars suspect that Aithanarit wrote during the Byzantine period.
2. Procopius, *History of the Wars* 6.15.16; Tacitus, *Germania* 46.3; Ian Whitaker, "Tacitus' *Fenni* and Ptolemy's *Phinnoi*," *Classical Journal* 75 (1980): 217.
3. Procopius, *History of the Wars* 6.15.25.

4. Tacitus, *Germania* 46.3.
5. Irmeli Valtonen, "Who Were the *Finnas*?," in *Ohthere's Voyages: A Late 9th-Century Account of Voyages along the Coasts of Norway and Denmark and Its Cultural Context*, ed. Janet Bately and Anton Englert (Roskilde: Viking Ship Museum, 2008), 106–7. The term *Finnas* eventually identified a range of Germanic peoples. Thus, for instance, the Battle of Finnsburg in the Old English poem *Beowulf* (lines 1068–1158) probably refers to Frisians, rather than Sámi.
6. Tacitus, *Germania* 46.3; Janne P. Ikäheimo, Juha-Pekka Joona, and Mikko Hietala, "Wretchedly Poor, but Amazingly Practical: Archaeological and Experimental Evidence on the Bone Arrowheads of the *Fenni*," *Acta Borealia* 21 (2004): 3–20.
7. John Weinstock, "The Role of Skis and Skiing in the Settlement of Early Scandinavia," *Northern Review* 25/26 (2005): 175.
8. Paulus Diaconus, *History of the Lombards* 1.5.
9. Procopius, *History of the Wars* 6.15.16. See the reasoning in Ian Whitaker, "Late Classical and Early Mediaeval Accounts of the Lapps (Sami)," *Classica et Mediævalia* 34 (1983): 290, 300–1 n. 42.
10. Although some readers may be more familiar with the terms "Laplander" or "Lapp," Sámi today regard these as derogatory and offensive.
11. Vitruvius, *On Architecture* 6.1.11. See also Strabo, *Geography* 6.4.2. We might also think of the *Umbilicus Urbis Romae* ("The Navel of the City of Rome"), a plaque that served as the city's symbolic center, from which all distance was measured. "All roads lead to Rome," after all.
12. Alluding to Tacitus' *Germania*. On environmental determinism in antiquity, see Isaac, *Invention of Racism*, 1–251.
13. Most Roman maps, like the *Tabula Peutingeriana*, omitted Scandia entirely. The original map was created in the fifth century CE, with a thirteenth century copy of the map surviving today.
14. Seneca the Younger, *Tranquility of Mind* 4.4.

15. Appian, *Foreign Wars* preface.1.7.
16. Strabo, *Geography* 6.4.2.
17. Lennart Lind, "The Monetary Reforms of the Romans and the Finds of Roman *Denarii* in Eastern and Northern Europe," *Current Swedish Archaeology* 1 (1993): 135–44.
18. E.g., Harold Barclay, *People Without Government: An Anthropology of Anarchy*, revised ed. (Seattle: Left Bank, 1990), 90–92; Gabriel Kuhn, "A Short Political History of Sápmi," in *Liberating Sápmi: Indigenous Resistance in Europe's Far North*, ed. Gabriel Kuhn (Oakland: PM Press, 2020), 6–7.
19. On the complex issue of when the Sámi domesticated reindeer, see Oula Seitsonen and Sami Viljanmaa, "Transnational Landscapes of Sámi Reindeer: Domestication and Herding in Northernmost Europe 700–1800 A.D.," *Journal of Field Archaeology* 46 (2021): 172–91. The account comes from the Old English adaptation of Orosius' *Seven Books of History against the Pagans*, which includes several unique additions absent from earlier versions of the text. See the relevant portion in Janet Bately, "Text and Translation," in *Ohthere's Voyages: A Late 9th-Century Account of Voyages along the Coasts of Norway and Denmark and Its Cultural Context*, ed. Janet Bately and Anton Englert (Roskilde: Viking Ship Museum, 2008), 45–46.
20. Niilas Helander, "Swimming, Indigenous Sovereignty, Anarchy, and Love," in *Sex Ecologies*, ed. Stefanie Hessler (Cambridge: MIT Press, 2021), 126.
21. E.g., Asta Mitkijá Balto and Gudrun Kuhmunen, *Máhttáhit: Re-Educate Them and Us! Sámi Self-Determination, Nation-Building, and Leadership* (Karasjohka: ČálliidLágadus, 2014).
22. In English see, e.g., Anna Afanasyeva, "Boarding School Education of the Sami People in Soviet Union (1935–1989): Experiences of Three Generations" (Ph.D. dissertation, Arctic University of Norway, 2018); Otso Kortekangas et al., eds., *Sámi Educational History in a Comparative International Perspective* (Cham: Palgrave Macmillan, 2019).

RADICAL ANTIQUITY

Chapter Five

1. Augustine, *Epistles* 185.15 (written 417 CE). See the helpful analysis of this letter in Geoffrey D. Dunn, "Discipline, Coercion, and Correction: Augustine against the Violence of the Donatists in Epistula 185," *Scrinium* 13 (2017): 114–30.
2. On Smangus, see Jon Burke, "Qalang Smangus: Successful Aboriginal Christian Anarchism in Taiwan," *Anarchist Studies* 32 (2024): 43–69.
3. For an accessible account of the "historical Jesus" as distinct from the "Christ of faith," see James G. Crossley and Robert J. Myles, *Jesus: A Life in Class Conflict* (Winchester: Zero, 2023).
4. Gospel of Mark 10:25; the now-lost *Gospel of the Nazoreans* also quoted this teaching (see Origen, *Commentary on Matthew* 15.14). Many people misconstrue this saying, claiming that Jesus was referring to a gate to the city of Jerusalem called "The Eye of the Needle" that a camel *could* pass through, albeit with difficulty. These efforts to de-radicalize Jesus' words crumble under the lightest scrutiny, since no such gate existed until a millennium after his death; see Agnieszka Ziemińska, "The Origin of the 'Needle's Eye Gate' Myth: Theophylact or Anselm?," *New Testament Studies* 68 (2022): 358–61. For some reasons why scholars think Jesus actually said this, see Robert W. Funk, Roy W. Hoover, and the Jesus Seminar, *The Five Gospels: The Search for the Authentic Words of Jesus* (New York: Macmillan, 1993), 91–93.
5. Gospel of Luke 13:30; cf. Gospel of Mark 10:31, *Gospel of Thomas* 4.2.
6. For an accessible discussion of early Christian diversity, see Burton L. Mack, *Who Wrote the New Testament? The Making of the Christian Myth* (San Francisco: HarperSanFrancisco, 1995).
7. See Gospel of Luke 6:20; *Gospel of Thomas* 54; contrast Gospel of Matthew 5:3. For extensive discussion of the history and later Christian revision of this saying, see Thomas Hieke, ed., *Q 6:20–21: The Beatitudes for the Poor, Hungry, and Mourning* (Leuven: Peeters, 2001), 4–215. Note that the Gospels in the

NOTES

Bible were originally anonymous, such that we do not know who wrote them. Later Christians attributed their authorship to the apostles (hence their titles of Matthew, Mark, Luke, and John).

8. Lactantius, *Divine Institutes* 3.22.
9. As quoted in Pliny the Younger, *Epistles* 10.97; translation from LCL.
10. Gospel of Matthew 10:33; cf. Gospel of Mark 8:38; Gospel of Luke 9:26, 12:9; 2 Timothy 2:12. Scholars generally doubt that Jesus actually said this, but by this time, the tradition had become codified in the Bible, rendering it part of Christian Scripture—regardless of what the historical Jesus may or may not have actually said.
11. The emperor Constantine marks an overlap of the Byzantine and Roman Empires. He founded a second capital for the Roman empire in 330 CE in the city of Byzantium/Constantinople (today's Istanbul). This marked the beginning of the Byzantine period; but the two formed a single legal regime whereby the laws of one empire were valid in those of the other for centuries afterwards.
12. On Christian refusal to participate in state violence before Constantine's reign, see Ronald J. Sider, *The Early Church on Killing: A Comprehensive Sourcebook on War, Abortion, and Capital Punishment* (Grand Rapids: Baker Academic, 2012).
13. There have been many other proposals: Zeev Rubin suggests that the Donatists had little to do with the Circumcellions, "Mass Movements in Late Antiquity: Appearances and Realities," in *Leaders and Masses in the Roman World: Studies in Honor of Zvi Yavetz*, ed. I. Malkin and Z. W. Rubinsohn (Leiden: Brill, 1995), 156–79; Noel Lenski suggests that Circumcellions were freelance enforcers hired by the Donatists to strongarm Catholics, "Harnessing Violence: Armed Force as Manpower in the Late Antique Countryside," *Journal of Late Antiquity* 6 (2013): 233–50; Brent D. Shaw suggests that the Circumcellions were not a distinct group, but an umbrella term applied to unrelated instances of violence, *Sacred Violence:*

African Christians and Sectarian Hatred in the Age of Augustine (Cambridge: Cambridge University Press, 2011).

14. Michael Gaddis, *There Is No Crime for Those Who Have Christ: Religious Violence in the Christian Roman Empire* (Berkeley: University of California Press, 2005), 107 n. 14, citing Augustine, *Exposition of the Psalms* 132.6. Also noteworthy are the military metaphors in the Donatist text *The Martyrdom of Maximian and Isaac* 3, 5.

15. Optatus, *Against the Donatists* 3.4, naming Axido and Fasir; Augustine, *Epistles* 108.14. This is consistent with what we otherwise know about Donatist ethnic demographics: David E. Wilhite, *Ancient African Christianity: An Introduction to a Unique Context and Tradition* (London: Routledge, 2017), 217–25. The Amazigh people were long called "Berbers," but this term is regarded as derogatory.

16. Optatus, *Against the Donatists* 3.4; see Shaw, *Sacred Violence*, 152, 634–5, 659–64.

17. Augustine, *Epistles* 35.2; Optatus, *Against the Donatists* 3.4.

18. See the discussion of Circumcellion apocalypticism in Jesse A. Hoover, *The Donatist Church in an Apocalyptic Age* (Oxford: Oxford University Press, 2018), 228–36.

19. *Codex Theodosianus* 16.5.52.

20. Augustine, *Epistles* 139.2; Optatus (*Against the Donatists* 6.8) likewise pointed out that "not only men but women" partook in Donatist violence, presumably referring to the Circumcellions.

21. Augustine, *Epistles* 35.2; cf. *Against the Letters of Petilian* 2.88.

22. On Augustine's misogyny, see Judith Chelius Stark, ed., *Feminist Interpretations of Augustine* (University Park: Pennsylvania State University Press, 2007).

23. Martine De Marre, "'Bad Girls'?: Collective Violence by Women and the Case of the Circumcellions in Roman North Africa," in *Piracy, Pillage and Plunder in Antiquity: Appropriation and the Ancient World*, ed. Richard Evans and Martine De Marre (London: Routledge, 2020), 154. But see the wild accusations against the Circumcellions in Augustine, *Against the Letters of Parmenian* 1.17.

NOTES

24. E.g., Possidius, *Life of Augustine* 10.1, *Epistles* 35.2. Of course, we can hardly overlook Augustine's hypocrisy on this point, as his youthful sexual transgressions were documented extensively; see Augustine, *Confessions*.
25. Brent D. Shaw, "Who Were the Circumcellions?," in *Vandals, Romans and Berbers: New Perspectives on Late Antique North Africa*, ed. A. H. Merrills (London: Ashgate, 2004), 227–58.
26. Although some historians believe they have identified inscriptions referring to Circumcellion or Donatist martyrs, these conclusions derive from dubious methods. This typically involves an epigrapher identifying phrasing that they think sounds self-righteous, then assuming that this phrasing reflects Donatists' feelings of superiority over Catholics. See, for instance, the discussion in Paul Lachlan MacKendrick, *The North African Stones Speak* (Chapel Hill: University of North Carolina Press, 1980), 267.
27. Augustine, *Epistles* 185.12; even more hyperbolically: Augustine, *Heresies* 69.4. See also Optatus, *Against the Donatists* 3.4.
28. Isidore, *Book of Heresies* 47; translation and discussion from Shaw, "Who Were the Circumcellions?," 245–50.
29. See, e.g., Valeria Graziano, Marcell Mars, and Moslav Medak, *Pirate Care: Acts Against the Criminalization of Solidarity* (London: Pluto, 2025); Andreas Malm, *How to Blow Up a Pipeline* (London: Verso, 2021); David Graeber, *Direct Action: An Ethnography* (Edinburgh: AK Press, 2009).
30. Optatus, *Against the Donatists* 3.4.
31. *Acts of the Carthaginian Conference* 3.258, omitting some names for the sake of brevity. Ultimately, Donatist bishops were banished as a result of the Carthaginian Conference. On the persecution of Circumcellions, see Optatus, *Against the Donatists* 3.3–8 and the heavily fictionalized accounts in *The Martyrdom of Isaac and Maximianus* and *The Martyrdom of Marculus*.
32. Augustine, *Psalms against the Donatists* 151–154, *Epistles* 185. Augustine could not help but rationalize the state's violence, despite deeming it inordinate.

33. Leslie Dossey, *Peasant and Empire in Christian North Africa* (Berkeley: University of California Press, 2010), 179; De Marre, "Bad Girls," 152; Shaw, *Sacred Violence*, 167–8.
34. Augustine, *Against the Letters of Parmenian* 1.17.
35. See Bruno Pottier, "Les Circoncellions: Formation d'une élite rurale monastique autonome dans l'Afrique du Nord des IVe et Ve siècles," [The Circumcellions: The Formation of an Autonomous Rural Monastic Elite in North Africa During the 4th and 5th Centuries] in *Revolte und Sozialstatus von der Spätantike bis zur Frühen Neuzeit*, ed. Philippe Depreaux (Munich: Oldenbourg Wissenschaftsverlag, 2011), 26, 33–34.
36. Dossey, *Peasant and Empire*, 281 n. 8 lists some examples: Augustine, *Epistles* 35.2, 105.2, *Against the Donatist Cresconius* 3.48.
37. See Augustine, *Against the Letters of Parmenian* 1.17, *Against the Letters of Petilian* 2.72, 2.143–146, *Epistles* 87.
38. Dean Spade, *Mutual Aid: Building Solidarity During This Crisis (and the Next)* (London: Verso, 2020), 7.
39. Analena Hope Hassbert, "Nurturing the Revolution: The Black Panther Party and the Early Seeds of the Food Justice Movement," in *Black Food Matters: Racial Justice in the Wake of Food Justice*, ed. Hanna Garth and Ashanté M. Reese (Minneapolis: University of Minnesota Press, 2020), 82–106.
40. Optatus, *Against the Donatists* 3.3.
41. See Jairus Banaji, *Agrarian Change in Late Antiquity: Gold, Labour, and Aristocratic Dominance*, revised ed. (Oxford: Oxford University Press, 2007).
42. Dossey, *Peasant and Empire*, 177–9.
43. *Codex Theodosianus* 11.27.2 (6 July 322 CE).
44. See the discussion in Claude Lepelley, "Liberté, colonat et esclavage d'après la Lettre 24*: juridiction épiscopale de *liberali causa*," [Liberty, Colonization, and Slavery According to Letter 24*: The Bishop's Jurisdiction of *liberali causa*] in *Les Lettres de saint Augustin découvertes par Johannes Divjak* (Paris: Editions Augustiniennes, 1983), 329–42.
45. Optatus, *Against the Donatists* 3.4.

NOTES

46. Augustine, *Against the Letters of Parmenian* 1.17.
47. Augustine, *Against the Letters of Parmenian* 3.18.
48. *Codex Theodosianus* 16.5.52.
49. Augustine, *Proceedings with Emeritus* 12.
50. Possidius, *Life of Augustine* 10.1, emphasis added.
51. Augustine, *Epistles* 185.12. To quote Augustine's brief story in full: "Sometimes they also provoked violence from judges they saw, hoping that they might be put to death by the executioners or by an officer of his court. And we thus have a story that a certain judge played a trick upon them: he ordered them to be bound and led away as though for execution, and so escaped their violence without injury to himself or them."
52. Theodoret, *Bad Tales of Heresy* 3.5 (written 451 CE); translation and discussion from Shaw, "Who Were the Circumcellions?," 242–4.
53. Contrast, e.g., Lenski, "Harnessing Violence."

Chapter Six

1. Diodorus Siculus, *Historical Library* 5.9; Pausanias, *Description of Greece* 10.11.3, 10.16.7; Thucydides, *History of the Peloponnesian War* 3.88; Strabo, *Geography* 6.2.10.
2. Diodorus Siculus, *Historical Library* 5.9; Livy, *History of Rome* 5.28; but see Robert J. Buck, "Communalism on the Lipari Islands (Diod. 5.9.4)," *Classical Philology* 54 (1959): 35–39.
3. Livy, *History of Rome* 5.28.
4. Diodorus Siculus, *Historical Library* 14.93.
5. Elena Flavia Castaginino Berlinghieri, *The Aeolian Islands: Crossroads of Mediterranean Maritime Routes. A Survey on Their Maritime Archaeology and Topography from the Prehistoric to the Roman Periods* (Oxford: BAR Publishing, 2016), 27–32, 79–91. On egalitarian burial customs, see: Thomas J. Figueira, "The Lipari Islanders and Their System of Communal Property," *Classical Antiquity* 3 (1984): 200.
6. Castaginino Berlinghieri, *Aeolian Islands*, 31.

7. See, e.g., Romolo Calciati, *Corpus Nummorum Siculorum: The Bronze Coinage*, vol. 1 (Milan: Edizioni I.P., 1983), nos. 4–8, 11–12, 20, 22, 25. These coins were minted 425–360 BCE.
8. Maria Clara Martinelli and Rosario Vilardo, "Through the Theatrical Mask: The Archaeological Museum of Lipari," *Mediterranean Journal of Clinical Psychology* 7, no. 1 Supp. (2019): 1–15.
9. Cnidus: Eric W. Robinson, *The First Democracies: Early Popular Government Outside Athens* (Stuttgart: Steiner Verlag, 1997), 101–3. Rhodes: Christian A. Thomsen, *The Politics of Association in Hellenistic Rhodes* (Edinburgh: Edinburgh University Press, 2020), 18–48. Before Rhodes' foundation, the island comprised a handful of small city-states.
10. See Philip De Souza, *Piracy in the Graeco-Roman World* (Cambridge: Cambridge University Press, 1999), 43–96.
11. On the reputation of maritime trade, see Livy, *History of Rome* 21.63. For more on the officers aboard such ships, see Wim Broekaert, *Navicularii et Negotiantes: A Prosopography of Roman Merchants and Shippers* (Rahden: Leidorf, 2013).
12. Demosthenes, *Orations* 33.4; translation from LCL, lightly edited.
13. Nicholas K. Rauh, *Merchants, Sailors and Pirates in the Roman World* (Charleston: Tempus, 2003), 135–68; Lionel Casson, *Ships and Seamanship in the Ancient World*, paperback ed. (Princeton: Princeton University Press, 1986), 328; De Souza, *Piracy*, 191–2.
14. Cicero, *Against Verres* 2.5.167.
15. On slaves laboring aboard merchant ships, see Julius Caesar, *Civil War* 3.14; Demosthenes, *Orations* 33.8–10, 34.10; *Digest* 4.9.7, 9.4.19, 14.1.1.
16. Synesius, *Epistles* 4.3–4.
17. *Codex Theodosianus* 14.4.9 (417 CE).
18. Dio Chrysostom, *Discourses* 72.1.
19. Petronius, *Satyricon* 105.
20. *P.Hib.* 2.198.86–87 (after 242 BCE); see the discussion in Roger S. Bagnall, "Some Notes on P.Hib. 198," *Bulletin of the*

NOTES

American Society of Papyrologists 6, no. 3/4 (1969): 86–87. Greeks and Romans commonly branded slaves in other contexts, too.

21. Plato, *Laws* 704d–705a; Aristotle, *Politics* 1256a–b.
22. Seneca the Elder, *Declamations* 1.2.10; Petronius, *Satyricon* 99; Horace, *Epodes* 17.20; Plautus, *Little Carthaginian* 831–835; Propertius, *Elegies* 49–52; Metagenes, *Fragments* 4 (Loeb).
23. Horace, *Satires* 1.5; translation from LCL.
24. See, e.g., fictional accounts of pirate recruitment in Chariton, *Chaereas and Callirhoe* 1.7; Achilles Tatius, *Leucippe and Clitophon* 2.17; Alciphron, *Epistles* 1.8; Philostratus, *Life of Apollonius* 3.24. Note also fishermen's plunder of shipwrecks in Petronius, *Satyricon* 114; *Digest* 47.9.10. Aristotle (*Politics* 1256a–b) and Heliodorus (*Ethiopian Story* 5.20) both observed the porous distinction between fishers and pirates; cf. *IG* 1.3.67.7–8: Athenians presumed that a community of fishermen regularly engaged in piracy.
25. See, e.g., *P.Tebt.* 3.802 (135 BCE), which documents a fight between the (landlubber) guard of one ship and the crew of another. For papyri recounting acts of theft aboard a boat, see *P.Heid.* 9.428 (158 BCE); *P.Mich.* 8.468 (second century CE).
26. *P.Hib.* 2.198.93–96. Scholars tend to assume that these sailors must have been part of the navy, though this seems unlikely; see Bagnall, "P.Hib. 198," 86–87.
27. Vincent Gabrielsen, "Economic Activity, Maritime Trade and Piracy in the Hellenistic Aegean," *Revue des Études Anciennes* 103 (2001): 221–2.
28. On pirate kidnapping, ransoming, and enslavement, see Anna Tarwacka, "Pirates' Captives in Light of Roman Law," in *Roman Law and Maritime Commerce*, ed. Peter Candy and Emilia Mataix Ferrándiz (Edinburgh: Edinburgh University Press, 2022), 41–55.
29. See Sencer Şahin, "Piratenüberfall auf Teos: Volksbeschluß über die Finanzierung der Erpressungsgelder," [Pirate Attack on Teos: The Referendum on Financing Extortion Money] *Epigraphica Anatolica* 23 (1994): 1–40.

30. See a Roman law detailing how these arrangements worked in *IKKnidos* 31.Dlph.
31. Plutarch, *Pompey* 24.3.
32. Respectively, Diodorus Siculus, *Historical Library* 37.16; Memnon, *Fragments* 37 (FGH); Cicero, *Against Verres* 2.5.37.
33. E.g., Cassius Dio, *History of Rome* 36.21.1; Appian, *Foreign Wars* 12.92.
34. E.g., Strabo, *Geography* 6.5.2.
35. Strabo, *Geography* 14.1.32; Ephorus, *Fragments* 36 (FGH); Alciphron, *Epistles* 1.18; Heliodorus, *Ethiopian Story* 5.20; Philostratus, *Life of Apollonius* 3.24.
36. This section builds upon Rauh, *Merchants, Sailors and Pirates*, 169–201; Nicholas K. Rauh, "Who Were the Cilician Pirates?," in *Res Maritimae: Cyprus and the Eastern Mediterranean from Prehistory to Late Antiquity*, ed. Stuart Swiny, Robert L. Hohlfelder, and Helena Wylde Swiny (Atlanta: Scholars Press, 1997), 263–83; Nicholas K. Rauh, Matthew Dillon, and T. Davina McClain, "*Ochlos Nautikos*: Leisure Culture and Underclass Discontent in the Roman Maritime World," in *The Maritime World of Ancient Rome*, ed. Robert L. Hohlfelder (Ann Arbor: University of Michigan Press, 2008), 222–7; Nicholas K. Rauh, "Coastal Highlands, the Sea and Dissident Behaviour on the Margins of Society," *Archaeological Dialogues* 26 (2019): 45–50; Robert C. Knapp, *Invisible Romans: Prostitutes, Outlaws, Slaves, Gladiators and Others* (London: Profile, 2011), 290–314.

    Rauh and Knapp draw upon research about radical self-organization in the Golden Age of Piracy (1690–1730 CE). See Marcus Rediker, *Villains of All Nations: Atlantic Pirates in the Golden Age* (London: Verso, 2004); Colin Woodard, *The Republic of Pirates: Being the True and Surprising Story of the Caribbean Pirates and the Man Who Brought Them Down* (Orlando: Harcourt, 2008); David Graeber, *Pirate Enlightenment: Or the Real Libertalia* (New York: Farrer, Straus and Giroux, 2023).

37. On the ancient equivalence between pirates and bandits, see De Souza, *Piracy*, 9–13.

NOTES

38. Arguing that these depictions were realistic: e.g., Keith Hopwood, "Bandits, Elites and Rural Order," in *Patronage in Ancient Society*, ed. A. Wallace-Hadrill (London: Routledge, 1989), 171–87; Ian Rutherford, "The Genealogy of the *Boukoloi*: How Greek Literature Appropriated an Ancient Narrative-Motif," *Journal of Hellenistic Studies* 120 (2000): 106–21. Arguing that these depictions were unrealistic: e.g., Thomas Grünewald, *Bandits in the Roman Empire: Myth and Reality*, trans. John Drinkwater (London: Routledge, 2004).
39. Diodorus Siculus, *Historical Library* 5.9. See the similar depictions in Apuleius, *Golden Ass* 7.9; Lucian, *The Ship* 28–29; Heliodorus, *Ethiopian Story* 1.19.
40. Notably, the office of "treasury protector," which was common on military and merchant ships, was combined with the captaincy among pirates (see, e.g., Apuleius, *Golden Ass* 7.10; *SIG* 3.521). This meant that the captain ensured fair distribution of the booty and negotiated exchanges with outsiders.
41. Heliodorus, *Ethiopian Story* 1.19. The Greek word for "comrade" commonly denoted equality between soldiers and their officers (e.g., Polyaenus, *Stratagems* 8.23.22; Synesius, *On Kingship* 13).
42. Heliodorus, *Ethiopian Story* 1.3, 5.31–32; cf. 1.19.
43. Cicero, *On Duties* 2.40; translation from LCL.
44. E.g., Heliodorus, *Ethiopian Story* 5.31–32; Achilles Tatius, *Leucippe and Clitophon* 8.16.
45. Apuleius, *Golden Ass* 4.6, 4.8.
46. This paragraph synthesizes several accounts, especially Apuleius, *Golden Ass* 6.32, 7.5, 7.10; Heliodorus, *Ethiopian Story* 1.19; Chariton, *Chaereas and Callirhoe* 1.10.
47. Plutarch, *Pompey* 28.1; Seneca the Elder, *Declamations* 1.6; Heliodorus, *Ethiopian Story* 1.19; Cassius Dio, *History of Rome* 36.22.4; Strabo, *Geography* 14.5.2.
48. Rauh, *Merchants, Sailors and Pirates*, 196.
49. E.g., Heliodorus, *Ethiopian Story* 5.31–32.
50. Augustine, *City of God* 4.4; Cicero, *On Duties* 2.40; Achilles Tatius, *Leucippe and Clitophon* 8.16; Heliodorus, *Ethiopian Story* 4.3.

51. Heliodorus, *Ethiopian Story* 5.31; translation from J. R. Morgan, "Heliodorus, *An Ethiopian Story*," in *Collected Ancient Greek Novels*, ed. B. P. Reardon (Berkeley: University of California Press, 1989), 469.
52. Chariton, *Chaereas and Callirhoe* 1.7–8; Xenophon of Ephesus, *An Ephesian Tale* 1.13; Strabo, *Geography* 14.1.32; Seneca the Elder, *Declamations* 1.2.8–10. Cicero alleged that one politician submitted to the sexual requests of the pirates who captured him (*Responses of the Haruspices* 4). We might also note that one archetypal character in ancient novels was the piratical seducer, who sought to marry a young woman he had captured; Nicolas Boulic and Françoise Létoublon, "Pirates in the Library," in *The Ancient Novel and the Frontiers of Genre*, ed. Marília P. Futre Pinheiro, Gareth Schmelling, and Edmund P. Cueva (Groningen: Barkhuis, 2014), 125–42.
53. Appian, *Foreign Wars* 12.92.
54. Diodorus Siculus, *Historical Library* 5.39, 43.4; Appian, *Foreign Wars* 10.8; *SIG* 581; Josephus, *Antiquities of the Jews* 14.43. This diversity was typical of merchant vessels as well.
55. Susanne Carlsson, *Hellenistic Democracies: Freedom, Independence and Political Procedure in Some East Greek City-States* (Stuttgart: Steiner Verlag, 2010), 162–84. No negative votes are recorded in any Iasos decree.
56. Strabo, *Geography* 14.2.5 with J. L. O'Neil, "How Democratic Was Hellenistic Rhodes?," *Athenaeum* 59 (1981): 468–73.
57. Carlsson, *Hellenistic Democracies*, 184–202.
58. Referring to the power of the *gerousia* (the aristocratic council of Jewish elders) vis-à-vis the high priest within Hellenistic Judaea, as indicated by 1 Maccabees 12:6 and Josephus, *Antiquities of the Jews* 13.166. See Martin Hengel, *Judaism and Hellenism: Studies in Their Encounter in Palestine During the Early Hellenistic Period*, trans. John Bowden (Minneapolis: Fortress, 1974), 25–27.
59. Geoffrey Poitras, *Equity Capital: From Ancient Partnerships to Modern Exchange Traded Funds* (London: Routledge, 2016), 27–69.

NOTES

60. Aristotle, *Politics* 1289b–1292b.
61. David Graeber, *The Democracy Project: A History, a Crisis, a Movement* (New York: Spiegel and Grau, 2013), 185–6. Cf. Peter T. Leeson, "An-arrgh-chy: The Law and Economics of Pirate Organization," *Journal of Political Economy* 115 (2007): 1049–94.
62. Heliodorus, *Ethiopian Story* 5.31–32.
63. See Marcus Rediker, *Between the Devil and the Deep Blue Sea: Merchant Seamen, Pirates, and the Anglo-American Maritime World, 1700–1750* (Cambridge: Cambridge University Press, 1987), 199–201.
64. Socrates as quoted in Plato, *Republic* 351c; Cicero, *On Duties* 2.40; translation from LCL in both cases.
65. Rauh, "Who Were," 273; cf. Rediker, *Between the Devil*, 267.
66. Graeber, *Democracy Project*, 178–9.
67. Ancient writers commonly accused pirates of sexual violence; see, e.g., Herodotus, *Histories* 6.16; Seneca the Elder, *Declamations* 1.2.8–10; Achilles Tatius, *Leucippe and Clitophon* 8.16; *Palatine Anthology* 5.161, 5.309; cf. Boulic and Létoublon, "Pirates in the Library." How accurate was this characterization? This mostly seems to be slander intended to horrify readers about the dishonorable behavior of the lawless lower-classes; observe, by contrast, how one fictional pirate claimed that respecting women prisoners was a desirable quality when choosing a captain (Heliodorus, *Ethiopian Story* 1.19–23).
68. This section draws especially upon Rauh, *Merchants, Sailors and Pirates*, 169–201; De Souza, *Piracy*, 97–148.
69. On archaeological evidence of the pirates harboring in Cilicia, see Nicholas K. Rauh, Matthew Dillon, and Richard Rothaus, "Anchors, Amphoras, and Ashlar Masonry: New Evidence for the Cilician Pirates," in *Rough Cilicia: New Historical and Archaeological Approaches*, ed. Michael C. Hoff and Rhys F. Townsend (Oxford: Oxbow, 2013), 59–86.
70. Appian, *Foreign Wars* 12.96; Florus, *Epitome* 1.41.2; Plutarch, *Sulla* 25; Cassius Dio, *History of Rome* 20.4.
71. Rauh, *Merchants, Sailors and Pirates*, 196.

72. Augustine, *City of God* 4.4; cf. Cicero, *Republic* 3.14. See the similar tale in Cassius Dio, *History of Rome* 77.10.7. The anecdote is almost certainly fictional.
73. Plautus, *Swaggering Soldier* 1176–1181, 1283; *Comedy of Asses* 69; *Persian* 154–157. Of course, clothing was preferable to the nudity they experienced when performing the same labor aboard merchant ships.
74. Plutarch, *Pompey* 24.4. Cicero (*Against Verres* 2.5.64) also observed how one pirate crew included six musicians; cf. Cicero, *Against Verres* 2.5.73; *Prophecy against Quintus Caecilius* 55.
75. Plutarch, *Pompey* 24.7; cf. Cicero, *Against Verres* 2.5.147.
76. E.g., Strabo, *Geography* 11.2.12 with De Souza, *Piracy*, 102–3. We might recall the Roman geographic chauvinism discussed in the Second Interlude.
77. De Souza, *Piracy*, 97–178.
78. Marcus Antonius: e.g., Obsequens, *Book of Prodigies* 44. Pompey: e.g., Cicero, *Pompey's Command* 33. Augustus: e.g., Augustus, *Res Gestae* 25. On the ritual celebrations known as Roman triumphs, see Mary Beard, *The Roman Triumph* (Oxford: Belknap, 2007).
79. *IGRRP* 3.718, 3.719, 3.721. Cf. Philo, *Embassy to Gaius* 146.
80. E.g., Cassius Dio (*History of Rome* 60.8.7) mentioned barbarian piracy upon the coast of Belgica in 41 CE.
81. *P.Mich.* 3.148. For other examples, see Catherine Wolff, *Les brigands en Orient sous le Haut-Empire romain* [Bandits in the East During the High Roman Empire] (Rome: École française de Rome, 2003), 159–61.
82. On crucifixion, see Suetonius, *Julius Caesar* 74; Sallust, *Histories* 3.9; Chariton, *Chaereas and Callirhoe* 3.4. There is also evidence of vigilante violence against pirates: *CIL* 3.1579.

Third Interlude

1. Gildas, *Ruin of Britain* 18–21. The causes of Rome's decline and fall have been discussed for over two millennia. See Edward J. Watts, *The Eternal Decline and Fall of Rome: The History of a Dangerous Idea* (Oxford: Oxford University Press, 2021).

NOTES

2. Patrick, *Confession* 1; *Letter to Coroticus* 10.
3. T. S. Brown, *Gentlemen and Officers: Imperial Administration and Aristocratic Power in Byzantine Italy A.D. 554–800* (Rome: British School at Rome, 1984), 31–34.
4. Paulus Diaconus, *History of the Lombards* 2.31–32.
5. See, e.g., Joshua J. Peck, "Status, Health, and Lifestyle in Middle Iron Age Britain: A Bioarchaeological Study of Elites and Non-Elites from East Yorkshire, Northern England," *International Journal of Paleopathology* 3 (2013): 83–94; Richard Hingley, "Egalitarianism in the Southern British Iron Age: An 'Archaeology' of Knowledge," in *Alternative Iron Ages: Social Theory from Archaeological Analysis*, ed. Brais X. Currás and Inés Sastre (London: Routledge, 2020), 109–26; Ian Armit, "Hierarchy to Anarchy and Back Again: Social Transformations from the Late Bronze Age to the Roman Iron Age in Lowland Scotland," in *Alternative Iron Ages: Social Theory from Archaeological Analysis*, ed. Brais X. Currás and Inés Sastre (London: Routledge, 2020), 195–217; Paul Sillitoe, "The Anthropological Imagination and British Iron Age Society," in *Archaeology and Anthropology: Past, Present and Future*, ed. David Shankland (London: Bloomsbury, 2013), 145–71.
6. E.g., Rob Wiseman, Benjamin Neil, and Francesca Mazzilli, "Extreme Justice: Decapitations and Prone Burials in Three Late Roman Cemeteries at Knobb's Farm, Cambridgeshire," *Britannia* 52 (2021): 119–73.
7. Robert Perry Stephan, "House Size and Economic Growth: Regional Trajectories in the Roman World" (Ph.D. dissertation, Stanford University, 2013), 87–125. The top quartile of house sizes exploded from 329 square meters in the pre-Roman period to 867 square meters in the Roman period (164 percent growth), whereas the bottom quartile of houses only grew from 76 square meters in the pre-Roman period to 112 square meters (47 percent growth).
8. Robin Fleming, *Britain after Rome: The Fall and Rise, 400 to 1070* (New York: Penguin, 2010), 30–60.

9. Robin Fleming, *The Material Fall of Roman Britain 300–525 CE* (Philadelphia: University of Pennsylvania Press, 2021), 6.
10. Scheidel, *Great Leveler*, 264–9; Simon Esmonde Cleary, *The Ending of Roman Britain* (London: Routledge, 1989); Chris Wickham, *Framing the Early Middle Ages: Europe and the Mediterranean, 400–800* (Oxford: Oxford University Press, 2005), 306–33.
11. Nikola Koepke and Joerg Baten, "The Biological Standard of Living in Europe During the Last Two Millennia," *European Review of Economic History* 9 (2005): 61–95. On the significance of height in identifying inequality, see Carles Boix and Frances Rosenbluth, "Bones of Contention: The Political Economy of Height Inequality," *American Political Science Review* 108 (2014): 1–22. Here we are speaking of large-scale demography. None of this implies any individual short person is less healthy than a tall person; there are innumerable factors that play into any one person's height. The point, rather, is that height changes in a single population are meaningful in a relative sense.
12. Fleming, *Material Fall of Roman Britain*, 34–50.
13. Stephan, "House Size," 87–125.
14. *The Ruin* 21–28; translation by Jack Watson, lightly edited.
15. Zosimus, *New History* 6.5.3.
16. See also Rhiannon Firth, *Disaster Anarchy: Mutual Aid and Radical Action* (London: Pluto, 2022). Firth discusses more recent examples of strong systems of mutual aid warding off state power amid social and natural disasters.

Conclusion

1. Plutarch, *Crassus* 11.7; Livy, *History of Rome* 97; Athenaeus, *Learned Banqueters* 273a; Florus, *Epitome* 2.8.14.
2. Appian, *Civil Wars* 1.120; translation from Brent D. Shaw, ed., *Spartacus and the Slave Wars: A Brief History with Documents* (Boston: Palgrave, 2001), 143.
3. Aldo Schiavone, *Spartacus*, trans. Jeremy Carden (Cambridge: Harvard University Press, 2013), 143.

NOTES

4. Ausonius, *Epigrams* 54, reworking *Palatine Anthology* 7.64. See the discussions in Chiara Di Serio, "The Catasterism of Diogenes the Cynic in an Epigram by Ausonius," *Studia Philologia Valentina* 25 (2023): 205–16; N. M. Kay, *Ausonius, Epigrams: Text with Introduction and Commentary* (London: Bloomsbury, 2001), 181–4. For further speculations about Diogenes' post-mortem hauntings, see *Palatine Anthology* 9.145; Ausonius, *Epigrams* 56.
5. Charles Dickens, *A Christmas Carol in Prose: Being a Ghost Story of Christmas* (London: Chapman & Hall, 1843).
6. Homer, *Iliad* 23.54–107.
7. Aeschylus, *Eumenides* 98–178.
8. Disaster: e.g., Valerius Maximus, *Nine Books of Memorable Deeds and Sayings* 1.8. Locations: e.g., Pliny the Younger, *Epistles* 27.5–11; Lucian, *Lover of Lies* 30–31; Plautus, *Ghost Play* 446–531. Revenge: e.g., Cicero, *On Divination* 1.57.
9. See the discussions in Deborah Felton, *Haunted Greece and Rome: Ghost Stories from Classical Antiquity* (Austin: University of Texas Press, 1999); Daniel Ogden, ed., *Magic, Witchcraft, and Ghosts in the Greek and Roman Worlds: A Sourcebook* (Oxford: Oxford University Press, 2002).
10. To be perfectly clear, this Conclusion does not advocate a "woo" understanding of ghosts, but uses them as a metaphor to rethink our relationship with exemplars of the past. See the helpful discussions in Avery F. Gordon, *Ghostly Matters: Haunting and the Sociological Imagination*, 2nd ed. (Minneapolis: University of Minnesota Press, 2008); Mark Fisher, "What Is Hauntology?," *Film Quarterly* 66, no. 1 (2012): 16–24.
11. See David Graeber, *The Ultimate Hidden Truth of the World: Essays*, ed. Nika Dubrovsky (New York: Random House, 2025), 184–6.
12. Here, I paraphrase Fisher, *Capitalist Realism*, 13.
13. David Graeber, *The Utopia of Rules: On Technology, Stupidity, and the Secret Joys of Bureaucracy* (Brooklyn: Melville House, 2015), 89.
14. *Greek Magical Papyri* 4.2006–2125.

15. On slavery, see Ellen Meiksins Wood, *Peasant-Citizen and Slave: The Foundations of Athenian Democracy* (London: Verso, 2015); Georgios Anagnostopoulos and Gerasimos Santas, eds., *Democracy, Justice, and Equality in Ancient Greece: Historical and Philosophical Perspectives* (Cham: Springer, 2018); Paulin Ismard, *Democracy's Slaves: A Political History of Ancient Greece*, trans. Jane Marie Todd (Cambridge: Harvard University Press, 2017).
16. Old Oligarch, *Constitution of the Athenians* 1.4.
17. Old Oligarch, *Constitution of the Athenians* 1.5.
18. See, e.g., Aristotle, *Politics* 1298a, 1303a. On this issue more broadly, see Bernard Mann, *The Principles of Representative Government* (Cambridge: Cambridge University Press, 1997), 132–60.
19. Polybius, *Histories* 6.
20. Plutarch, *Morals*; Aristotle, *Politics*; Plato, *Laws*. In his *Laws*, Plato advocated a very different system from the philosopher-king system delineated in his *Republic*. See also Cicero, *Letters to Atticus* 13.32; Diogenes Laertius, *Lives of Eminent Philosophers* 7.32; Dionysius of Halicarnassus, *Roman Antiquities* 2.7.7. This chapter as a whole draws upon Graeber, *Democracy Project*, 150–207.
21. Russell L. Hanson, "Democracy," in *Political Innovation and Conceptual Change*, ed. Terence Ball, James Farr, and Russell L. Hanson (Cambridge: Cambridge University Press, 1989), 68–89. On similar French and Canadian conceptions of democracy around this time: Francis Dupuis-Déri, "History of the Word 'Democracy' in Canada and Québec: A Political Analysis of Rhetorical Strategies," *World Political Science Review* 6 (2010): 10.1–24. A more nuanced view of America's founding period will emerge below.
22. Thucydides, *History of the Peloponnesian War* 4.105.
23. Ober, *Political Dissent*, 52–121. Nowadays, historians understand Thucydides as more ambivalent to democracy than Hobbes did; see, e.g., Ryan K. Balot, "Thucydides on Democracy and Other Regimes," in *The Cambridge Companion to*

NOTES

Thucydides, ed. Polly Low (Cambridge: Cambridge University Press, 2023), 198–214.

24. See further Clifford W. Brown, Jr., "Thucydides, Hobbes, and the Derivation of Anarchy," *History of Political Thought* 8 (1987): 33–62, discussing Thomas Hobbes, *Eight Bookes of the Peloponnesian Warre Written by Thucydides the Sonne of Olorus* (London: Seile, 1629).

25. See Luca Iori, "Hobbes, Thucydides and Athenian Democracy," in *Brill's Companion to the Reception of Athenian Democracy: From the Late Middle Ages to the Contemporary Era*, ed. Dino Piovan and Giovanni Giorgini (Leiden: Brill, 2021), 153–78.

26. Quoted from the translation in Maurice Pope, "Thucydides and Democracy," *Historia* 37 (1988): 276.

27. John Adams, *The Works of John Adams, Second President of the United States* (Boston: Little and Brown, 1851), 6.481. Adams claimed that the masses consistently seek out an autocratic leader as soon as something goes awry in democracies, pointing to Julius Caesar as an example. On Hobbes' influence, see, e.g., Gary L. McDowell, "Private Conscience & Public Order: Hobbes & *The Federalist*," *Polity* 25 (1993): 421–43.

28. I. H., "Mess. Drapers," *Massachusetts Gazette*, 12 Dec 1765, 2.

29. Anonymous, "Remarks on the New Constitution of Pennsylvania, in 1776," *New-York Gazette: and the Weekly Mercury*, 12 October 1778, 1, lightly edited.

30. James Madison, "The Federalist X," *The Independent Journal or, the General Advertiser*, 23 Nov 1787, 2.

31. Carl J. Richard, *The Founders and the Classics: Greece, Rome, and the American Enlightenment* (Cambridge: Harvard University Press, 1994), 123–68; Roberts, *Athens on Trial*. Cf. Michael J. Klarman, *The Framers' Coup: The Making of the United States Constitution* (Oxford: Oxford University Press, 2018).

32. Cato, "To the People of Pennsylvania: Letter VIII," *Pennsylvania Packet*, 29 April 1776, 1, 4.

33. There were multiple Roman politicians named Cato. Another, this one called Cato the Elder (234–149 BCE), was a conserva-

tive politician who expressed his support for a mixed system of governance (Servius, *Commentary on Virgil* 4.682).

34. See the influential characterization in Polybius, *Histories* 6.4.9.
35. Thomas Jefferson, "III.23: To Samuel Kercheval," in *Jefferson: Political Writings*, ed. Joyce Appleby and Terence Ball (Cambridge: Cambridge University Press, 1999), 210–17.
36. Benjamin L. Carp, *Rebels Rising: Cities and the American Revolution* (Oxford: Oxford University Press, 2007).
37. Terry Bouton, *Taming Democracy: "The People," the Founders, and the Troubled Ending of the American Revolution* (Oxford: Oxford University Press, 2007), 238.
38. Appius, "Letters of Appius to the Citizens of South-Carolina, No. III," *City Gazette & Daily Advertiser*, 4 August 1794, 2.
39. William Murray et al., "(Circular) to the Citizens of Kentucky," *National Gazette*, 12 October 1793, 1. On the Lexington Society, see Eugene Perry Link, *Democratic-Republican Societies, 1790–1800* (New York: Columbia University Press, 1942), 152–3.
40. David Lefer, *The Founding Conservatives: How a Group of Unsung Heroes Saved the American Revolution* (New York: Penguin, 2013), 134–6. To be clear, Lefer writes this as a criticism of Pennsylvania's 1776 Constitution.
41. Gordon S. Wood, *The Creation of the American Republic 1776–1787* (New York: Norton & Company, 1969), 49.
42. Carl J. Richard, *Greeks and Romans Bearing Gifts: How the Ancients Inspired the Founding Fathers* (Lanham: Rowman and Littlefield, 2008), 49–128.
43. For example, in the early 1840s, Thomas Dew—a professor of history and political law—looked to Athens for a model of democracy, since "Athens was the instructress of Greece, and every citizen seemed capable of dedicating his faculties to the most multifarious objects with dexterity and grace. ... Slaves were better treated there than in any other city of Greece." Thomas R. Dew, *A Digest of the Laws, Customs, Manners, and Institutions of the Ancient and Modern Nations* (New York: Appleton, 1853), 208. Dew argued that Athens provided an

appropriate template for America, whose democracy meant little more than the right of a small class of citizens to regard themselves as equals and govern those under their patriarchal authority however they pleased. Dew sought to implement the worst aspects of Greek democracy in the American South: the institutional enforcement of slavery, gender inequality, and xenophobia. For more on this development, see Carl J. Richard, *The Golden Age of the Classics in America: Greece, Rome, and the Antebellum United States* (Cambridge: Harvard University Press, 2009), 41–82.

44. Quoted in Berna González Harbour, "Mary Beard: 'The Roman Empire Emboldens Self-Absorbed Macho Men'," 14 November 2023, https://english.elpais.com/culture/2023-11-14/mary-beard-the-roman-empire-emboldens-self-absorbed-macho-men.html.

45. Mark Bradley, ed., *Classics and Imperialism in the British Empire* (Oxford: Oxford University Press, 2010); C. A. Hagerman, *Britain's Imperial Muse: The Classics, Imperialism, and the Indian Empire, 1784–1914* (London: Palgrave Macmillan, 2013).

46. Johann Chapoutot, *Greeks, Romans, Germans: How the Nazis Usurped Europe's Classical Past*, trans. Richard R. Nybakken (Berkeley: University of California Press, 2016).

47. On racism in the study of antiquity, see Denise Eileen McCoskey, *Race: Antiquity and Its Legacy* (London: Taurus, 2012); Donna Zuckerberg, *Not All Dead White Men* (Cambridge: Harvard University Press, 2018).

48. I do not mean to suggest that either the founding period of the U.S. or Mediterranean antiquity are uniquely useful resources for contemplating radical governance. Indeed, there is much to be gathered from other histories, like that of the Indigenous peoples of the Americas; many Native people regularly adapted their political systems to ensure an egalitarian way of life, which was decimated by European settlers.

Index

Alexander the Great 1, 78–80, 96, 99, 186, 192–3
Alexandria xii, 53, 61–3, 71
American democracy
  direct action in early 222–5
  early aristocratic critics of 216–21, 225–6
  early popular democracy in 221–8, 233–4
  slavery and 226–7, 286–7
anarchy
  as distinct from anarchism 16–17
  as distinct from anarchists 15–16
  as a form of democracy 9–10, 14, 20, 226, 235
  definition of 18–21, 240
  Greek term *anarchia* 9–10, 238
Antisthenes (see also Cynicism) 86–90, 93, 98
aristocracy (see also mixed governance) 212–13
Aristotle 9, 88, 98, 135, 178, 187, 212, 216, 238
asceticism (see also celibacy; poverty) 59–61, 68, 70, 86, 96, 105, 127, 151, 249
Athens xii
  aristocratic critics of 8–10, 98–101, 211–17

consensus-based decision-making in 2, 6–7
democracy of 1–10, 86–7, 187, 211–17
popular critics of 86–94, 99–102, 186, 214–15
use of ostracism 7–8
Augustine of Hippo (see also Catholic Christianity)
  on Circumcellions 147–8, 155–7, 160, 165, 167–70
  on Cynics 254
  on Donatists 147–8, 154, 160, 239
Augustus 14, 62, 144, 194, 227
Axido and Fasir (see also Circumcellion Christianity) 158–61, 163–4, 233

Beruriah (see also Judaism) 51–2, 66, 73
Bible (see also Christianity; Jesus of Nazareth; Judaism)
  Circumcellions' interpretation 152–3, 155
  depiction of Jesus 149–51, 268–9
  Philo's interpretation 67–8
  Therapeutae's interpretation 53–4, 64–8, 71–2

INDEX

Britannia xii, 197–204
  egalitarianism within 200–2
  personification of 44–5, 199
  Roman abandonment of 197–204

cash-cropping 117, 164–5, 201, 203
Catholic Christianity 197, 207
  asceticism within 59–60, 69, 103, 151
  development of 148–54
  Roman support for 104–5, 148, 152–5, 159–60, 163, 165–70, 232–3
  Roman suppression of 151–2, 232–3
celibacy (see also asceticism)
  among Christian monks 59–60, 69
  among Circumcellions 156
  among Essenes 52, 57, 68–71
  among Therapeutae 52, 68–70
  and patriarchy 52, 68–72, 156
charity (see also mutual aid) 162–5, 233
Christianity (see Catholic Christianity; Circumcellion Christianity; Donatist Christianity; Jesus of Nazareth)
Circumcellion Christianity 147–71, 207
  Catholic vilification of 147–8, 155–60, 167–70
  celibacy among 156
  direct action of 158–67, 170
  leaderlessness among 160, 209
  mutual aid among 161–7, 170, 233
  relationship to Donatism 154, 159–61, 165–6, 269–70
  social status of 154–6, 160–1, 163–7
  women among 156, 160, 171, 270
citizenship (see also cosmopolitanism)
  among Cynic philosophers 94, 97, 99
  Athenian 2, 4–7, 86–7, 92, 101, 186–8, 212–14, 219, 236–7
  Roman 25, 44, 46, 69, 101–3, 236–7, 256–7
  Sasanian 115–17
  Spartan 134–6, 219
city-state (see *polis*)
clothing
  among Cynics 95–6
  among Essenes 56, 58–60
  among pirates and sailors 177, 190, 193
  among Therapeutae 59–60, 70
communal child-rearing 109, 130–5, 138
communal meals
  among pirates 174
  among Therapeutae 54

communal ownership
  among Essenes 55–6, 97
  among Mazdakites 109–11, 115, 123, 134–8
  among pirates 172–4
  among Therapeutae 55, 97
consensus-based decision-making
  today 6, 230
  within Athens 2, 6–7
  within Hellenistic city-states 174, 186
  within pirate crews 173–4, 183–5, 188
cosmopolitanism
  among Cynics 86–9, 92–3, 99–102, 105, 107
  among pirates 185–7, 233
core and periphery 11, 55, 60–1, 140–6, 197–8, 247
Crates (see also Cynicism) 85, 89–90, 93
Cynicism 85–108
  chreia as storytelling 94–6, 98, 101, 105
  clothing of 95–6
  cosmopolitanism within 86–9, 92–3, 99–102, 105, 107
  critics of 100–1, 103–5
  Hellenistic 98–102
  pacifism within 97
  Roman 102–5
  shamelessness within 87–94, 102–5
  women within 89–90, 96, 105, 255

democracy (see also American democracy; Athens; voting)
  definition of 14, 20, 216–17
  direct democracy 6–8, 20, 173–4, 183–6
  elections within 7–8, 214
  within mixed governance 215–17, 220, 225
Diogenes of Sinope (see also Cynicism) 85, 87, 90–2, 94, 96, 98, 104–6
  afterlife of 206–7, 209, 211, 228–9
direct action 19–20
  among Circumcellions 158–67, 170
  among Mazdakites 119
  among pirates 179
  definition of 158
  in the early United States 222–5
dispute resolution
  among Mazdakites 134
  among pirates 187–9
Donatist Christianity (see also Circumcellions) 12–13, 147–71
Drimachus 27, 33, 39

egalitarianism
  in post-Roman Britannia 200–2
  in Phrygia 78, 80–3
Epictetus (see also Stoicism) 22–3, 94–5, 103

INDEX

Essenes 52, 55–61, 63–73
  celibacy among 52, 57, 68–71
  clothing of 56, 58–60
  communal ownership 55–6, 97
  diet of 56
  distinction from Dead Sea Scrolls group 56–7
  gender among 68–71, 231
  labor among 55–6
  leaderlessness among 55–9, 63–4
  literacy among 66–8
  pacifism of 55, 57
  social status of 55, 63–5, 97
  voting among 56
Erotis (see also slavery) 1–6, 236

First Servile War 25–9, 32–3, 39
  coinage within 28–9, 34, 39
  King Eunus/Antiochus 26–9, 32–3
  leadership during 28–9, 32–3

gender non-conformity 70, 73, 87, 89–90, 93, 96, 110, 124–33, 138, 156
ghosts 205–11, 234
Graeber, David 187–90, 210

harems (see non-monogamy)
heretics
  Circumcellions as 147–8, 154–5, 157–8
  Donatists as 147–8, 152–5, 157–8
  Mazdakites as 109, 121, 126–7, 131–4
  Mazdakite tolerance of 134
heroes (see ghosts)
Hipparchia (see also Cynicism) 89–91, 93, 96
Hobbes, Thomas 17, 218–19
honor and shame (see also shamelessness) 87–91, 94, 102–5, 110, 113, 136, 175–9, 189, 211

Islands of the Sun 57–9
in-kind payments (see also money and coinage; taxation) 36–7, 80, 116–18

Jesus of Nazareth (see also Bible; Christianity) 149–52, 155, 206, 268–9
Judaism (see also Bible; Essenes; Jesus of Nazareth; Therapeutae) 51–74, 103, 149
  Jerusalem Temple xii, 64–8, 80–1, 250
  women within 51–2, 66, 68–73

!Kung people 40–1

leaderlessness
  among Circumcellions 160, 209

among Essenes 55–9, 63–4
among Mazdakites 134
among pirates 181–5
among Therapeutae 52–5, 70, 72
as a feature of anarchy 18–20
at Thurii 39–43, 46, 48–9
in the early United States 221–4, 233–4
Lele people 127–31, 133–4, 263
leveling mechanisms (see also leaderlessness)
among !Kung 40–1
at Thurii 40–3, 46
clothing as 56, 58–60, 70, 95–6
literacy
among Essenes 65–8
among Therapeutae 65–8
rates of, in antiquity 13
rejection of, in Phrygia 77, 80–4

maps xii, 56–7, 140–5
Mazdak 110, 115–23, 137, 227–8
Mazdakism 109–39
before Mazdak (see also Zaradusht) 110–15
communal ownership 109–11, 115, 123, 134–8
direct action of 119
dispute resolution 134
doctrines 111
during the life of Mazdak 115–21

Khurrami iteration 122–3, 131–3
leaderlessness within 134
pacifism within 109, 111, 114, 120, 122–3, 127
polyandry within 109–10, 115, 124–38, 232
poverty within 115–9
relationship to Zoroastrian priesthood 110, 115, 121–2, 137
religious pluralism 123, 264
social status of 115–19
vegetarianism 109, 123
mixed governance 215–17, 219–21, 224–6
elections as a part of 214–15
in antiquity 212–17, 219–21
today 224–6
money and coinage
alternatives to (see also communal ownership; in-kind payments; prohibition of money) 34–9, 116–17, 145–6, 243–4
barter and 243–4
effect on inequality 36–7
in Cynicism 93–4
in First Servile War 28–9
in Gaul and Thrace 37–8
in Jewish Wars 244
in Phrygia 81
in Sápmi 143–6
in Sasanian taxes 116–17
invention of 35–6

military-industrial-coinage complex 34–6
mutual aid (see also charity)
  among Black Panther Party 162–3
  among Circumcellions 161–7, 170, 233
  among Essenes 55, 60
  among Hellenistic associations
  among Mazdakites 110–11, 115–22, 138
  among pirates 189
  among Therapeutae 55, 60
  definition of 161
  in rural contexts 36–7
  state appropriation of 121–2, 162–3, 261–2

nomos and *physis* 97–100, 232
non-monogamy (see also communal child-rearing; sex work)
  fraternal polyandry, definition of 109–10, 124
  polyandry among Lele 127–31, 133–4
  polyandry among Mazdakites 109–10, 115, 124–38, 232
  polyandry among other ancient cultures 132, 264
  polyandry among Spartans 134–7
  polygyny in the Sasanian Empire 111–13, 116, 124–5, 128, 131, 136, 262

obliviousness to empire 75–6, 84, 252

pacifism 19
  among Cynics 97
  among Essenes 55, 57
  among Mazdakites 109, 111, 114, 120, 122–3, 127
patriarchy 51–2, 68–71, 89–91, 111–14, 124–5, 127, 137–8
  marriage and 68–71, 112–13
Paul and Macarius (see also Catholic Christianity) 159–61, 163–4, 233
Philo of Alexandria (see also Judaism) 56–7, 67–8, 70
Phrygia xii, 75–84
  egalitarianism within 78, 80–3
  rejection of literacy within 77, 80–4
pirates 172–96
  clothing of 177, 190, 193
  communal ownership 172–4
  consensus-based decision-making of 173–4, 183–5, 188
  constitutions of 182–5
  cosmopolitanism among 185–7, 233
  direct action of 179
  dispute resolution 187–9
  leaderlessness among 181–5, 277
  poverty of 175–81
  recruitment of 178–9, 275

shamelessness among
175–81, 193
support for injured 183–5
trickery of 49, 180–1
voting among 172, 181–8
Plato 8–10, 16, 91–2, 99, 177–8
polis 62–3, 86–8, 90, 92–3,
97–102, 136, 186–8
polygamy (see non-monogamy)
poverty
among Catholics 59–60
among Circumcellions 154–6,
160–1, 163–7
among Cynics 87–94, 102–5
among Essenes 55, 63–5, 97
among Mazdakites 115–19
among pirates and sailors
175–81
among Therapeutae 55, 97
in Phrygia 78–81
in post-Roman Britannia
200–2
vows of 59–60, 160
power, types of 18–19

redistribution of wealth
at Thurii 34–9
by Circumcellions 161–7, 170
by Essenes 55–6
by Mazdakites 109–11, 115,
123, 134–8
by pirates 179–84
Roman Empire xii
fall of 197–204

sailors (see pirates)

Sámi people 140–6
as beyond imperial reach
140–5
non-monetized economy
143–4
Sápmi, homeland of xii, 141,
146
Sasanian Empire xii
Kavad I, emperor of 112–15,
124–5
Khosrow I, emperor of 115–22
polygyny within 111–13, 116,
124–5, 128, 131, 136
support for Mazdakism
111–15
suppression of Mazdakism
119–22
taxation policies of 116–18
Scott, James C. 76–8, 83
Second Servile War 26, 28–9,
39, 46
sex work 68–9, 89–91, 103, 178,
185
sexual violence
accusations against Catholics
160
accusations against
Mazdakites 124–7, 137–9
accusations against pirates
278–9
accusations against Thurii
31–3, 246
against slaves 44–6, 68–9
in Roman artwork 44–5, 199
under the reign of Kavad
112–15

INDEX

shamelessness
  among Cynics 87–94, 102–5
  among pirates 175–81, 193
slavery
  among Circumcellions 155–6, 160, 165
  among Cynics 85, 91–2, 100, 103
  among rebels at Thurii 27–8, 30–40, 42–50
  among sailors 175–9
  ancient opposition to 25–6, 57, 230–1, 242
  and American "democracy" 226–7, 286–7
  at Qumran 57, 248
  identity as slave 25–7
  pirates and 179–80, 191
  sexualization of (see also sexual violence; sex work) 26, 43–6, 68–9, 112–13
Socrates (see also Plato) 88–9, 98–100, 189, 212
Sparta xii, 134–7
Spartacus (see also Third Servile War; Thurii) 24, 30–2, 34, 39–40, 42–3, 47–50
  afterlife of 205–6, 209–11
state, definition of 19, 236, 241
Stoicism 15–16, 22–3, 103, 143, 241
Symeon the Holy Fool (see also Cynicism) 103

taxation
  as exploitation in antiquity 116–18, 163, 200
  collection 37, 75, 80, 145, 163, 200
  in-kind 37, 80, 116–18, 145, 200
  monetization via 37, 116–18
Therapeutae 52–5, 59–74
  celibacy among 52, 68–70
  clothing of 59–60, 70
  communal ownership 55, 97
  diet of 53–4
  gender among 52, 68–70, 73, 231
  leaderlessness among 52–5, 70, 72
  literacy among 65–8
  social status of 55, 65–8, 97
Third Servile War (see also Spartacus; Thurii)
  federated armies of 42
  gladiators in 24, 30, 32, 35, 43
  Spartacus' role within 24, 30–2, 34, 39–40, 42–3, 47–50
Thurii (see also Spartacus; Third Servile War) xii, 22–50
  leaderlessness at 39–43, 46, 48–9
  leveling mechanisms at 40–3, 46
  prohibition of money at 34–9, 231
  women at 27, 31, 43–6, 49
Tiberius Gracchus 25

utopias in ancient literature 15–17, 57–9

voting
  among the Essenes 56
  among pirates 172, 181–8
  in American democracy 216–28
  in ancient militaries 186–8
  in Athenian democracy 2, 6–8, 214–17, 220, 225

women (see also gender non-conformity; sexual violence)
  in antiquity 234–5
  in Circumcellion Christianity 156, 160, 171, 270
  in Cynicism 89–90, 96, 105, 255
  in Hellenistic associations 1–6
  in Judaism 51–2, 66, 68–73
  in Mazdakism 109–10, 112–15, 124–38, 232
  in pirate communities 178, 183–5, 191, 279
  in Sámi culture 140
  in the Sasanian Empire 111–16, 124–8, 131, 136
  in Thurii 27, 31, 43–6, 49
  sexual regulation of 51–2, 68–9, 89–91, 110, 112–16, 124–7, 136

Zaradusht (see also Mazdakism) 110–12, 114–15, 118, 123
Zeno of Citium (see also Stoicism) 15–16, 240

The Pluto Press Newsletter

Hello friend of Pluto!

Want to stay on top of the best radical books we publish?

Then sign up to be the first to hear about our new books, as well as special events, podcasts and videos.

You'll also get 50% off your first order with us when you sign up.

Come and join us!

Go to bit.ly/PlutoNewsletter